BECOMING A WHITE ANTIRACIST

Advance Praise for
Becoming a White Antiracist

"Brookfield and Hess offer a highly accessible step-by-step guide for those who seek to foster discussion and create curricula related to systemic racism. As a woman of color, I found their frameworks useful to my teaching about antiracism within a predominantly white institution."—**Hetty Cunningham**, *Associate Professor and Associate Vice Chair for Education and the Learning Environment, Department of Pediatrics, and Director for Equity and Justice in Curricular Affairs, Vagelos College of Physicians and Surgeons, Columbia University*

"As a white antiracist educator, this book was exactly the resource that I needed to sharpen my craft. Brookfield and Hess honor the rigor this important topic deserves, while also creating an accessible entry point for readers at varying levels of development. This is just the right book for just the right time."—**David Scherer**, *Artist and Educator with JUSTmove Consulting*

"For those stepping up to the critical work of teaching and learning about how to live into antiracist white identity, Brookfield and Hess will help them gain critical footing as they wade into the fray."—**Katherine Turpin**, *Professor of Practical Theology and Religious Education, Iliff School of Theology*

"*Becoming a White Antiracist* removes the mask of white innocence and raises a painful and disagreeable mirror to white people. Brookfield and Hess share James Baldwin's rejection of love in the American sense of infantilism or just being made happy. Rather, the book that you hold deploys love as a painful process whereby it is unequivocally demanded that white people see themselves as they are; it is a powerful text that is steadfast in its pedagogical, conceptual, and discursive passion and courage to lay bare the lie and the mythopoetic structure of white identity. In doing so, the text effectively creates a robust dialogical space for profound *generative* white discomfort, disorientation, and loss. *Becoming a White Antiracist* is a daring book that demands action, that instructs white people to be in danger, to risk themselves, to undo their power and privilege, and to rethink the category of the 'human' outside the white order of things."—**George Yancy**, *The Samuel Candler Dobbs Professor of Philosophy at Emory University*

BECOMING A WHITE ANTIRACIST

A Practical Guide for Educators, Leaders, and Activists

Stephen D. Brookfield and Mary E. Hess

1996-2021 25ᵀᴴ ANNIVERSARY

Stylus
PUBLISHING, LLC.

STERLING, VIRGINIA

COPYRIGHT © 2021 BY STYLUS PUBLISHING, LLC.

Published by Stylus Publishing, LLC.
22883 Quicksilver Drive
Sterling, Virginia 20166-2019

Library of Congress Cataloging-in-Publication Data
The CIP data for this title have been applied for.

13-digit ISBN: 978-1-62036-858-9 (cloth)
13-digit ISBN: 978-1-62036-859-6 (paperback)
13-digit ISBN: 978-1-62036-860-2 (library networkable e-edition)
13-digit ISBN: 978-1-62036-861-9 (consumer e-edition)

Printed in the United States of America

All first editions printed on acid-free paper
that meets the American National Standards Institute
Z39-48 Standard.

Bulk Purchases

Quantity discounts are available for use in workshops and for staff development.
Call 1-800-232-0223

First Edition, 2021

Stephen dedicates this book to his late friend and colleague Dr. Elizabeth Peterson of National Louis University, Chicago.

Mary dedicates this book to her late friend and colleague Jeannie Hess, coordinator of community service programs at the Harvard Medical School.

CONTENTS

A s this book was being written, the United States exploded in outrage against the murder by police of people of color across the country. Corporations, branches of state and local government, and educational institutions all pledged to work for racial justice, and the Black Lives Matters movement moved into the mainstream as people from multiple racial and class identities pledged their support to its message. Diversity initiatives abounded, mission statements everywhere were changed to incorporate references to racial justice, and the rampant anti-Blackness endemic to U.S. culture was brought strikingly to the surface. Everywhere, it seemed, white people were looking to learn about race. This was true even in the face of the Trump administration stopping federal training from using critical race theory and the term *white privilege* and branding antiracist education as un-American.

But even as white people seemed eager to move into a serious engagement with this topic, the two of us noticed the apologetic wave of guilt and shame that often overtook them as they came to understand the pervasive nature of white supremacy in the United States. Conversations turned into confessions as folks lamented the fact that eyes had been blinkered, and hearts had been sealed, for so long. At the same time, they were desperate to know how to move past this guilt and take action based on their new awareness of enduring, endemic racism. "What do we do?" "How can we help?" These were the cries we heard most frequently from those whites whose consciousness of racism was being raised.

This book is our answer to those cries. It's grounded in what colleagues and friends of color have often told us—that white people need to start with themselves, with understanding that they have a white racial identity. Once you've learned about what it means to be white in a white supremacist world, the answer to "What can I do?" becomes clear. You work in multiracial alliances to organize and press for genuine social, political, and economic equity and you work with white colleagues and friends to unearth and combat the white supremacy that lives within you and that supports the everyday enactment of racist structures, policies, and habits. In this book we explore what it means for whites to move from becoming aware of the extent of their unwitting collusion in racism toward developing a committed antiracist white identity. We create a road map, or series of paths, that people can consider traveling as they work to become white antiracists.

We focus particularly on the dynamic of white leaders, educators and activists working with white members of mostly white organizations. When a white person introduces race in a room full of white people, it's a very different situation than when a person of color does the same thing. White teachers and leaders are seen as being in the same racial "club" as their audience. Consequently, they have an inbuilt advantage (at least at the outset) when trying to help other whites consider what it would look like to develop and live out a white identity focused on fighting racism. Rarely are they accused of playing the race card or pursuing a "narrow" racial agenda.

If you're white you're already an expert in knowing how white supremacy is learned and transmitted via a daily diet of racist messages received from family, friends, media, work colleagues, and leaders. When whites tell us that they know nothing about race, we usually reply that actually they're racial *experts*, at least on how white supremacy is absorbed and lived. No one knows better than them how biases and stereotypes worm their way into white consciousness; no one has more experience of receiving the benefits of a white supremacist system. Once these processes have been uncovered and challenged, white people's distinct contribution is to share how the benign, yet supremely powerful, socialization into whiteness takes place. The next stage is to challenge, and do their best to dismantle, the destructive white supremacist system that has formed them.

A white identity always involves a level of self-awareness, but its most important dimension is a commitment to action. The purpose of this book is to take readers along the developmental path of convincing those who see themselves as "good" whites to understand how white supremacy has inserted itself into their consciousness and plays itself out in their racialized actions. Our intent is to take readers to the point where white people view taking purposeful action to dismantle racism as a fundamental part of who they are, as a central part of what it means to be white. Along the way we show readers how to move beyond a color-blind perspective to live an antiracist life. We show how to challenge stock, official stories of racial progress and how to develop counter-narratives. We explore how to run discussions on race that get people to think structurally and systemically about racism, and how to use your power as a teacher and leader to empower others. We urge attending to the history of antiracist struggle and examine how best to respond to the inevitable pushback you'll encounter when developing an antiracist identity. And, of course, we keep examining, and problematizing, what it means to be a white ally or accomplice.

Audience

Our primary audience for the book is anyone who is working with mostly white groups to help them become aware of, and then seek to dismantle, racism and white supremacy. Much of the book is organized around the idea of an antiracist white identity, because for us the concept of identity is so fundamental to how we live life. An identity entails not just a sense of who we are but of who we want to become. It embeds our commitments and is lived through our actions. And for us it is the taking of action that is the crucial and most important dimension of becoming a white antiracist. Certainly, we want people to have a fully developed awareness of the different ways that white supremacy structures how the economy, health-care provision, education, government, and incarceration mechanisms all function in the United States. But mostly we want to explore how that awareness can translate into action in communities, organizations, movements, and political parties.

We hope that the book will be useful to anyone trying to create conversations around race, teach about white supremacy, arrange staff and development workshops on racism, and help colleagues explore how to create an antiracist culture or environment. This work happens in schools, colleges, and universities, and we suspect many readers will be located in K–12 and higher education. But we also know from our own consulting that helping white people become antiracist is a project that occurs in corporations, congregations, community groups, health care, state and local government, arts organizations, and the military. So we have tried to make this book as accessible as possible to those working in these locations. Essentially, if you have an interest in helping the whites you interact with become antiracist, then this book is written very specifically for you.

Chapter Summary

Our introduction begins with us telling something of our own stories of struggling to move to an antiracist white identity. If readers know something about the two of us, then they can better judge whether or not our advice is worth considering.

Chapter 1 states our conviction that developing an antiracist white identity is a task that's missing from most diversity, equity, and inclusion initiatives. We argue that although it's obviously important to bear witness to the testimonies of BIPOC (Black, indigenous, and people of color) whites really need to focus on understanding their collusion in, and enactment of, white supremacy.

Chapter 2 outlines components of an antiracist white identity, proposes an epistemology of antiracist thinking, and introduces the concept of brave (not safe) space. We warn of the dangers of whites demonizing other, less racially aware, whites and the importance of bearing witness to BIPOC testimonies of racism.

Exactly what constitutes a white identity is a mystery to many, so in chapter 3 we name some common elements of white racial identity—a colorblind view of the world, denying one has a racial identity as a white person, and choosing when to deal with race and when to ignore it.

In chapter 4 we offer a template of how to help white people become aware of their racial identity. We describe a series of steps we take to scaffold the kind of transformative learning that becoming aware of whiteness entails. Some of these steps involve adjusting our notion of what counts as success, researching how people enter learning environments, modeling extensively our own struggle with white supremacy, using scenario analyses as an initial learning activity, moving into structured discussion protocols, and responding to whites' resistance to being told they have "privilege."

The use of personal stories and digital narratives is the focus of chapter 5. We both feel strongly that sharing stories is a useful starting point in the journey of becoming a white antiracist. We offer ground rules for storytelling groups, share some narrative prompts, and describe activities such as the power flower, the four corners exercise, story circles, and titling the story.

Helping people embrace the discomfort of examining their own white supremacy and moving to a different conception of what it means to be a "good white" is the focus of chapter 6. We stress again the importance of modeling and explain how to begin sessions with a meditative pause. Then we describe how to respond to racist comments when they're expressed. We explore in some detail the beliefs and behaviors exercise and urge engaging visual, musical, and dramatic senses to open people up to different ways of thinking about race.

Chapter 7 explores how to run discussions about race that are structured to be both inclusive and expansive. We describe how social media can be used as both a prompt for, and a productive interrupter of, racial discussion, and then propose five specific discussion protocols that we have found especially helpful—circle of voices, chalk talk, circular response, Bohmian dialogue, and appreciative pauses.

One of the biggest barriers to developing an antiracist white identity is the difficulty of shifting your understanding of racism away from a focus on individual moral failings or personal thoughtlessness to seeing it as a structural and systemic phenomenon. In chapter 8 we propose activities such as the privilege walk and the deconstruction of personal stories as a key to thinking structurally. We also show how to do a power analysis and how to conduct ideology critique.

How teachers and leaders can exercise their own power in a responsible, ethical, and effective manner is the focus of chapter 9. We distinguish between being authoritarian and being authoritative in the ways we set necessary boundaries in antiracist work, how to leverage white privilege, and the need to create productive dissonance designed to disrupt and transform.

Chapter 10 shows how we can draw on the history of antiracist work to ignite interest in becoming an antiracist white. We provide numerous examples of written, spoken, visual, and musical resources that are freely available to help people develop their own sense of individual and collective agency.

Anyone trying to uncover and challenge white supremacy will sooner or later encounter serious institutional pushback. In chapter 11 we advise readers on how to understand the contexts in which they're working and we provide some basic do's and don'ts in responding to resistance.

Chapter 12 asks what it means to be a white ally and accomplice while pointing out the problematic aspects of that idea.

Who Wrote What?

Our process was as follows. Stephen Brookfield took the responsibility of writing the first drafts of chapters 1, 2, 3, 4, 7, 8, 9, and 12. Mary Hess wrote the first drafts of chapters 5, 6, 10, and 11. We then read and revised each other's chapter drafts several times and met frequently to discuss and respond to edits. Brookfield then did a final rewrite of the whole book to ensure a consistency of tone.

ACKNOWLEDGMENTS

Stephen Brookfield would like to acknowledge Mary Hess, without whom this book would never have seen the light of day. She has been a powerful influence on his work and practice for the last 2 decades and was a wonderfully creative and supportive writing partner. He would also like to acknowledge Lucia Pawlowski, the director of the WORD writing studio at St. Lawrence University (Canton, NY) for helping frame an early version of this book.

Mary Hess would first like to acknowledge Stephen Brookfield. She has never before encountered such a gracious yet challenging partner in learning and writing. He pushed her far beyond the scholarly, footnoted voice she was comfortable with and into a space of saying clearly what she meant in ways that could be practical. Beyond that, she gives thanks to Mary Boys, who first introduced her to Brookfield's work decades ago. Further, the many, many women of color who mentored, challenged, prayed, and cried with Hess over the years: Shi, Mary, and Melissa, college roommates; Addie, Boyung, and Elizabeth, learning partners in a PhD program; Vivian, longtime scholar/teacher collaborator extraordinaire; and finally, though it may sound strange to ears tuned within secular contexts, infinite gratitude to the woman she reverences in her Catholic being—Mary, the unwed, dark-skinned peasant woman, the refugee fleeing empire, the woman who proclaimed the justice of God as she carried and birthed, raised, and buried the Incarnate One.

INTRODUCTION

Our Racial Stories

Throughout this book we stress the importance of narrative disclosure as a way of building trust and setting a tone for "real" conversation on race. A story can clearly illustrate what often seems like an abstract idea—that the ideology of white supremacy secures the continuance of a racist system—by situating that idea in specific events and incidents. We would never dream of giving any suggestions or guidance on how to become a white antiracist or ask anyone to reveal how they had learned white supremacy without initially disclosing some of our own experiences of our collusion in, and enactment of, racism.

So in this introduction we want to tell readers something about how we came to this work, how we think about our own racial identity, and what we continue to struggle with. If you choose to skip this section and get to what you might consider the "real" stuff in the chapters after this one, please remember that skipping narrative disclosure is a rookie mistake that we, and others, have often made as we go into an antiracist effort. So please—*never* ask anyone to talk about how they've experienced or enacted racism until you've done this first in front of them.

Stephen's Story

What drew me to this work? Why would I strive to be a white antiracist if I know my learned racism will always be inside me? If I accept, as I do, that during my 7 decades on the planet I have internalized a white supremacist ideology at a very deep level, what is the point of trying to push back against all that conditioning?

I still believe a moral tenet that I learned early in life and that has always seemed clear and obvious to me—you should strive to treat people as you would like to be treated. If you take this "'golden rule" seriously, then you have an automatic imperative to make sure no one is thought of as less than fully human because of their race or any other identity marker. In conversations,

1

workshops, and classes I often start by asking people what they think about the golden rule, because it seems a benign idea that most people support. Then I broaden the conversation out so we can talk about what it would look like to live by that rule in a multiracial world. This simple rule is also connected to the socialist ideal of fairness, which is extremely powerful for me. At an early age I would complain, "That's not fair," when I saw power being used in an abusive, arrogant way. That same sense of outrage still sits at the center of my moral consciousness.

However, this outrage took a long time to be framed in racial terms until some pivotal events in my 30s and 40s really brought that issue into focus. In the 1980s, I remember being challenged by people of color as to why I wasn't speaking in groups on racial matters. When I explained I felt that white males had taken up too much space and needed to stay silent, I was told that whites staying silent is an exercise of power, leaving the people of color in the room wondering exactly what that silence signifies—approval, condemnation, confusion, disinterest? It was also pointed out to me just how condescending it was for me to stay silent if I thought that my quiet was a way to "bring people into voice." The implication seemed to be that I thought my voice was so powerful and authoritative that people of color would be intimidated by me and afraid of challenging or contradicting me.

In the early 1990s a white colleague asked me why my work was so race-blind at about the same time that a colleague of color told me that she saw *everything* through the lens of race. She was so convincing and impassioned that from then on I assumed that every person of color shared that perspective. It's proved to be an excellent guiding principle. Around then I also began a decade-long period of adjunct work and consultancy with a doctoral program in Chicago (at National Louis University) that allowed me to coteach with African American colleagues (Scipio Colin Jr. III and Elizabeth Peterson) influenced by very different traditions from Afrocentric philosophy to critical race theory. But in the 1980s and 1990s I felt so ignorant and naïve in my understanding of race that I determined I would not publish anything about it until I'd spent at least 10 years working in that area. So my first pieces dealing with race did not come out until the early 2000s (Brookfield, 2003a, 2003b).

I have always believed that compassion is the highest human virtue and it's the quality I value most in others. And the more I learned about racism and power, the more I realized that you can't act compassionately toward anyone you regard as "other." That meant that acting compassionately entailed exercising empathy toward those who struggle with the effects of racism.

But this raises two problems for whites like me. First, no matter how hard I try, I can never know what it's like to be marked for physical and symbolic violence in the ways experienced by members of a racial minority. Second, I must honestly admit that I find it very hard to exercise empathy for those in positions of power who perpetrate racism. I believe that evil exists and am quick to condemn, quick to rage, and quick to identify who are my enemies. There is a perverse and seductive pleasure in savoring a righteous condemnation of those you regard as evil fools, and it's one I savor.

If coming to an awareness of one's white identity is a developmental learning process, as I believe it is, then I need to remember that those whites I quickly condemn and despise have the possibility of growth and redemption within them. I live at the Manichean nexus of two contending voices, both of which have truth and meaning for me. One is an activist voice that says, "You can't wait for people to learn to be antiracist—they're perpetrating too much hurt right now, so your duty is to stop them having any influence." The other is an educator's voice that says, "You can't expect people to learn on your timetable; you have to start where they are and bring them along as best you can."

In a typical day I enact both of these voices. In meetings, union business, or grassroots organizing I heed my activist voice. I try to be strategic in organizing resistance by playing with organizational symbols to embarrass those in power, building alliances, and preaching the power of collective solidarity. In these moments my duty is to outwit those in authority. But in classes and workshops I hear my educator voice. I try to focus on the dynamics of learning and to play the long game. I find out as much as possible about those I'm working with, try to create bridges between the knowledge and experiences they bring and their readiness for learning, and seek to move them, often incrementally, toward an antiracist identity.

Ultimately, I think that in a racially diverse world there is no other option but to develop a form of racialized communicative action (Habermas, 1987)—that is, to find common ground on which people of very different racial backgrounds and identities can negotiate how to live in a world in which we press up against each other and in which common agreements need to be reached.

I wish I could claim to have a fully developed antiracist identity, but I don't think that lies in my future. The best I can hope for is to work toward that end, knowing it will never be attained. This is because the white supremacist ideology I've been brought up in is just too deeply embedded in me. Ever since I was old enough to perceive how the world worked, I've assimilated a set of paradigmatic assumptions that have seemed to me to represent such obvious, commonsense reality that I've mostly regarded them as empirical truth rather than assumptions. Chief among these are the following:

- Leadership is white.
- Intelligence is white.
- Objectivity is white.
- Rationality is white.
- History is white.
- Geography is white.

These assumptions comprise the essence of white supremacy. Why do whites seem to end up in leadership positions making decisions for the rest of us? Because, according to white supremacy, whites have a greater facility for thinking clearly and logically about what comprises the common good and how that should be achieved. So it would seem to make natural sense for them to be leaders. I also grew up accepting patriarchy. Not only did I accept that most leaders should be white, I also thought of them as obviously male. Just as I never questioned that whites should be in leadership positions because of their intelligence and rationality, so I never challenged the notion that men's clarity and greater objectivity meant their decisions were to be trusted over those of women who were more likely to be swayed by emotion, particularly compassion. I was an excellent little student of the white patriarchy so clearly described by Rebecca Traister (2018).

I would still be living in a totally unraced way had it not been for other people pointing out the meaning of my white identity to me. Now I'm paying their work forward. In this book I want to explore how educators, activists, and leaders can bring the fact of whiteness to the attention of those who exhibit and live it, yet don't give it a second thought.

Of course I had many Black heroes as a teenager in the rock and roll music I loved—Little Richard (whom I later met), Chuck Berry, and Jimi Hendrix. But the trope that it was cool to be a Black musician because "they" had "soul" actually supported my enmeshment in white supremacy. Soul and spontaneity was great for rock and roll, but to be an effective leader you needed to be a white man soaked in rationality. I spent my formative years as an "unraced" person in a racially homogenous world. Even though my home city was Liverpool (England), a bustling port with merchant seamen from across the world, my parents, friends, brothers, neighbors, and teachers were all white. Diversity was having a best friend with Scottish parents and race was something that "foreigners" had, particularly those who were Black and brown.

It was only once I got to college, made Pakistani friends and had Caribbean roommates, that I had any awareness of racial diversity. All the authority figures in my life—university teachers, administrators, police, doctors, politicians—were still white, of course. In fact, until I was in my 40s, no one who had any formal authority over me was other than white. So what counted as normal for me, the universal standard against which strangeness or deviance was measured, was whiteness. My way of making meaning of the world was centered squarely in what Feagin (2013) described as the white racial frame—the learned worldview that legitimizes white supremacy and makes permanent racial inequity seem unremarkable, normal, just the way things are.

But even bathed in white supremacy, I had moments of ideological interruption. One pivotal event happened at the age of 17 when I was being beaten up by a gang of white youths (they were "rockers"; I was a "mod") in Banbury High Street one Friday night. Banbury is a country town in Oxfordshire, England, not far from the Upper Heyford Air Force Base then served by many U.S. personnel. A Black American GI from there crossed the street and broke up the fight, telling us "everybody's got to be cool now." That man saved me from potentially severe injury. I was being whipped with metal chains and on the verge of falling to the floor as the GI intervened. Being born in Bootle (Liverpool) I knew that once you were on the floor things got a lot worse, because then people could kick you in the kidneys and head. That event formed what critical race theory calls a counter-story that disrupted the white supremacist script forming in my head saying Black people are violent and start fights and white people are peacemakers who sometimes have to use force to rein in Black instigators of violence. Here was a stunning role reversal that made a big impression on me.

Another was when I was in college in Chelsea (London) and Michael X, the Jamaican activist, addressed our student group. He came in flanked by bodyguards and I remember thinking that I was now hearing the authentic voice of Black revolutionary experience. That day when I got home, I spoke excitedly to my Afro-Caribbean roommate, Terry, about the session, anticipating that he'd be equally enthused. Instead, he got alarmed for my safety and asked me, "What are you doing listening to that rabble rouser? He's nothing but a troublemaker." It was an early introduction for me to the danger of thinking that simply being Black implied a shared, monolithic perspective or experience. It would never have occurred to me that all whites thought alike or experienced the world the same way, yet here I was ascribing only one shared reality based on melanin and phenotype.

Over the years I've done all the "right" things to show my antiracist identity. I marched against apartheid and the treatment of undocumented people, I've joined antiracist coalitions and been to antiracist conferences, and I've tried to support colleagues and students of color by leveraging my white privilege whenever possible. But I still see the identity of a "good white person" (Sullivan, 2014) claiming its self-congratulatory hold on me. It's so easy to fall into thinking that now I'm one of the good guys who's rid himself of racist conditioning and that my work is done. I have to remind myself constantly that racial awareness is something I can opt into or out of as I wish, the complete opposite of the reality experienced by people of color.

So if I see the impossibility of my ever embracing a fully antiracist identity, why would I even try? Well, not to do something is unacceptable. That sense that there is no option other than acting has hardened and deepened over the years the more that I see racism in action. It really is no simpler than that, at least for me. To treat people as if they are less than human is wrong, so if you see it happening you have to try to do something about it. If something is unfair, it must be identified as such and remedied. I hate racism in myself and I hate to see it in the world around me. I have anger and outrage and I nurture that flame as a positive force for action in my life. Trying to become a white antiracist is just the right thing to do.

Mary's Story

It feels like a daunting task to share my story after Stephen's. He is the scholar whose work I have revered and hungrily read for years. His analyses drew me deeply into my field, and have sustained me long since. The stories he just shared here underline what we are about in this book in so many ways. Rather than try to replicate his "voice," he has urged and encouraged, in some cases frustrated and challenged me, to speak from my own place. So that's what I will do here.

I grew up in Oshkosh, Wisconsin, on the shores of Lake Winnebago. I was 5 when we moved there, and my mom still lives in the house I grew up in. Place matters. Place teaches. And the names of these places echo through me these days—not simply as places I knew as a child, but as the names of native peoples forced out of that territory.

Back when I was growing up these names only meant home to me. It wasn't until much later in life that I learned about Chief Oshkosh of the Menominee nation, and of the Winnebago or Ho-Chunk nation, let alone other stories of the native peoples pushed out of Wisconsin. Back then the people living in my home town were white.

I grew up learning about race as something "other" people had. I learned that there were certain words I should never speak out loud—even though my grandfather used them—because they would earn harsh discipline from my mom. But I also learned that race wasn't something I should worry about; it wasn't part of "my" identity.

In sixth grade I had my first best friend, someone who cared about the same things I did, someone who loved to read, who was great at math, who pondered questions about God and religion. That friend was also someone with dark skin, who frequently told people, "I'm not Black!" I knew, on some deep level, that the distinction between being the child of parents from India who had come as professors to the local university campus and not "one of them" (that is, someone who was Black) mattered, but I didn't understand why.

The distinctions that made the most impact on me were economic ones—who could afford to buy the latest fad in jeans, who had what brand of sneaker, who could easily go on the school trips that were offered. I was not one of those fortunate ones. Instead I was the child growing up in a single-parent home, the child who wore hand-me-downs, who flinched when my mother had to use food stamps at the grocery store, who knew that money was something you never talked about but always had to think about.

I grew up knowing that small distinctions make big differences, and that I wanted to escape from the constant nagging worry about money. I also learned that community mattered, and that even though I had to wear hand-me-downs, at least I had them. I knew that the people in our church may have felt sorry for us, but they also valued us. I learned that the world was not fair, but that we could and should strive to make it so. Those values grew deep roots in my soul, and when I left Oshkosh for the East Coast, to attend the rarified epitome of scholarship that was the Yale of my imagination, I brought them with me.

My first year at Yale I had four roommates, two of whom were Jewish, one of whom was Korean American, and one of whom was white like me. I was transformed by Yale in ways I doubt that that institution intended. I learned early on that privilege and private school education didn't guarantee fairness or openness. I learned that there were whole worlds I had no experience with or even knowledge of, and that some of those worlds looked like nothing I had imagined. I encountered all sorts of power, and learned that access to power could bring with it the smallest and meanest of actions.

But I was also very lucky. My 1st-year roommates had distinguished parents who were highly successful in their fields. Fortunately for me these parents had taught their daughters about fairness and openness. I never quite "fit in" but I was always welcomed by them, and in the tumult of that 1st year my roommates provided a safe space for me.

Looking for some place at Yale that felt like home, I finally fell in with the Chaplain's Office and an organization that had space on campus but was not owned by Yale. Dwight Hall was the offspring of an old student

YMCA, and it beat with the heartbeats of justice, equity, and action. In the early 1970s Dwight Hall had provided neutral ground when conflicts with the Black Panthers raged across New Haven. The chaplain at that time was William Sloane Coffin, and his legacy of activism for peace and justice lived on into the '80s when I arrived. Dwight Hall became my home and, alongside of the many centers of power and wealth that operated at Yale, it introduced me to people who were using their access to power and wealth as a lever to open up other possibilities for everyone.

By the time I entered my sophomore year I found myself deeply immersed in the challenges facing New Haven, which at that time was the seventh poorest city of its size in the United States. The economic disparities I had grown up with were deepening across that city in the early years of the Reagan administration, and I searched desperately for ways to make sense of the injustices I was encountering alongside of the immense wealth and power that was Yale. I knew somehow deep in my soul that there had to be ways I could still be committed to openness and fairness. I knew that as a "Yalie" I had no real idea of what the people of New Haven were living with, but I also felt like I had more in common with them than I did with the bulk of the student body.

My sophomore year roommates were yet another set of vivacious and fascinating women. Two of them were Black, from very different contexts. One had grown up in the heart of the Black community of New York, and along with her elegant stride and passionate diction she introduced me to her Rastafarian boyfriend. The other had gone to elite private schools that were majority white, and her father was a pilot for Air France. Both of these young women had access to wealth and social strata that I had no experience with. I lurked around the edges of their vivid debates, enjoying the compelling ways they argued about what it could mean to build a just and open society and learning viscerally that what it means to be Black in the United States cannot be contained in any one story. These were my first close friends who were Black, and their brilliance, compassion, and integrity were a revelation to me. So, too, were the everyday hurts they endured.

Up until that point I had had no awareness of the mundane ways in which people of color are constantly reminded that they are not white. I slowly began to learn small things, such as how walking into a Yale dining room for my roommates meant immediately scanning the room to see if anyone else of color was there. I was deeply blessed that they were willing to share their stories with me, but I was also deeply perturbed at how utterly ignorant I was. I knew how much it hurt when I couldn't do the things someone else was going to do because I didn't have the funds to do so—but I had no idea that there were whole other worlds of pain all around me to which I was completely oblivious.

I didn't like that feeling. I had grown up knowing I was smart, and that had been a personal bulwark against the slights I felt around money. But here I was learning how stupid I was, how ignorant and unthinkingly cruel I had been. Having borne the brunt of other people's unthinking stupidity around poverty, I did not in any way want to cause such pain to anyone else for any reason. Of course, simply becoming aware was no guarantee of good action, or of even having the first clue as to what I could do with such awareness.

My two other roommates that sophomore year, both of whom were white, had also lived comfortably and enjoyed elements of Yale that were foreign to my experience. They began to be drawn into other parts of Yale, and I grew more and more uncomfortable with the place.

Three of us moved off campus the next year—my two Black roommates to a downtown apartment and I to a co-op house of activists. Our paths diverged at that point, as I became more and more caught up in systemic analysis of the economic privileges Yale enjoyed, and more involved in resistance to Reaganism. My last 2 years at Yale were spent deep in the study of mass movements and social change. I had stumbled into both the American Studies Department—at that time the only bastion of Marxism left at Yale—and the Divinity School, whose faculty in those years included Cornel West, Letty Russell, and Margaret Farley (three central theologians in the movement for justice within Christian community).

Analyses of race, economic power, sexuality, and gender were the conceptual frameworks that energized me. I grew further and further away from Yale as a school and more and more into the activism of the streets. We fought for a clerical and technical workers' union, we fought against apartheid, we walked with people in the early stages of the HIV/AIDS epidemic, we spent time getting arrested in an effort to shed light on the Reagan government's actions in Central America. It was an energizing and vivid time in my life, and the work of collective solidarity and communal hope has remained with me through all the following years.

When I graduated from Yale in 1985 I vowed I would never go back to school, never put a book on a dusty shelf that no one would ever read, and always work for justice. Thirty years later I find myself a professor of educational leadership in a Christian graduate theological school.

The story of how that came to be is probably longer than makes sense to share in this brief introduction, but the heartbeat throughout all of it has been my deep desire to live in a just world, to live in ways that do not bring hurt or shame to people, to embody the fairness and openness that took root in me in my childhood. Yale taught me, perhaps against its institutional commitments, that injustice is rampant in our world, and that power over people—whether that power is exercised structurally through hierarchies, politically through narrow targeted organizing, therapeutically in how *health* and *wellness* are defined within white supremacy, or symbolically in all of the content of all of the stories of dominance that swirl around us—being able to exert power over people is central to many of our most "cherished" notions of what it means to be American. My family, my roommates, my fellow activists in New Haven taught me that there is power in shared action, and that a first step toward growing such *power with* (rather than power over) is acknowledging the realities of the world through listening to, and really hearing, the stories of those most hurt by specific systems.

My eyes often hurt as I open up to the stories of people who inhabit much different contexts and experiences than those I grew up with, as I "see" them more fully and come to know how I am implicated in their pain. Audre Lorde was one of the first authors to invite me to see in this way, and the writing of women of color continues to be a profound resource in my learning journey. She was not writing to or about me. Yet her vivid imagery and passionate convictions about love, anger, justice, and hope gave me something upon which to base my nascent feeling that there was more to the world than the stories of success and domination that fueled my undergraduate environment.

Audre Lorde (1978) taught me that there is something deeply grounding and powerful about connecting to other human beings—indeed, to all of creation—in ways that help us to "re-member" each other. I am a theologian and at the heart of that vocation, at least as I understand it, is the journey to become ever more deeply aware of human interdependency, of all the ways in which we belong to each other, even those whom we may fear as enemies.

James Baldwin (1984) once wrote, "I imagine one of the reasons why people cling to their hates so stubbornly is because they sense, once hate is gone, they will be forced to deal with pain" (p. 101). I work to dismantle racism because there is so much pain embedded in that system. I have learned over time that the anger many white people express when issues of race are brought up is precisely what Baldwin was pointing to—a mask that is placed over deep pain. And I want to bear witness here to that pain—both the unending pain of people of color experiencing the sharp end of the stick that is systemic racism and the pain of white people who have had to submerge and deny their awareness of interconnected relationship in order to remain complicit with racism. I also want to bear witness, however, to the hope and the joy that lives on the other side of acknowledgment, that lives in the energy of shared collective action in pursuit of justice, that is embodied in uncovering the lies of racism and leaning into the truths of shared human being.

My heart has been broken many times over the last decades as I listen to, learn from, and encounter the many ways in which human beings can hurt each other. Still, I keep striving to have my heart broken open—to adapt Palmer's (2011) language—rather than broken into shards. Learning what it means to be white in the racialized United States has given me a great deal of pain, but that pain has opened me up more thoroughly to joy and love and justice than anything else I have ever done.

My hope in the pages to come is that Stephen and I can continue to bear witness to racism and the struggle to dismantle it in ways that enliven, energize, and embody living justly in this world.

I

WHY WE NEED WHITE ANTIRACISM

Writing 60 years ago, James Baldwin observed that for whites to lose their innocent belief that they live in a humane country, they had to experience an upheaval in their universe that profoundly attacked their sense of their own reality. Even those whites who saw through the idea of white supremacy found it difficult to act on that awareness. In Baldwin's (1962) always prescient words: "To act is to be committed, and to be committed is to be in danger. In this case, the danger, in the minds of most white Americans, is the loss of their identity" (p. 9). This book invites you into danger, into thinking through what it means to lose an unconscious, unwitting white supremacist white identity and embrace a new one, a proudly antiracist white identity.

We need this book. By "we," we mean the two of us, your two authors. Both of us have spent many years addressing white supremacy and racism in different contexts and struggling to find a way through all the contradictions, dilemmas, and emotions inherent to such work. We have worked with many schools, colleges, and universities, but also with seminaries, community groups, health care, congregations, arts organizations, social movements, nonprofits, the military, corporations, businesses, and many other settings. Because of where we live—St. Paul, Minnesota—we have almost always found ourselves doing that work in predominantly white environments. Over the years we have noticed that most of the institutional members, learners, and participants in community organizations we encounter (and also many of their leaders, staff developers, and teachers) see race-based work with whites as focusing mostly on understanding the benefits of diversity and inclusion, and on trying to support the BIPOC minority in the organization. There's usually a strong emphasis on cultural competency, on working in ways that are sensitive to different cultural traditions.

We heartily support efforts at inclusion and culturally responsive practice. But we are also struck by the fact that much diversity, equity, and inclusion (DEI) work does not focus on whiteness—particularly on understanding what it means to have a white racial identity, how whites learn and enact white supremacy, and the way white supremacy ensures the continuance of racism. It's quite possible, in our experience, to attend a diversity training event and never hear the words *racism, white supremacy,* or even *white racial identity.* In the work we've done we've found that when we shift the focus onto racism, white supremacy, and white identity, our primarily white audiences often become skeptical and bemused.

Consequently, we've had many conversations where we've asked each other for advice and for leads on good resources. When we do this we usually end up decrying the lack of a book, written from the perspective of learning, that focuses on how to help white people develop an antiracist identity. Both of us are educators, and although we both engage in antiracist work outside our professional roles, we are always interested in the dynamics of learning. But we've never been able to find the book we really needed—a book that explores how to help whites learn what an antiracist white identity entails, and that details what it means to enact that identity in everyday actions and practices in both individual and collective ways.

So, quite simply, we decided to write the book that we needed! As it turned out the years we spent writing it—2019 and 2020—were incredibly tumultuous ones involving catastrophic climate change, a global pandemic, and economic collapse. For us, though, the most significant upheavals were those around racial justice. We were inspired by the Black Lives Matter movement, outraged by the growth of anti-Blackness in the United States, and staggered by the way it became legal to tear immigrant families apart at the U.S. border and imprison children like animals in cages. Each week brought further instances of the slaughter of people of color and the demonization of anyone not of white European descent. The murders of Philando Castile in the St. Paul suburb of Falcon Heights and of George Floyd in Minneapolis brought things home to our doorsteps and we became used to police helicopters over our houses, looters running through our yards, constant demonstrations, and the smell of smoke and tear gas.

When we would tell friends, family, and colleagues about the book we were writing on creating an antiracist white identity, people would say, "We need that book!" Then, as word of the book spread and we were invited to teach courses, run workshops, speak to community groups and congregations, people would ask, "When's it coming out? We need it!" For a while we felt the pressure to hurry the book up but then we realized that whether or not the book was published 2 months or 2 years in the future was really immaterial. It wasn't as if racism was going to go away! And we kept telling ourselves that the events and outrages that were foremost in our minds as we were writing specific chapters would be replaced by many others, equally murderous and violent, by the time the book appeared in print and online.

Why a Book on an Antiracist White Identity?

Many best sellers on race and racism are written by people of color who chronicle the lived experience of being on the receiving end of racism. Acclaimed experts on race and racism, and most professionals in charge of DEI offices and initiatives, are also people of color. So it's not surprising that most whites typically look—as the two of us often do—to people of color when we're trying to figure out what being antiracist really means. There are, of course, exceptions to this—witness the enormous popularity of Robin DiAngelo's (2018) work on white fragility.

But we feel there are traps in automatically turning to people of color to educate whites like us about racism. First, this instinctive and seemingly obvious choice underscores the mistaken notion that race is a problem of people of color. Our position is that *race is really a problem of white people.* That's because racism is the process by which one racial group entrenches its power over all other groups by enforcing the idea (through policies, institutional practices, and cultural habits) that the dominant racial group deserves its position of superiority. In the United States, the dominant racial group is white.

Whites maintain their racial power by persuading all racial groups to internalize a view of the world that accepts this situation as normal and natural, as just the way that things are. This view of the world is the core of white supremacy, the idea that, because of their supposedly superior intelligence and greater capacity to use logic and reason to come to objective decisions, white people should naturally be in positions of power and authority. As long as whites have an unexamined white supremacist worldview lodged in their consciousness, they won't see the need to involve themselves in any effort to bring about sustained change. Why would they? After all, in their minds it's not their problem, is it? So understanding how white supremacy is learned, how it becomes so deeply internalized, is crucial to dismantling racism.

Second, always turning to people of color to take on the work of teaching whites about racism, while the same time they are trying to negotiate a white supremacist world, is an unfair division of labor. Fighting everyday racism takes an enormous psychic and physical toll and requires constant networking, collective organizing, and the provision of emotional sustenance (Solomon & Rankin, 2019). To survive in a war against white supremacy takes everything you have and leaves you bone tired, even when faith and community lift you up. So it's exhausting for BIPOC individuals to be asked to devote effort to educating whites about their racial cluelessness. Those people of color who do find the time and emotional energy to work with whites in this way are committing an enormous act of generosity.

Perhaps even more troubling, though, is that expecting people of color always to take the lead in educating whites about racism removes any responsibility from the shoulders of whites of having to think through the next steps they should take. Too often we've seen whites turn to people of color and ask, quite innocently, "What should we do?" And, equally frequently, we've seen people of color reply, often exasperatedly, "Work it out for yourself." When pressed further they will usually say, "Find out about what it means to be white. Become aware of your own white identity and how that affects how you navigate the world." So we need books that help white people think through what it means to have a white racial identity and how to get other whites involved in developing an antiracist white identity.

The biggest problem to achieving any measure of racial justice, however you define that slippery and contested term, is the continuing existence of the ideology of white supremacy. As long as the idea that whites are innately superior flourishes in people's consciousness and is enacted in institutional behaviors, cultural messages, and political policies, racism will continue largely intact. So for us, helping whites become aware of the ideology that legitimizes their power is a major antiracist project.

Of course, becoming aware of one's whiteness and what that means for your life is the start, not the end, of developing an antiracist identity. We don't think you can be seriously antiracist without a thorough understanding of how your whiteness benefits you, of how it means you don't have to deal with the consequences of being perceived as a person of color in the United States. But too often we've seen whites (including ourselves) think that by simply becoming aware of white privilege they have somehow transformed themselves into becoming white antiracists. Just being aware of racism, and deploring and condemning it, doesn't mean you are antiracist. As a white person you can quote W.E.B. Du Bois, Paul Robeson, Rosa Parks, James Baldwin, Angela Davis, Malcolm X, and Audre Lorde. You can wear Black Lives Matter caps and T-shirts. You can send around videos of Kimberly Latrice Jones, Alicia Garza, or Opal Tometi. But as you do those things your whiteness means that the system still continues to advantage you and you can continue enacting multiple racial microaggressions without being aware of that fact.

Understanding how racism and white supremacy work allows you to see the system in action and is a helpful precursor to getting involved in changing it. But an antiracist identity is only truly realized when you take individual and collective action to challenge white supremacy. An antiracist white identity is inherently activist.

Why Confronting Racism Is Necessary for White Mental Health

When white people are asked why they are interested in becoming antiracist, they typically cite the need to stop the violence and cruelty enacted against people of color. They will talk of the need for racial justice; of the loss of life, hope, and talent represented by mass incarceration and police murder of unarmed people of color; and the corrosive effects of not challenging a political economy built on slavery and genocide.

When the two of us speak of these antiracist motivations, we typically get a lot of approval from white colleagues, students, and friends who consider themselves "woke" or who think of themselves as trying to live a better, antiracist life. Sometimes people of color also express appreciation, although it's often tinged with an unspoken sentiment: "Duh! How did it take you so long to see what's going on in front of your eyes?" A dynamic we've often observed in multiracial settings is whites earnestly striving to testify to their commitment to antiracism, while people of color are forced to sit and listen to a series of confessionals along the lines of "I used to be racist but now the scales are lifted from my eyes and I see injustice everywhere."

Our advice is that you should assume that people of color are tired of having to confer blessings and absolution on whites who desperately need to know that people of color see them as allies, as good white people (Sullivan, 2014). BIPOC folks have probably been burned by countless instances in which white folk profess a commitment to antiracism and then don't follow through with the daily hard work of calling out white supremacy whenever they see or enact it.

When explaining why you as a white person are interested in becoming antiracist, we advocate considering taking a different tack that may seem at first to be counterintuitive—the tack of selfishness, of personal interest. Following the advice of two white men—Tim Wise in *White Like Me* (2011) and Chris Crass in *Towards Collective Liberation* (2013) and *Towards the "Other America"* (2015)—we suggest that people of color will be far more likely to take your antiracist expressions seriously—at least initially—if you talk about the fact that you're doing this for yourself, that it's in *your* own best interest to do so.

In many ways, striving to become an antiracist white person is motivated by a concern for your own mental health as much as anything else. This is because if you accept the myth of white supremacy, then at some deep level you know that you're living a lie. And living this way is deeply alienating. You know that who you really are—a fallible, imperfect being struggling to make sense of the contradictions and complexities of daily existence—is not who white supremacy has told you that you are. White supremacy tells you that you're superior to people of color and that that's why you deserve your relative wealth, power, and privilege. Your supposedly elevated intelligence and ability to make calm, logical decisions mean that you, or people like you, should quite naturally control the levers of power. White supremacy also tells you that people of color should be kept marginalized and barred from positions of influence because of their imputed volatility, emotionality, and irrationality.

But every day you encounter clear empirical evidence that white people are *not* inherently more humane, rational, intelligent, or reasonable than people of color. Equally, you see the reality of humanity, compassion, strength, resilience, and a clear-eyed focus on the prize of racial justice among colleagues and friends of color. You see video of trigger-happy cops, rousting people of color and responding to benign and compliant actions by emptying their magazines into Black bodies. Processing this either forces you to a 180-degree reconsideration of the identity narrative you've been sold—whites are calm and reasonable and people of color are unpredictable and violent—or it triggers a convoluted reordering of the truth you've witnessed whereby cops' actions are always justified by a real and immediate threat to their lives.

So in many ways, being white means you're at war with yourself. On the one hand, you've been conditioned to think that your racial identity as white means that you, and others like you, constitute the norm of how a human being should think, feel, and act. On the other hand, the world constantly illustrates to you the insanity of that belief.

When you live a life as a white person based on racial lies, you have to spend a lot of emotional energy maintaining an untenable fiction. It's almost a form of racial schizophrenia. Your socially constructed racial DNA tells you that you constitute the preferred norm, that you represent the universal standard of how people should behave. Your daily reality, however, teaches you the opposite. So deconstructing the myth of white supremacy is really necessary for your mental health. That's why thinking through, and acting on, the need to be a white antiracist is really a selfish act of personal survival. If you don't try to do this, you'll go crazy.

There's another selfish reason why you need to try to develop a white antiracist identity. If you accept the myth of white supremacy, then you live in a state of constant fear. When you're accused of racism, you have to expend a lot of emotional energy explaining it away by insisting that you're really a good person, that your actions and words didn't mean anything or intend to harm, and that you've been misunderstood or misinterpreted. Every time you witness righteous anger expressed by people of color, white supremacy tells you this is further evidence of "their" volatility and emotional instability. You start thinking about buying a gun, about preparing for the race war that must be coming.

Living in this state of constant fear is a psychosocial cancer that eats away at your well-being. Being constantly afraid of coming disruption and planning how to respond when it happens is exhausting.

Of course, living with the very real fear of death is the lifelong reality of so many people of color. For them reaching inside your jacket gets you killed. Talking back gets you killed. Not complying quietly and immediately with commands gets you killed. And sometimes complying with those same commands gets you killed anyway. White fear is exhausting but the two of us don't live our lives knowing that we're marked by law enforcement as potentially unstable and uncontrollable, liable to explode into irrational violence at any moment.

Finally, living with learned racism is an act of self-denial, of cutting yourself off from pleasure. Living in fear of a BIPOC planet means you forego access to the alterity of experience. The project of life, and the chief social learning task of adulthood, is understanding that your experience, no matter how varied and multifaceted that might be, is still only that—*your* experience. Coming to the realization that you share space with people who experience life in a bewildering variety of ways is sometimes threatening, particularly if that realization means that your assumptions about how the world works are shattered. But it's also beautifully sensuous. It opens you up to new realities and to the joy of complexity. Human growth and development are premised on the promise of transformation, of coming to understand that the world is not settled and that the future is in fact open to your invention. Living with a white supremacist consciousness, in which the category of whiteness constitutes the settled standard for how to live life, stops you in your tracks and prevents you from exploring the sensuous shades of experience the world offers.

What's So Important About a *White* Antiracist Identity?

This is a book about one particular racial group that we refer to as "white." This term is a shorthand description of a racial category and is, like all such terms, problematic, porous, and inconsistent (Bazelon, 2018). For example, in the United States, those who are thought of as white has changed over time (Painter, 2015) and debates have always existed about who can be considered authentically white (Yancey, 2003). And, of course, to lump everyone that a particular classification considers white into one generic category and assume an essential similarity or shared identity between them is crazy. Just like any other group, those of us considered white on a census form or job application have multiple other identities and exhibit enormous differences.

When we use the term *white* we use it to mean Americans of European descent, even though they may refer to themselves by their nationality (Italian, Swedish, Irish) or ethnicity (Jewish). Those in this broad category of "white" typically don't think of themselves as raced, because to them racial identity is usually associated only with people of color. Whites will often say they know nothing about race, never think about race, and are therefore unqualified to enter into a conversation about it. But white people have specific characteristics that set them up for a particular role in race talk.

First, whites are the experts on white supremacy. For example, the two of us (like almost every other white person we know) can speak with some experiential authority about how white supremacy is learned and transmitted. We can testify to the power of stereotyping and the way we learn to do that via family stories and jokes with peers. We know the ease of slipping into casual white-on-white racism and how hard it sometimes is to interrupt racist talk in gatherings where racism is allowed, even encouraged and celebrated. In particular, we know how whites "other" people of color by speaking of them as exotic or dangerous, by highlighting their physical prowess or possession of "soul." Othering does not necessarily involve denigration. Whites can admire the sporting and artistic achievements of people of color in a way that positions these as delightful deviations from the generally accepted inferior and unsophisticated norm.

Second, your identity as a white person means that you occupy a particular position within antiracist work. You will be mistrusted by people of color as a tourist enacting optical allyship, as someone looking for the affirmation of people of color so that you can think of yourself as a "good white person" (Sullivan, 2014). But you have the privilege conferred on you by your whiteness of being able to say and do things that would bring much harsher penalties down on the heads of people of color. If you choose to make race an issue in a community meeting, workshop, class, or casual conversation, you won't be accused of playing the race card or of having a narrow racial agenda. And you will probably make further unchallenged inroads into white centers of power while still being taken seriously, compared to a person of color. So one of the things you will have to figure out as a white person is how to leverage the privilege and strategic advantages you have as you work for racial justice.

Third, your whiteness means you have the specific task within antiracist work of focusing on teaching other whites. Whites teaching other whites about whiteness has its own very particular dynamics, and you will need to understand these as you go forward. You will probably spend a lot of time learning how to model critical reflection on your struggles to work, act, and practice in antiracist ways. As a white person your unique mission is to help other intimidated white friends and colleagues engage in antiracist action, while simultaneously revealing and analyzing how you are constantly screwing up, committing multiple racial microaggressions, and feeling naïve, unqualified, and uninformed.

Why We Need to Understand Racism as Systemic, Not Individual

We want to make sure that we introduce in this chapter a clarification of what we mean by *racism*. When we teach courses and workshops, or when we lead meetings, we often find white folks interpreting being antiracist as the project of ridding themselves of the implicit biases and racial stereotypes they hold as individuals. They see being antiracist as an act of personal cleansing, of ideological detoxification. In their minds the end result will be their emerging with a new identity in which they will commit no more racial microaggressions and be free of racist instincts and impulses.

Of course, these are important projects and we wouldn't want to dissuade organizations and institutions from running programs that promote these purposes, or individuals from pursuing them. But we do want to underscore what for us is a central truth of racism—that it should always be understood as systemic.

Racism is a system that is designed to perpetuate the power of one particular racial group over others. This system is maintained by laws and policies and supported by state, judicial, and paramilitary power. When the system works as it's designed, it has the effect of disproportionately benefiting one racial group who are at the top of the American caste system (Wilkerson, 2020). In the United States that group is white people. This is why, when white critics say the system is dysfunctional, people of color will often reply with the opposite sentiment—the system is extremely functional in the terms it sets itself. The system works very well to keep the dominant white group in power via a whole set of institutional disparities—what Lipsitz (2018) described as the possessive investment in whiteness.

So, for example, redlining mortgage policies ensure that people of color cannot get loans to purchase property in areas that are predominantly white. People of color live in the poorest areas where property taxes are insufficient to fund good schools and proper health care. The higher levels of education correlated with professional jobs are thus closed off, meaning that minimum wage jobs in the service economy are disproportionately filled by people of color. When people of color find themselves in supposedly integrated public schools, the racist stereotype that they are less academic and less intelligent ensures a de facto resegregation whereby they are much more likely to be automatically placed in groups, classes, and streams that have low academic expectations. Environmental law allows for the dumping of toxic waste in poor areas that are inhabited disproportionately by people of color. The securing in the public mind of the innate criminality of black, brown, and indigenous people means that they are then targeted for arrest and conviction, resulting in the school-to-prison pipeline.

The individual behaviors mentioned earlier—holding and acting on racial biases, subscribing to stereotype threat, making racist jokes—are all reflections of this system. If we focus only on eliminating these individual behaviors, we're not tackling their cause, that is, of course, the wider racist system. So, although working on individual enactments of racism is important, it's only one part of the story. Organizing to change the system is the real way you live out a commitment to white antiracism.

Where Is White Supremacy in All This?

How is it that the system reproduces itself successfully for most of the time? Well, that's because people accept it as the natural way the world is ordered. Having people think a certain way, without their even being aware that this viewpoint is constructed, secures and legitimizes white power. This is because the ideology of white supremacy is in place.

White supremacy is the ideological bulwark of racism. It's a simple idea, a worldview that becomes accepted as obvious and commonsense, a way of explaining and justifying the racial disparities we see around us. White supremacy turns these humanly created and enforced disparities into a law of nature, as detached from, and impermeable to, human intervention as the weather.

At the heart of white supremacy is the idea that white people, because they are supposedly more intelligent than other racial groups, should be in positions of power and authority. White supremacy holds that whites deserve to be in these positions because they use reason at a higher level than BIPOC folk. Whites are deemed to be better at staying calm in a crisis and making good, objective decisions based solely on evidence. Under white supremacy, "logic assumes a historical posture that grants eternal objectivity to the views

of elite Whites and condemns the views of non-Whites to perpetual subjec-
tivity" (Bonilla-Silva & Zuberi, 2008, p. 17). The ability to think and act
logically is conflated with white racial identity. People of color are deemed
to think anecdotally, to rely on personal experience and exercise an undue
amount of emotion in decision-making, in contrast to whites' capacity to use
clear, calm, cold, remorseless logic.

White supremacy also contends that people of color can't be trusted
with power and authority and shouldn't occupy positions of responsibility,
because they are too volatile and unpredictable. They are seen as governed
not by reason, but rather driven by animalistic instinct that will, if not kept
in check, undeniably turn violent. Their decision-making is viewed as fundamentally flawed because it is held to reflect personal predilection, rather than
an objective assessment of data. Most ironically, whites argue that decisions
should not be handed over to people of color because any decisions they
make will reflect their racial interests and further a racialized agenda. This
despite the fact that white supremacy has ensured that policy and practice
since the founding of the Republic of the United States has furthered a racial
agenda of cementing white power and authority so as to make it appear as
the natural state of the universe.

This idea is the glue that holds systems in place. If the stereotypes of
white supremacy are broadly accepted, then all the educational, economic,
health, penal, and environmental inequities mentioned earlier are seen as
completely explicable. When the two of us use the term *white supremacy*, we
don't use it to describe its most extreme and violent manifestations in white
power and white nationalist groups. We use it instead to refer to the broadly
accepted idea of innate white superiority and the way that outlook legitimizes the continued existence of massive racial disparities.

We should point out that it is possible for someone to say that they're
antiracist while also being in thrall to white supremacy. The two of us are
living examples of that apparently contradictory state. We both strive to
change a racist system in institutional and individual ways, but we both have
the legacy of white supremacist consciousness within us. We can fight against
it and be more alert for its presence, but it will never be completely erased.
This consciousness has been so deeply sedimented in us that it makes it hard
for us to notice the daily interactions with, and enactments of, racism that
we encounter on a daily basis. Sometimes we don't notice them for what they
really are because we've been very successfully socialized into assuming that
that's just the way the world works.

Finally, it's important to understand the economic context for white
supremacy. Although white supremacy appears to be concerned only with
race and race hatred, it's actually just as much an economic tool to justify,

first, slavery, then Jim Crow, and now the miseducation of people of color to staff the service economy of low-paid, part-time jobs with no security or health care. It's an ideological con trick to stop a working-class movement developing that organizes for fairly paid jobs, education, and health care. As Crass (2015) observed, white supremacy tells the white working class that people of color

> are cheats and criminals . . . who are stealing from white America directly or have pulled a con and are stealing from white America collectively— through welfare, food stamps, or by taking unionized public sector jobs or spots in college away from more qualified whites through Affirmative Action. (p. 23)

This divide-and-rule strategy is one way to blunt the development of a working-class movement.

Our Five Basic Understandings

So there you have it, our initial justification as to why we need this book! To sum up, our text is premised on five basic understandings:

- We need as white people to confront racism because it's morally wrong, but also because it's in the interest of our own mental health to do so.
- We need to take responsibility for doing the work of white antiracism and not asking people of color to educate us about how racism works.
- We need to work out how best to use the strategic advantages conferred on us by a white identity to push for change and racial justice.
- We need to understand racism as a system that works to secure the continued dominance of one particular racial group, rather than the expression of individual prejudice.
- We need to challenge the way that the mythical but powerful idea of white supremacy keeps this system in place by explaining it as a "natural" ordering of the world.

2

WHAT IS A WHITE ANTIRACIST IDENTITY?

In recent years the overt expression of white supremacist ideas has become an acceptable part of political discourse. White men in particular "continue to construct and reproduce an array of sincere fictions about white America and white Americans" (Feagin & O'Brien, 2003, p. 93), such as that whiteness itself is a disadvantage and that, like dinosaurs, white men are becoming extinct. At the heart of these fantasies is "the idea that whites are victimized by other racial groups" (Rodriguez, 2008, p. 124). More than any other time in the lives of the two of us, racism and its ideological handmaiden—white supremacy—have been legitimized by the words and actions of politicians, policymakers, elected officials, police, and major media outlets.

Yet, contradictorily, we hear more and more calls to embrace diversity. Corporations that need to maximize profits by expanding markets, colleges that need to attract students from diverse racial backgrounds in order to stay afloat, and nonprofits bound by antidiscrimination law, all seek to establish programs that proclaim the benefits of diversity and inclusion. These efforts present themselves as being inspired by the need to acknowledge the value and dignity of every human being, and the recognition that diverse human experiences enhance intellectual, community, and political life. Predominantly white organizations and institutions often create special offices of diversity or inclusion, typically staffed by the only person of color in the senior leadership team.

The two of us celebrate the alterity of experience and the benefits of communicating across difference. We both share a commitment to diversity that emphasizes the valuing of all human individuals and an acknowledgment that difference illuminates and expands our understanding of the human experience. We both subscribe to Habermas's (1990) contention that

24

the signal that you're entering into adulthood is when you stop universalizing your own experience. Diversity workshops that encourage people to broaden their intercultural awareness and to recognize their implicit cultural biases are good things to have in any institution.

But as leaders and participants in many diversity and inclusion initiatives, we have a pretty cynical view of the assumptions informing these efforts. Despite the sincere intentions of those involved, we find that diversity and inclusion are all too often flattened into an equal embrace of all views and all people. The emphasis is placed on individuals embracing alternative perspectives rather than the need for collective mobilization to push back against racist systems and structures. In diversity efforts whites are often placed as the central actors who learn to open themselves up to other racial experiences. In this way diversity efforts often *underscore* the power of whiteness. Rarely are white people in the institution "explicitly talked about as a group in the same ways that students, faculty, and staff of color are" (Kendall, 2013, p. 168).

Missing from many of the efforts we've observed is attention to the power attached to different racial identities, the manner in which a racist system acts as a very real enforcement mechanism designed to benefit one racial group—Euro-Americans or, more simply, whites. Oluo (2018) wrote that "if you are white in a white supremacist society, you are racist" (p. 216). An antiracist identity built on an awareness of how whiteness is accorded greater material power and enhanced status is conspicuously absent from too much diversity, equity, and inclusion work. If developing an antiracist identity were at the center of diversity initiatives, then we would be analyzing inclusion and equity through the lens of power. We would be examining the process by which different racial identities are accorded different valuations judged against the universal standard of whiteness. This is why Outlaw (2004) proposed that whites becoming aware of their racial identity should be the chief antiracist project they undertake.

An antiracist orientation begins by focusing on how whiteness has come to be entrenched as the de facto way of assessing what it means to be human. It then moves to examining ways to challenge the unquestioned idea of white superiority and to interrupt the power of whites to be automatic gatekeepers, moralists, and policymakers across multiple institutions. Right now diversity education often focuses on whites learning about people of color. By way of contrast, antiracist education focuses on whites examining how the notion of innate white superiority is weaponized to ensure that people of color are kept from material, educational, and political advancement. An antiracist education teaches how to take action to challenge and dismantle white supremacy on both individual and collective levels.

How Diversity Is "Managed" to Avoid Antiracism

When predominantly white institutions are challenged by external pressure to address race—perhaps because of community outrage or legal mandate—a very predictable process ensues by which they manage threats to their authority and legitimacy. Instead of trying to oppose the threat to their legitimacy directly by discrediting those issuing the challenge or minimizing the nature of its importance, institutions respond in a far subtler and ultimately more effective way. They appear to take the challenge seriously by creating working parties, task forces, and advisory committees to document the racial grievances being brought to their attention. They make changes to their institutional functioning that appear substantive and important. For example, when accused of racist practices or a lack of diversity, they strive for greater representation of people of color in the images and materials they present to the world as depicting what the institution is about. This is usually followed by an effort to recruit more members of color into the organization. In higher education this means diversifying the student body, staff, and faculty. Often there are high-profile appointments of one or two people of color to the senior leadership team or the creation of a special diversity office.

But all these measures can be taken without any fundamental change to the structures of power within the organization. Whites will still be overwhelmingly in positions of institutional authority and, ensnared by the ideology of white supremacy, can continue to act in racist ways. To take just one small example, faculty of color are often hired specifically to teach the courses dealing with diversity and race in predominantly white universities. Their performance of this responsibility is at least partly assessed via student evaluation of teaching forms that ask students to rate how effective, clear, and responsive instructors have been in delivering content, explaining difficult material, addressing questions, and providing feedback. The results of these forms are then factored into reappointment and tenure decisions.

In a predominantly white institution the courses that are often most feared or disliked by white students are those dealing with race and diversity. Yet, to meet a diversity requirement, a certain number of these need to be taken. Faculty members of color show up and are deemed immediately by many students to be "playing the race card" in teaching this content and regarded as being intent on shaming, embarrassing, and making white students feel guilty for things they had no control over way back in history. As the class engages with more and more contentious issues, students feel like they are being forced to admit to being racist and that instructors of color are singling them out unfairly. Consequently, on the end-of-term evaluations of teaching they hammer the instructor for what they judge to be his or her pursuit of an unjustified and unrelenting focus on fictional racism. The faculty of color then has to justify poor teaching evaluations that have been occasioned by them simply doing their job—teaching the inherently raw and contentious topic of race. In this case all the power is in the hands of the white students filling out the forms and the white department chairs or deans reading them. White administrators will view faculty of color as "failing" because their teaching scores are poor. They are then quietly counseled to leave before tenure decisions become due and replaced by new hires who just repeat the cycle.

This whole process has been nicely described by Marcuse (1965) as repressive tolerance, the strategy by which organizations appear to change while still maintaining the status quo. On the surface it looks as though a major new institutional initiative has been launched. But the way this is implemented means that dominant ideology is unchallenged and white supremacy continues to frame daily practices, routines, and habits.

In this chapter we want to examine how to help whites in predominantly white institutions develop an antiracist identity. This involves thinking and acting in fundamentally different and more purposeful ways than those entailed by just embracing diversity. Of course, learning to develop and enact an antiracist identity is a journey that is never fully realized. As whites we are always *becoming* antiracist, never quite there. Racism is a system that has become so much a part of daily life that we who benefit from it, we who are complicit with it, have been taught not to see it. But at the outset of this book we think it's helpful to suggest a number of indicators or markers that would be in place if such an identity was being developed. These markers will be examined in much more detail throughout the chapters that follow, so for now we review them only briefly.

Antiracist Content and Curriculum

By *curriculum* we mean the typical content that would be the focus of any workshops, courses, or training institutes that might be offered in an antiracist program. Such a curriculum would emphasize the following:

- Moving people from an understanding of racism as committing acts of individual privilege and personal hatred or bigotry to seeing it as the way a system privileges the continuing power of one racial group.
- Understanding white supremacy as a dominant ideology that frames how people experience and act in the world. This ideology holds that because whites are judged self-evidently to be more intelligent, rational, objective, and logical than other racial groups, they should have the power to make decisions on how society's resources should be used for the good of all.

- Making clear how the stereotyping of people of color as emotional, unstable, unpredictable, less intelligent, and more unable to deploy rational thought keeps white superiority intact.
- Learning how whiteness is conceptualized as the universal and highest end point of human development. This idea informed how Christians of all denominations justified slavery. If slaves were believed to be subhuman, then treating them as if they were animals was no abomination. Contemporary racism enacts this same belief in overt and covert ways.
- Studying how the idea of white superiority outlined previously becomes broadly internalized and accepted as normal, natural common sense so that it informs how the institutions and systems in our society function. At a university, for example, recruitment efforts, admissions policies, standards for what counts as superior academic work, the racial makeup of the faculty and student bodies, disciplinary procedures—even something as basic as how people talk (or don't talk) about race—all take place within a frame where whiteness is the standard by which "human-ness" is assessed.
- Helping colleagues examine how the standards and procedures for assessing what counts as reliable knowledge—what Foucault (1980) called the regime of truth—reflect the dominance of white academic gatekeepers. For example, what are the racial identities of journal editors, handbook editors, conference overseers, and other disciplinary gatekeepers and how do they enforce specific conceptions of disciplinary intelligence and expertise?
- Developing structural thinking through which people are encouraged to analyze the connection between how institutions and systems operate and their own individual actions. This is where work on implicit bias and microaggressions comes into play.
- Understanding whiteness as a particular racial identity.
- Moving to develop a positive white identity in which feelings of shame, guilt, or resentment are replaced by an acknowledgment of whiteness as a racial identity like any other that can join in the common project of dismantling white supremacy.
- Helping white people focus not on the sins of their ancestors or their personal complicity in past racism, but on how they can help build institutions and communities that strive for racial equity.

Antiracist Practices in Organizations

By antiracist practices we mean the actions that people engage in as they enact living an antiracist identity. These might include the following:

- Calling out when repressive tolerance diverts attention away from structural change and into superficial indicators of improvement, thus neutralizing antiracist efforts.
- Illuminating how antiracist efforts are sabotaged by those whites who either believe racism is a myth or who fully understand how it benefits them.
- Developing procedures and protocols to hold individuals and institutions accountable for their enactment of racism.
- Learning how to stay constantly alert to the way racism still moves within us.
- Developing strategies to talk about racism in ways that keep the conversation going and help people live with the inevitable tension of realizing that fundamentally different ways of seeing the world coexist in groups, communities, and organizations.
- Bearing witness to the testimony of people of color.
- Learning how to organize collective efforts—small and large—to call out racism and push for racial equity.
- Deliberating collectively about what a racially equitable and inclusive community would look like and how it would function.
- Organizing and running conversations that focus on how racism manifests itself in everyday life.
- Learning how to analyze institutional and systemic practices and policies to reveal their racist dimensions.
- Organizing resistance to racism through institutional initiatives and community movements.
- Challenging white superiority and white normativity when it structures decision-making, policies, and practices.
- Calling out institutions and individuals for their explicit, but also their unacknowledged, racism.
- Holding ourselves accountable for our explicit, but also our unacknowledged, racism.
- Enacting antiracist change, both small and large scale, in specific environments.

How We Think as Antiracists

Antiracism is not just a set of things we study and a collection of practices. It also represents an epistemology, a way of seeing the world and judging how to assess what is truthful. Epistemology is the study of how we know what we know, and an antiracist epistemology focuses particularly on studying how patterns of thinking based in white supremacy, white privilege, and white normativity become accepted as truthful representations of the empirical world. We propose the following as elements of an antiracist epistemology.

Knowing That Race Is Not Real but Racism Is

A fundamental element of antiracist epistemology is the realization that race as a biologically determined category is a complete illusion. Race is not real, even as racism is very real. Racism benefits from the pseudoscientific sheen created around discussions of cultural conditioning that conflate culturally learned habits with biologically determined, essential differences. This is not to deny the existence of observable physical differences; clearly there are variations across humankind evident in skin color and phenotype in the shape of eyes, the texture of hair, the color of skin, structure of facial features, and so on. The problem is that under racism those insignificant biological differences are ascribed completely fictional genetic identities. So understanding that racial difference is a social construction is a fundamental marker of an antiracist way of thinking.

Along with recognizing the myth of biologically innate genetic differences goes the acknowledgment that pervasive racism is the enduring reality of American life. An antiracist epistemology spends no time debating whether or not racism exists—acknowledging that racism is real is the *sine qua non* of an antiracist consciousness. This is, of course, the backbone of a critical race theory perspective (Delgado & Stefancic, 2017) and it has significant implications for the conduct of antiracist practice. In diversity training white participants frequently express a color-blind view of the world, arguing that they don't see color, only actions, or that the past election of a Black president means that we are now living in a postracial world. Facilitators then have to counter that with personal testimony, documentary evidence, research, and statistics.

However, in antiracist training, the enduring permanence and pervasiveness of racism should be the taken-for-granted starting point. Trainers and leaders must refuse to go down the rabbit hole of proving to skeptics that racism is real, and instead reassert the purpose of the workshop as developing an antiracist identity and practice. Even though some participants are invariably disgruntled, the leader must assert her belief that we are here to combat racism, not to debate its existence. For us this is an ethical use of teacher power and authority.

How you assert the reality of racism differs, of course, depending on context. Insisting that discussing the possibility that racism doesn't really exist is off the table is *much* easier if you're overseeing an antiracist training event where people have volunteered to attend. At such a gathering you may never in fact hear such a viewpoint expressed. After all, if people have come to learn how to be antiracist of their own volition, it would be surprising indeed if they felt that racism wasn't actually real.

However, if you're running a mandatory attendance event in a predominantly white institution where people are coerced into attending, you'll possibly be facing many whites who flat out deny the existence of racism. They'll say (or feel) that race isn't a problem anymore, that talking about whiteness is unpatriotic, and that your session is a politically correct waste of time. In such a situation you can't just tell people they're wrong. Their experiences, their cultural conditioning, and the authority figures they trust and revere have all combined to convince them that racism isn't a problem. Dismissing these as inaccurate and wrongheaded means you're dismissing their whole beings, their identities, their cultures. Do this and you've just lost the chance for learning to happen.

As we emphasize throughout this book, people have a right to their deeply felt beliefs and opinions, even if you know in your core that these are the result of racist ideological manipulation. So, through anonymous social media tools such as Sli.do, Tweedback.de, and backchannelchat.com, we'll often start an event by giving participants the chance to express their resistance and convictions. We want them to know that we take what they believe seriously, and will allow them to explain why they hold the "racism doesn't really exist" viewpoint.

But then we as educators, leaders, and activists have a right to present our counter-narrative. We do this by modeling our own struggles with the white supremacy that lives within us and by presenting personal and digital narratives and testimonies from people of color and whites. We'll try to explain racism as structural, not personal, and show how being white historically constitutes a permanent structural advantage in the United States (Lipsitz, 2018). We may use terms such as *white advantage* if we judge that saying *white privilege* or *white supremacy* will initially cause people to switch off mentally for the duration of the training or meeting. We'll introduce some scenarios in which race is a central factor and ask people to interpret what's going on. Then we'll move them into various discussion protocols, all the while doing quick check-ins to see how they're reacting to the presentation of data that represents a 180-degree difference in how they think the world works. And, when people don't appear to change their thinking on the spot, we remind ourselves that transformative learning is usually initially rejected, takes a long time to happen, and typically occurs incrementally. All of these ideas and practices to help people become white antiracists will be examined much more thoroughly in the pages to come.

Recognizing White Supremacy as a Dominant Ideology in the United States

White supremacy—now there's a term guaranteed to ignite contention! For most people the term is associated with the KKK, lynching, cross burnings and angry white men carrying Tikki torches, or white nationalist militias "policing" Black Lives Matter demonstrations. Depending on context, the two of us may use alternate terms such as *white advantage* (Lipsitz, 2018), *white superiority* (Saini, 2019), *white privilege* (McIntosh, 1988), *white normativity* (Essed et al., 2018), *implicit bias* (Nordell, 2017), or the *white racial frame* (Feagin, 2013). But eventually we get around to the terminology of *white supremacy*, which to us communicates the twin notions of white superiority and the systemic enactment of white power.

White supremacy is both an idea and a practice. The idea is that whites, because of their innate ability to think clearly and logically about what comprises the common good, should be in positions of leadership. The practice is the reproduction of this idea in the way that organizations, institutions, and systems function. White supremacy blends spurious biology and pseudoscience to argue that those born with white skin are more intelligent, more rational, and also capable of more sophisticated thought. It's the idea "that white equals better, superior, more worthy, more credible, more deserving and more valuable" (Saad, 2020, p. 14). In the United States a strong element of anti-Blackness (Mosley et al., 2020; Ross, 2020) is embedded in this ideology.

As is true with any dominant ideology, the point is to retain the ability of a particular group—in this case, whites—to keep control of commonly shared resources and decide how such resources should be allocated. This is accomplished by ensuring that people of color remain on the margins of decision-making processes. If leadership is seen as white, if history is written by whites, if the judiciary, the penal system, the police, housing policy, health care, and education all function to the disadvantage of racial minorities, then white supremacy is clearly in place. And if that situation is accepted as normal, as just the way things shake out, then the ideology of white supremacy is left intact to ensure that an historically constructed arrangement is seen as being a somehow universally appropriate way to arrange human affairs.

The culture and epistemology of white supremacy are widespread and pervasive, soaking our worldviews and framing our actions. Ideologies like white supremacy "tend to disappear from view into the taken-for-granted 'naturalized' world of common sense" (Hall, 2003, p. 89). When we speak what are really ideologically constructed truths we feel we are presenting something so obviously accurate and authentically personal it elides any critical questioning. White supremacy ensures that a particular system of meaning-making becomes accepted as a universal, empirically accurate norm. A white racial frame comprising a "set of racial stereotypes, prejudices, ideologies, interlinked interpretations and narratives, and visual images" (Feagin, 2013, p. xii) serves to justify and explain the continued subjection of racial minorities. Okun (2010) and Jones and Okun (2001) have outlined a series of habits of mind, such as perfectionism, individualism, objectivity, the worship of profit, and binary thinking, that are drawn from white European enlightenment epistemology. Similarly, Paxton (2010) described a white epistemological paradigm of compartmentalization, rationality, individualism, competition, positivism, logic, scientism, and dualism.

But at its heart, white supremacy is about power, specifically about ensuring that the structural dominance of white people is viewed as unremarkable, normal, and correct. As with all dominant ideologies, if you can get people to think in a certain way, then systems and structures can continue to function in clearly iniquitous ways without people complaining. An antiracist identity foregrounds the existence of white supremacy, identifies its presence in the interactions of everyday life, and seeks to disrupt its smooth operation.

Thinking Structurally

Diversity and inclusiveness training often focus on the importance of bringing multiple individuals into play, of making sure everyone gets a chance to contribute, of giving everyone a voice at the table, and of becoming more aware of racial and cultural differences. The focus for participants is usually on changing individual behavior: How can I be less racist, less subject to implicit bias, and more culturally competent? How can I develop protocols that don't exclude people because of their cultural habits? These are undoubtedly important tasks. However, missing from such questions is a focus on the structural and systemic ways that racism operates.

The story of reformed white supremacist Derek Black is noticeably heartening to many whites (Saslow, 2018). Black attended college, was outed as a white power broadcaster, and changed his views because of conversations with members of groups he deemed evil and/or inferior. He represents the possibility of change through reflection and education, precisely the story that the two of us love to discover. We, just as much as anybody else, need to read about hope and witness transformative possibility. But we also need to be wary of getting stuck at the level of individual journeys such as those taken by Black. Racism is structural and systemic and individual choices and actions around race are inevitably framed by the wider ideology of white supremacy. For us the imperative is always to move beyond skill sets of cultural competence and code shifting and to see becoming antiracist as entailing collective efforts for change.

Thinking structurally is a major part of antiracist identity formation. As Eddo-Lodge (2017) wrote, "We need to see racism as structural in order to see its insidiousness. We need to see how it seeps, like a noxious gas, into everything" (p. 222). But shifting to structural thinking is complex, difficult, and takes time. Furthermore, "the implication that White students are themselves 'racist' is a big part of what they are likely seeking to avoid through resistance" (Kernahan, 2019, p. 61). So as we work to encourage this shift we need to give people hope that, even though structural racism is pervasive, that does not mean we can't take any individual antiracist actions. In her classic and highly influential book *Why Are All the Black Kids Sitting in the Cafeteria? And Other Conversations About Race*, Beverly Tatum (1997) talked about acknowledging one's own sphere of influence as an antidote to hopelessness. She wrote, "I can't fix everything, but some things are in my control . . . everyone has some sphere of influence in which they can work for change" (p. 204).

If we start thinking this way, then we refocus our task from changing individuals to changing structures. Thinking structurally "places this agency within a larger political framework and recognizes the multiple ways that people struggle within and against larger structures of domination" (Mangino, 2008, p. 40). Seeing the systemic and structural ways in which racism has become embedded in our society helps illuminate the road in front of us. For example, when choosing how best to deploy what energies and other resources we have available to us, the two of us always look for actions that will change structures. Changing individual hearts and minds is important, of course; but by the same token those hearts and minds are formed structurally. Racism is learned as we negotiate systems and structures and it's not something that's innate to consciousness. So a major antiracist priority is dismantling and rebuilding in more equal ways the structures that form who we are and how we live.

Thinking structurally is one of the hardest disciplines to learn, particularly if we have bought into the Horatio Alger myth of individuals pulling themselves up by their bootstraps. Rugged individualism and the frontier mentality are heavily entrenched in narratives of American identity. Allied to this is an ideologically learned mistrust of collectivism as communistic control and the denial of personal creative expression. So when you think structurally you have to reject some powerful ideologies of individualism and anticollectivism. In their place you need to constantly ask, "Who most benefits from a suggestion, programmatic change, or new policy?" Equally, you ask, "Who is most disadvantaged by these changes and policies?" You get into the habit of focusing on the levers of control that exist in any organization, the sites where decisions are made, and the communication patterns that determine the flow of information.

One consequence of thinking structurally is helping you to move past the guilt and shame produced by realizing that you have been acting in racist ways, enacting microaggressions, or supporting racist systems. It's easy to become consumed with guilt and embarrassment as you review your unacknowledged collusion in racism. Whites like us experience an alarming fall from grace as we realize we are not the good white people (Sullivan, 2014) we imagined ourselves to be and we can quickly spiral into an arc of self-recrimination and self-loathing.

Thinking structurally helps keep this tendency in check. If people can understand that racist instincts, impulses, and actions are learned as part and parcel of moving through the systems and institutions in which they live their lives, then they will see it would be remarkable for them *not* to have learned racism. Part of thinking structurally is getting people to see they are socially formed, that when you're surrounded by a frame of white superiority it is normal to grow up assuming that leadership, history, and expertise all look white.

In this sense we believe that it is important to normalize racism—that is, to get people to see it as a normal thing to have assimilated racist ideology in a white supremacist world. If people understand that it's normal to have breathed in and internalized the racism embedded in the air surrounding us, then this stops them picking at the scab of their supposed moral failings of doing racist things and having racist thoughts. As we shall stress throughout this book, we both believe in modeling and disclosing our own daily enactments of white supremacy to help normalize its existence.

Embracing Brave Spaces

Part of becoming a white antiracist is recognizing that the work ahead will be raw, bruising, and tense, but still being ready to embrace that reality. It won't be conducted in a safe space in which people agree to disagree, everyone's experience is recognized as equally valid, and emotions are kept at a safe distance or controlled by a facilitator who "doesn't let things get out of hand." As we move into embracing a white antiracist identity we must enter brave rather than safe spaces, because "authentic learning about social justice often requires the very qualities of risk, difficulty, and controversy that are defined as incompatible with safety" (Arao & Clemens, 2013, p. 139). Of course, we both acknowledge that when people of color bear witness to experiences of racism that their testimonies must be shared in a safe space where their stories won't be dismissed as unfounded, partisan, or playing the race card. But in mostly white spaces developing an antiracist identity means signing up for danger and recognizing the need for courage.

In her description of how she builds brave space classrooms Pawlowski (2019) writes of how she explains to her students that safe spaces work to privilege whites by never letting them confront their own racism directly. She asked her learners to enter a brave rather than safe space in which they will be open to challenge, be exposed to the expression of raw emotion, and not expect to leave an encounter with a sense of resolution. She pointed out how being honest about one's experiences, actions, and thinking inevitably involves saying the "wrong" thing and making so-called mistakes. She emphasizes how she shares her own many "mistakes" in racial dialogue as a way of giving permission for her students to stop worrying about being politically correct or nonracist.

Part of entering a brave space involves reappraising the bourgeois decorum that hooks (1994) identified as the norm in white academic conversation. White notions of respectful conversation are that it is calm and "reasonable," an even-tempered analytical exchange in which expressions of anger or crying are signs that things have gone out of control. The culture of whiteness privileges cognitive frameworks that rule expressing strong emotions as out of order—unless of course they are the purview of dominant groups. There are numerous tropes circulating in our cultural spaces—the angry Black woman, the threatening Black man, the sensual, spontaneously emotional Latina— that create derogatory and denigrating perceptions of emotional displays that in white people are more likely to be viewed as appropriate. People who feel angry, sad, fearful, or guilty should not have to strive to remain calm as their bodies are shaking and their hearts racing.

One sign that the work of developing an antiracist white identity is succeeding is when whites embrace the full humanity of participants in dialogue, with all the emotions and frustrations this generates. Bryan Stevenson (2014) pointed out that embracing discomfort is a key element of transformative change. There is hard work involved in recognizing one's own complicity in causing pain to other people. Living into connected activism brings a whole range of emotions with it and requires finding ways to embrace discomfort constructively.

Detecting Demonization and Avoidance

Anyone doing antiracist work with whites should be aware of the very common traps of avoidance and demonization. Some whites will do anything to avoid having the focus of attention on themselves, a phenomenon sometimes referred to as white fragility (DiAngelo, 2018). One diversionary strategy is to turn themselves into emotional victims whose displays of fraught emotion as they confront their collusion in white supremacy become a problem to be "fixed." Okun (2010) noted the

> "acting out" of feelings that students and workshop participants use to avoid actually dealing with class content, to remain the focus of attention, to take up space while the rest of us, uncomfortable with someone in distress, spend our collective energies trying to make the emotive person feel "better." (p. 154)

Another tendency evident in white groups exploring antiracism is to create a binary between good "woke" whites and those with a supposedly inferior level of racial cognizance. This creates a "call out culture" "in which White people try to one-up one another or shame one another, a culture that ultimately alienates more people than it persuades" (Michael, 2015, p. 110). Those who think they are woke demonize the "bad whites" in the room and then shaming and blaming each other takes up all the energy. In a study of white student leaders who wished to become racially conscious leaders, Foste (2020) noted how the enlightenment narrative of moving toward greater cultural competency and antiracist mastery via performative tasks that can be measured and checked governed their understanding of becoming antiracist. The desire to show that they had become good whites who could then educate colleagues who were less "woke" than them was "fundamentally at odds with the vulnerability, humility, and uncertainty necessary to meaningfully critique and unlearn whiteness" (p. 40).

An allied approach is to demonize rural and working-class whites outside the room as too ignorant or dumb to realize their own bigotry. The focus is then shifted to the great "they" outside the workshop, training, or class who are too unsophisticated to "get" racism in the way that those inside an event are doing. Sullivan (2014) described this as

> the middle-class dumping of responsibility for racism on lower and working-class people, who are posited as the true source of ongoing racial injustice. Lower-class white people allegedly are the bad white people who are too unintelligent or unenlightened to know that people of color aren't inferior to white people. (p. 6)

Similarly, whites retreat into distancing themselves from a racist, slaveholder past so that "whoever the real racists are—white slaveholders, white supremacists, poor white people—they are over there, not here where the middle-class white people are" (Sullivan 2014, p. 8).

Finally, a recurrent avoidance strategy is to turn the classroom into a confessional for the purging of white sins. People assume that if you detail the various ways you have been guilty of unintentional racism that you will be "cleansed." Others will marvel at the depth of your immersion in white supremacy and celebrate your epistemological release from all the blinkered and constrained ways of thinking that have blocked you in the past. As Kernahan (2019) wrote,

> Students, especially White students, can simply view feel themselves as better people if they have 'confessed'. Having admitted that they are personally privileged or that they feel guilty, they are free to exempt themselves from the larger system of institutional racism. (p. 117).

Obviously, we want people to come to this awareness and to feel a necessary degree of guilt. But in becoming a white antiracist we focus on what we do with those feelings and emotions, with how they can propel action and commitment.

Bearing Witness

In empirical studies of transformative learning (Cranton, 2016; Mezirow & Taylor & Associates, 2009; Taylor & Cranton & Associates, 2012), a key indicator to changing one's worldview is exposure to a disorienting dilemma— an event that throws one's previous reading of the world into productive confusion. For whites in brave spaces one such dilemma is hearing accounts of a reality they thought they understood being presented in a totally different way. For example, whites may think they've been working within a multiracial group that has built a history of good, trustful relationships in which everybody gets along. It is healthily disorienting for them to hear people of color in the group describe how they have experienced their voice constantly being marginalized. We have both experienced the ways in which organizations and communities that pride themselves on their smoothly rational humanity are shattered by narratives from members detailing sustained and pervasive racism.

Critical race theory (Delgado & Stefancic, 2017) has long insisted on the power of counter-narratives that challenge the stock stories (Bell, 2010) of racial progress. Bearing witness to testimonies of racism—listening intently with empathy to raw hurt—is a crucial step in developing an antiracist white identity. We distinguish here between sympathy and empathy. Sympathy conveys a feeling inspired by having experienced the same situation. It is "feeling—with." Empathy is deeper and more complex. It comes from a realization that although you will never fully experience what someone else is feeling, you can still be drawn into compassionate response. You can search your own life for situations in which you have experienced a flicker of something analogous. So, as a cisgender woman, Mary Hess knows much of what it means to be disadvantaged by the misogyny and sexism that permeates our society. But as a white person, she does not know what it means to live at the sharp end of the stick of racism. Both of us think that it is possible to have compassion for those who are situated differently from ourselves. And both of us have a deep interest in and desire for learning about racism, in part because that helps us understand the permanent frisson of fear and suspicion that lurks in our consciousness regarding the unruly "others" we fear will kill us in a race war. Racism advantages whites but it also harms them, separating them from the experience of a common humanity and placing them in a constant state of anxiety.

Becoming a white antiracist means you can never skip this step of bearing witness. Rationally you can accept as a white person that people of color have been subject to a continuous lifelong assault on their personal dignity and life chances, and you can vow to do your bit to change that reality. But that effort must be underscored by trying diligently to get inside another person's experiences of daily hurt, frustration, and deep anger. It's true that as a white person you can never understand what it's like to live as a person of color. But while acknowledging that, you must still try to draw on whatever memories you have of being abused by dominant power to find the best place inside yourself to understand what it must be like to be on the receiving end of sustained racism.

Sitting with a story of racism told by a person of color often prompts a number of reactions from whites like the two of us. Inevitably we want to offer comfort, to let people of color know that we're allies and that they're not alone in their struggle. We want to show them we are doing our best to empathize with their stories by linking them to our own. All these strategies can backfire disastrously as they become seen as white attempts to take over the narrative and recenter whiteness. Our experience is that it is best to listen quietly and intently; to wince, cry, and shake with emotion and righteous anger; and to show that you are visibly affected. It's fine to offer brief and heartfelt recognitions of pain and to acknowledge that as whites you can have little real understanding of what people are describing. But you must resist the call of European epistemology to "fix" the problem, or the call of your own conscience to keep letting people of color know you're an ally. Don't try to take over the narrative with examples of all the worst experiences of white racism you're witnessed. Just focus on doing your best to appreciate what it must feel like to live the life of the storyteller.

One other thing. There is a danger of whites turning testimonies of racism into only narratives of victimhood. Your feelings of guilt and shame can cause you to miss the narratives of resistance inevitably woven into accounts of racialized experience. In most testimonies there are rich descriptions of pushing back, of finding solace in community, of developing solidarity to fight white racism and drawing on family, faith, wellsprings of courage, and the wisdom of elders. We who are white need to notice, and be as moved by, these elements as we are horrified by the destructive reality of white racism. And we need then to work within white spaces, so that we can express our own deeply painful feelings without fatiguing those with whom we walk in solidarity.

Building Collective Action

And so we come to the whole point of developing an antiracist identity—to build collective action that works to dismantle racist institutions, practices, and behaviors. To paraphrase Marx's 11th thesis on Feuerbach (Marx & Engels, 1998), it is not enough to understand how racism works; we must seek to change it. Becoming a white antiracist entails a lifelong commitment to work for racial justice, to identify and push back against racism in multiple settings, and to change the structures that keep racism intact. Sometimes our eye is on a short-term goal such as fighting to reverse a specific policy or practice that is harming people we know personally. But our eye should always be on the long-term prize of creating a more racially equitable world. It's fine and appropriate for our actions to be locally focused in our sphere of influence (Tatum, 1997). Much of the time we will be working with particular classrooms, teams, or departments caught in an unacknowledged perpetuation of racist practices. But that work must also be viewed as part of a regional or national movement for political change.

Although we both recognize that intrapersonal work is valuable and that it's always necessary to work on identifying how white supremacy lives within you as a white person, our core commitment is to collective action. Individuals can always influence events, and particularly charismatic individuals can embody the spirit and character of a broader movement and serve as an inspirational conduit for the efforts of thousands. But it is always the movement, the collective, the group, that ultimately changes things over the long run.

We both invoke the term *solidarity* to encapsulate what we're striving for. Because of sustained efforts to discredit unions over the last several decades, and because of the de facto media ban on any language that smacks of socialism, the term *solidarity* is pretty much restricted these days to grassroots organizing. But an effective antiracist movement is founded on the principal of multiracial solidarity. Although there are times when different racial groups need their own space to share their own experiences with each other and to strategize together, lasting structural change usually comes from a strong multiracial alliance. It is important that this movement *not* be led by whites. Developing an antiracist white identity means heeding the leadership and direction of the people most directly harmed by systems of racial exclusion.

Of course that caution does not excuse whites from exercising leadership from the back and the side, and occasionally from the front. Leadership can, after all, be enacted by anyone. It is a process, not a person-specific phenomenon. As whites we can leverage our privilege in predominantly white institutions to draw attention to shameful practices. We can say critical things without being accused of playing the race card. We can point out racist policies and behaviors without being seen as pursuing a narrow racial agenda. We can show that it is the responsibility of whites to dismantle racism, and keep saying that racism is primarily a white problem caused by a blindness to the way the world is organized in favor of people like us.

Final Comment

In the rest of this book we examine how to develop a disciplined focus on becoming a white antiracist who is committed to changing the world. The markers we offer in this chapter are signposts on a road the end of which we cannot yet see. Many religious and mystical traditions tell us that the journey is really the goal and adaptive action scholars remind us that complex changes result from unknown forces acting unpredictably to bring about surprising outcomes (Eoyang & Holladay, 2013). The journey to an antiracist white identity is one rooted in a sense of history, attentive to the present, and always looking to the future. It is one of the best examples of what it means to embody "lifelong learning."

3

WHAT IT MEANS
TO BE WHITE

Becoming aware of whiteness is the beginning of creating an antiracist identity for whites. This is because whiteness as an identity is connected to power—in particular, the way that a learned blindness to the fact of one's whiteness helps maintain a system that exhibits structural exclusion and normalizes brutality. As George Yancy (2018a) wrote, racism is *not* the process of individually demeaning or diminishing others, "a site of individual acts of meanness" (p. 74); rather, it's being "implicated in a complex web of racist power relationships . . . heteronomous webs of white practices to which you, as a white, are linked both as a beneficiary and as co-contributor to such practices" (p. 75). Because our whiteness constantly benefits the two of us, and because that benefit accrues to us because we're defined in relation to the stigma of Blackness, we are structurally racist. We don't go about hurling racial epithets but we are "embedded in a pre-existing social matrix of white power" (p. 76) that gives us advantages of which we have only an occasional awareness. For example, to feel safe is our norm, to be "systemically *racially* marked for death" (p. 102) is Yancy's.

This is an important point so we want to say a little more on this. Structurally, the United States is set up economically, socially, and politically to preserve the power and advantage of white people and to keep BIPOC communities relegated to low paying, service economy jobs, often part-time with no health benefits. In other words, the United States is structurally racist; that is, the system is designed to keep one racial group in control of most resources and to provide them with first "dibs" on education, employment, and health care. Much of the time this structural fact is unnoticed by whites like us. We go through our days consumed with the problems, joys, and crises of work, family, friends, and recreation. As we choose schools, juggle work and parenting, deal with relationship problems and try to care for aging parents, we are not thinking explicitly racist thoughts, nor do we make explicit racial jokes or deliberately engage in racial stereotyping.

At the same time as these life events are happening, we benefit from our racial identity in ways that usually pass us by. Our whiteness means we are much more likely to get loans, be perceived as nonthreatening by law enforcement and have our children automatically streamed into nonremedial classrooms. Because our earning power is higher, we are better placed to afford child care. Because we are in salaried jobs, we will probably have health care provided as part of our employment package. We probably won't have toxic waste close to our homes. Our children are much more likely to graduate high school and then go on to college. They are also much less likely to be targeted by law enforcement and the penal system as criminally threatening.

So, given that we continually benefit from a racist system, we are structurally racist. Even when we march, demonstrate and organize against racism, we still benefit from it. As we write books like this one and teach courses, run workshops or deliver training on antiracism, we are still structurally racist. To paraphrase the sign in Bill Clinton's 1992 election war room, "it's the structure, stupid!"

One fatal mistake we have noticed in some antiracist training is for leaders and instructors to assume, in our view wrongly, that when white folk are told that they are racist because they benefit from a racist system, they will understand that argument pretty quickly. Not so. In our experience, beginning with this argument causes more problems than it solves. Whites who don't tell racist jokes (or if they do, believe genuinely that these have no ill intent) and who insist that they don't see color, will feel attacked and unfairly insulted. Far better to begin with some autobiographical modeling. Tell some stories of how you as a white person benefit from your racial identity, talk about how difficult it is for you to understand that, and then describe some ways you act on that awareness with colleagues, students, and friends. Starting with narrative positions you're better to then move to helping people to think structurally about race.

In some ways we would love to begin a workshop saying that everybody white in the room should consider themselves as racists because they all benefit from white supremacy. This might be possible at a Showing Up for Racial Justice (SURJ) meeting or an antiracist conference. But say this in mandatory antiracist training sessions in a mostly white environment and you're not thinking as an educator. You might feel a self-congratulatory activist thrill go through you, but you've just created barriers to learning. You can't force white people to an antiracist consciousness simply by blaming and shaming them. They need to be persuaded, to be led to that conclusion, so that they claim as their own truth the reality of how they have benefitted unwittingly from white racism.

Beginning Strategies for Identity Work

Over the years people of color have consistently told us that the most helpful thing whites can do in terms of fighting racism is to become aware of what it means to be white. They say it's much more important for whites to learn that they have a particular racial identity, and to examine how that identity operates in the world, than it is for them to learn about the cultures of racial minorities. When we act on that advice and explore the elements of white identity, we typically face accusations from those whites we work with of reverse racism, of unfairly singling out whites for their supposed sins, and of white bashing. This is, of course, very predictable.

So we'll often open up an analysis of whiteness by saying we want to look at the importance of identity and then introduce race as one of its many defining elements. If we anticipate that the audience has probably not considered their white identity as being at all significant, then we'll often sneak it in the back door. If we use the "I am from" exercise (Klein, 2019), we make sure that "I am from . . . race" is one of the prompts. Sometimes we'll start by asking people to tell us what it means to them to come from a particular class background, a particular place, or a particular culture. And then we'll ask what it means for them to come from a particular race.

In response to these questions we're often told that race has no importance at all. When we ask why people's racial identity isn't significant, they'll often say that because everyone else around them is white, there's no reason to focus on race. This then allows us to talk about our own upbringing in overwhelmingly white settings and how for many years we never thought about racial identity. We can then smuggle in the insight that one of the chief markers of a white racial identity is thinking that race is not that significant if you're white, never being aware that one is raced.

For many of us whites it's as if whiteness is an invisible force field, a wall (Lara-Villanueva, 2018), or an ocean—something that surrounds us so completely that it goes unnoticed. Yep (2007) described teaching about whiteness to whites as the pedagogy of the opaque, an effort to reframe something completely familiar and ordinary as something totally surprising and extraordinary. If one of the strongest indicators of white identity is being unable to see that whiteness constitutes a racial marker (Sullivan, 2006; Tochluk, 2010), then we need to think through very carefully how we can bring that reality to other whites' attention.

Developing a white antiracist identity starts with the enormous step of getting people to be aware that being white *is* a racial identity. Then, we need to follow that up with the equally significant project of helping them see the power attached to that whiteness. We want white colleagues, students, and peers to understand that irrespective of your social class or level of income, the simple fact of being white means you don't have to worry about overcoming racial stereotypes held by employers or teachers that create barriers to getting work or education. So although we may begin a discussion of racial identity by using a diversity framework (everyone has a racial identity and there are lots of identities in the world out there), we try to move as quickly as we can to an antiracist framework (whatever one's racial identity is, it's connected to power).

Doing this is like walking a tightrope in a gale force wind. We want to get people to think about race as a defining marker of who they are, but we don't want them to think that we are trying to shame them or make them feel guilty for their whiteness. This is less of a problem in settings where people have voluntarily signed up to do antiracist work. But when we have to run any kind of mandatory training, where we know that many whites will feel they're wasting their time in attending an unnecessary, politically correct attempt to "bash" them, then we have to convince them that being white is actually a matter of significance. Yet we need to do that while leading them to a position of taking *pride* in being white, to create a sense that being white means standing up for fairness. If people feel they are being led down an alley that begins with their being assumed to be motivated by racial animus and ends in their confessing the sin of white racism, then few will sign up for that journey. Their bodies may be present because they're required to attend, but their minds will most definitely be absent.

Using the Concept of Fairness

So how can you get whites to start taking pride in standing against racism? One way is to frame what you want to talk about using the term *fairness*. Do you know how in the process of a spring thaw a small drip of water becomes a trickle, which creates a rivulet, which becomes a stream, which then starts to penetrate the ice? Before you know it, the frozen sheet that covered your pathway is breaking up. Well, because *social justice* as a term seems threatening to many forced to attend an antiracist event, we will often begin instead with the word *fairness*. It's our initial mental droplet that we find starts to thaw the icy resistance to contemplating race that many whites who attend compulsory antibias training are feeling.

"That's not fair" is a phrase that most whites are quite comfortable with using and, if you ask people to describe something that seems unfair to them, they'll usually focus on the fact that someone is being denied an opportunity that everyone should have access to, usually because of some arbitrary characteristic or behavior. We often hear white participants saying something along the lines of "It's not fair that he or she should have that, just because of who they are, or who they know. That's an unfair advantage. They don't deserve it." This kind of comment is music to our ears because it pries open an opportunity to take the words people have used and reframe it in explicitly racial terms. If people take seriously the idea that it's unfair to get special treatment not because of something you've done but because of who you are, or because of your network of connections, then our stream becomes a river washing away the winter ice.

If we focus on fairness, then the next step is to link it to white power and white privilege. But with a reluctant audience forced to attend a training we often hold off on talking about white privilege, a term many working class whites have an understandable knee-jerk reaction against. A white high school dropout who works two or three menial service jobs to pay the bills, who has no union, no health care, and can be laid off by their employers at a moment's notice, will bridle against hearing themselves described as privileged. So, at least initially, we tend to use the term *white advantage*. We want to build on the notion of an unearned advantage that so many whites regard as basically unfair, but this time link it to racial advantage. When skeptical white participants talk about how affirmative action discriminates against whites, they're very relaxed about using terms like *reverse racism* or *antiwhite discrimination*. That at least gets us in the door, terminologically speaking.

When people start throwing around words like *racism* and *discrimination*, that allows us then to provide factual data from official reports and government agencies on how racism *really* works to disadvantage communities of color. For example, Lipsitz's (2018) work on the possessive investment in whiteness carefully documents the myriad ways that "whiteness is not so much a color as a condition, a structured advantage sustained by past and present forms of exclusion and subordination" (p. xxii). In health, finance, residence, education, and incarceration, whites profit from "opportunity hoarding" (p. xxii), the ability to participate fully in civil society at a fuller and more prosperous level than their BIPOC counterparts. Of course, if research like this or government data are then refuted as untrustworthy "fake news," the product of deep state agencies controlled by those who want to turn the United States into a socialist or communist state, then we have another related set of problems to deal with!

Developing a Positive Antiracist White Identity

Heightening awareness of the quotidian and mundane nature of everyday racism and making it the object of analysis requires a number of different approaches. One possibility is to teach about different models of white and BIPOC racial identity development (Helms, 2019; Racial Equity Tools, 2020). For whites struggling to understand what constitutes a racial identity, seeing it charted in stages in which they can locate themselves can be reassuring and helpful. They can recognize elements of their past and anticipate what waits in the future. Another is to focus on how scholars of color such as Yancy (2004, 2012) throw whiteness into sharp relief by seeing it from a different racial perspective.

Both approaches are helpful. When elements of whiteness are highlighted by people of color, we learn particularly about how white supremacy operates to circumscribe and devalue their lives. On the other hand, when whites examine whiteness together, they learn how these norms are transmitted among themselves, how challenges to these norms are deflected, and how groupthink operates to stop efforts to identify what whiteness means. The two of us would both still be living in a totally unraced way had it not been for other people—both colleagues of color and other whites—pointing out the meaning of our white identity to us.

Early on it's important to point out to white colleagues, friends, students, and community members that the point of learning about whiteness is not to embarrass or humiliate. We'll say that nobody wants to volunteer for being exposed to an experience of sustained disgrace concerning something they can't control—their racial identity. (We'll often follow that comment by observing how that's often the lifelong reality for communities of color.) Then we'll emphasize instead that we're trying to develop a white identity that people can take pride in. Katz (2003) described this as the project of helping people become "antiracist racists" (p. 179)—that is, helping whites "live their whiteness in ways that actually challenge white domination" (Sullivan, 2014, p. 152). Rather than only feeling shame or guilt, whites need to work out what constitutes a positive white racial identity. This identity work can focus on how to leverage the privilege one has to work for racial justice (Warren, 2010), how to be an interventionist bystander (Sue et al., 2019), and how to confront racism at the individual, group, and systemic level (Michael, 2015).

A positive white identity is best developed in groups in our view. Whites need other whites to support and share stories and experiences of struggling to be antiracist. Only with such a support group in place can whites "develop a spiritually healthy form of self-love" (Sullivan, 2014, p. 149). Given that making mistakes and feeling out of your depth is a constant reality in white antiracist work, it can't be done alone. Even if we act as discrete individuals in a particular setting, we need a collaborative space in which to problematize and debrief our actions with others who are engaged in similar struggles. Otherwise, we fall victim to the myth of the lone hero described by Barnett (2013) who, as a white woman struggling to connect with her Black students at a school in Bedford Stuyvesant, did

> what I had been socialized to do as a good White woman: suffer silently, turn the rage inward, and strive for perfection. Resent those around you for not seeing your suffering, but don't ask for help. *Never* ask for help. To ask for help is to admit weakness, to admit that you—*gasp!*—have needs. Let the resentment grow. I kept my struggles to myself. (p. 148)

Feeling like this is a harbinger of the demoralizing death of antiracist activism.

Finally, those whites who have spent time trying to work in antiracist ways need to go public about that experience. They need to do this not as an act of heroic self-glorification but as an attempt to provide a range of possible models of what white antiracism might look like. Crass (2015) quoted the Reverend Anne Dunlap of Denver's United Church of Christ on this as follows:

> White folk are longing for some white models for racial justice and solidarity, and so we need those of us more practiced at it and/or willing to "be public" to continue to do that, and encourage more folks to try it . . . being public about our questions and wrestlings, being public about our mistakes, being public about the resources we find helpful, being public about our horror at what is continuing to be done in our name. (p. 154)

When meeting with mostly white groups to introduce the topic of whiteness we usually begin by identifying three core elements of white identity:

- A conviction that you don't see race, that you have a color-blind view of the world
- A belief that being white does not constitute a racial identity because only people of color are raced
- The opportunity to opt in and out of engaging with race

Color-Blindness

Bonilla-Silva (2003) names color-blindness as the enactment of racism without racists. A color-blind view of the world appeals to many whites for its emphasis on the fundamental humanity shared by all people. It is a conscious adoption of Dr. Martin Luther King Jr.'s dictum that we should judge people not by the color of their skin but by the content of their character. Whites are often very proud of saying that they don't see color, that they take people as they come, give everyone the benefit of the doubt, and then make individual judgments about people that are unaffected by race as they interact with them in particular settings. A majority of the contributors to a recent anthology on teaching race (Brookfield & Associates, 2019) identified the enduring permanence of the color-blind perspective as the biggest pedagogic challenged they faced.

Why should color-blindness be a problem? Isn't it admirable to avoid stereotyping people and to put learned prejudices aside so you can focus instead on the unique humanity of each individual you encounter? Well, if this were truly what was happening then both of us would be overjoyed. But the color-blind perspective has two major flaws. First, it implies that whites can indeed quickly learn to stop stereotyping, bracket their biases, and see people in an unraced way. Second, it assumes a level playing field is in place in which whites interact with people of color as moral and political equals.

Let's take the issue of being able to detach yourself from a race-based view of the world. Our position is that the ideology of white supremacy is so all enveloping that only hermits permanently cut off from all human interaction and all media could escape its influence. So, despite whites saying that they see only people, not color, we don't believe this to be true. To take ourselves as examples, we have both been socialized in a world in which white supremacy underscores how we think people should behave and institutions should function. Even though we have spent decades trying to uncover this ideology in ourselves, and to identify racism in the contexts through which we move, we are still held hostage to our white supremacist conditioning. We hope we've got better at detecting its influence and in calling it out when we see it in play. But its frame will never leave us and we come smack up against it every day of our lives.

Now let's think about the fact that racial exchanges don't happen in a flat, neutral terrain. Even if the two of us could remove all biases, stereotypes, and prejudices from our mental frameworks, we would still be moving through an asymmetrical world. Access to jobs, health care, and education are so disproportionately advantaged in favor of whites that the "breaking news" cable TV headline that we *should* see every day ought to read "Revolution has still not broken out despite massive racial inequality." Across the country incarceration rates for Black and brown people are astoundingly disproportionate and the last few years have highlighted regular shootings of people of color by white police, with no accountability being exercised. There is clear racial segregation in housing, and even in "integrated" public schools in our own city of St. Paul a color line clearly exists. Add to this the demonization of Black and brown immigrants as disease-ridden terrorists, rapists, and hardened gang criminals, and it seems impossible for whites not to realize they live in a deeply racist world in which they are disproportionately advantaged. So what keeps intact the idea of American democracy as a level playing field in which hard work ensures that all, irrespective of color, have equal access to the same opportunities? Two words—ideological manipulation.

Dominant ideologies are what secure consent to structural injustice and what stop revolution breaking out when objective statistics and personal life experiences combine to present a world that is clearly unequal. Capitalist ideology promotes the idea that anyone can go from rags to riches if they show enough entrepreneurial spirit and if they work hard enough. Democratic ideology proclaims we live in a world where people's opinions direct legislative acts, where everyone has free speech, and where the people's will is always enacted. And white supremacy supports the view that continued white dominance is just a fact of life because, let's face it, whites are just more intelligent, calm, rational, and objective than people of color. Whites think better and make better decisions, so it's natural that they should end up occupying positions of power and authority.

When whites say to people of color that they don't see race, they will come across as naïve in a world where institutions and systems are *structured* around ensuring the continued dominance of one racial group. We have both worked for predominantly white institutions that proclaim a valuing of every person's dignity and we're happy to aspire to that value. But we have also pointed out to those institutions that because of the white supremacy embedded in the way they function, the dignity of institutional members of color can only be enacted if there are radical structural changes in admissions, financial aid, assessment systems, governance, curricula, and performance appraisal.

We believe that a white person who tells people of color that they don't see color is making a mistake it's hard to recover from, particularly if that person thinks that now they will be seen as a trusted ally. As a white person you may feel the world is unraced, but you should assume that a person of color sees it in exactly opposite terms, that *everything* is seen through the lens of race. One of the most damaging dynamics we've observed in multiracial groups is whites saying that they're nonracist and expecting people of color to take them at their word—and then bristling at any suggestions that they lack a full awareness of their racism. Even though we write books like this, give presentations, try to leverage our privilege, work on consciousness raising, demonstrate, advocate, mentor, and teach courses around racial issues, neither of us expects to be trusted by colleagues of color.

We always counsel those whites we work with not to get hung up on assessing how much they are trusted by folks of color. Instead, they should have as their starting point an expectation of *not* being trusted. They should accept that, like the two of us, they will make many mistakes, say the wrong things, and act in racist ways. How could they (and we) *not* do this having been raised under white supremacy? If somewhere down the line a person of color tells you they trust you, then accept that as a recognition of your good work. But don't think you're not being effective if that acknowledgment never comes.

Whiteness Is *Not* a Racial Identity

When we ask white people about the moment when they first become aware of their white identity, we are often met with bemusement. Equally, the questions "What does it mean to be white?" or "What role does your whiteness play in your life?" are viewed almost as nonsensical. This is because many whites don't believe they have a racial identity and that whether or not they are white has absolutely nothing to do with where they are in life or how they conduct themselves.

The belief that whiteness does not constitute a racial identity is a building block of white supremacy. It's part of what is often referred to as white normativity, the idea that the norms and standards by which we judge what is acceptable in the world are colored white. And it's something that whites don't usually think about unless, like the white parents of children of color who have to navigate norms of whiteness (Chandler, 2016; Smith et al. 2011), something in your experience requires you to do so. Under white normativity race is something exhibited only by those with skin not colored white. This is because whiteness is viewed as the universal standard, the de facto center, the commonsense way the universe should look when it's working as normal. Under white supremacy leadership looks white, authority looks white, experts look white, and what counts as legitimate knowledge and acceptable logic are all constructed by whites. The power of white supremacy is making this seem unremarkable, obviously correct, and just the way things are.

If you accept this perspective on life, then race is not something you need to attend to. If being white means you don't have a race, then it's easy to compartmentalize any discussion of race as something appropriate only for people of color. In this way it's quite possible to attend a training on diversity, inclusion, or cultural competence without ever really thinking about what it means to be white. You can leave such a training thinking that race is something that others have. If you spend your life in predominantly white environments surrounded by people who look like you, then it's not surprising that you'd think that race is something "out there," evident in neighborhoods you don't frequent, streets you don't walk on, and company you don't keep.

This perhaps explains why in so many predominantly white environments the "experts" who come to run workshops and do training around diversity are people of color. Whites assume that the only people who can teach about race are people of color, because they're the only ones with a racial identity! The fact that whiteness is itself a racial identity is never considered. This is probably also why diversity offices in predominantly white organizations are typically headed by the only person of color in the senior leadership team. If race is something you see only people of color having, then it makes sense to have such a person in charge of diversity because they have the "race" that they're going to teach whites (who don't have race) about.

We both feel that diversity initiatives are best run by a multiracial team in which whites are involved. This allows the team to talk in public about their own racial dynamics, thereby demonstrating that whites are just as raced as any other group. We believe that because whiteness is a racial identity and because that identity is generally supported in a racist world, whites need to be in the mix whenever conversations about race are held.

Opting In and Out of Race

Whites who don't believe themselves to be raced and who live mostly in white environments can in effect decide when to opt in or out of thinking about, or dealing with, race. This is a luxury denied most people of color who have to navigate a white world for large portions of every day. So the problem of race is a *white* problem. White racist structures, policies, and practices continue to endure partly because whites don't see how those structures are maintained to disadvantage people of color. The race "problem" is obviously a problem of the systematic marginalization and diminishment of people of color, but it's just as much a problem of how good white people (Sullivan, 2014) who consider their actions to be prompted by morality and compassion don't see how white supremacy keeps racism in place.

Thinking that you can move in and out of dealing with race is partly a reflection of the individualistic mythology so much a part of American culture. It's easy to push thinking about race to the corners of your world if you think that being racist is all a matter of individual choice. Unless you put structural racism at the center of your analysis, you can view racism as a matter of personal conduct, of whether or not you have bad thoughts, say bad things, and treat people unfairly. Many of the diversity and inclusiveness trainings we've attended, and no doubt some we've conducted ourselves, have fallen into this trap. Attention focuses on catching the implicit biases, prejudices, and stereotypes you carry in your head that structure your interactions with people, or the microaggressions (Sue, 2010) you enact that, without you intending it, demean people of color. We both think such trainings can be helpful and have led them ourselves. But without an awareness of structural racism, their effect is limited. People could attend a diversity institute and come away with a determination to purge elements of racism from their personal behavior but with no awareness of how systemic racism is maintained.

If you believe that you're a moral, compassionate person and that racism is all a matter of individual choice, then you can think you have an antiracist identity without doing any of the heavy lifting to fundamentally restructure the world in which you live. You can feel virtuous about addressing the learned racist stereotypes and instincts you discover in yourself without engaging in the fundamentally necessary collective organizing that brings about change. This is why helping people to think structurally, not individualistically, is so crucial. A structural worldview always seeks to understand individual personal experience as being at least partially socially formed. To adapt two well-known slogans, a structural perspective holds that the personal is structural and that we should think locally and act structurally. The two of us try to prioritize our efforts to spend the greatest time and energy working for structural changes. This is because in the institutions we have worked for people constantly change, but habitual practices and policies endure. As educators we love to see individual hearts and minds change, but as activists we believe the most important thing is to force structural change.

4

HELPING PEOPLE BECOME
AWARE OF THEIR WHITENESS

I n this chapter we outline the basic steps we've found helpful in getting
people in overwhelmingly white environments to be aware of their
whiteness. The typical setting we're imagining is one where an organization, institution, or community has experienced a traumatic incident or
series of events in which racism is clearly evident. This could be anything
from a slogan scrawled on a BIPOC student's dorm room door, to an
alumnus shooting at Black Lives Matter protesters, to the expression of
pain, outrage, and anger at the state-sanctioned police murder of unarmed
people of color. We have experienced all of these in our own institutions.

The aftermath of such events sees the organization concerned struggling to address race and racism seriously as a community, possibly for the
first time in its existence. Through 10-point action plans and other initiatives, the institution hopes to move swiftly and purposefully in addressing the problem of racism. Typically, they would love to show the world
how major transformative change happens overnight. But the nature of
how transformative learning happens is much more incremental. People
struggle to ease themselves into what is going to be a major perspective
change, a whole new way of thinking about how the world works. Their
willingness to change is based on seeing people they trust doing the work
in front of them and showing that they are not out to induce shame,
seek confessions, or denigrate those for whom thinking about race is a
new project.

The logic of this kind of learning means it has to be allocated the time
it needs. Transformative learning around race and racism is built on trustful
relationships, on believing that those inviting you into this work see you
for who you really are, not for who they assume you are or want you to be.
And this trustfulness cannot be forced. It needs time to germinate and that

time can't be artificially foreshortened. People need to see you walk the talk and practice what you preach. And then, once a serious reappraisal of their racial assumptions begins, and people start to consider a 180-degree different version of the world, they need time to think, to process, to mull over what the dramatically altered picture of life they're exploring means for them and their future actions.

So in this chapter you'll see that we adopt a scaffolding approach that begins with a lot of modeling and then moves incrementally to get people more and more comfortable with scrutinizing their own assumptions and actions. In doing this we follow work on how people learn to think critically. But we need to point out that in other settings we might work in a far different, much more direct, way. We both subscribe to Myles Horton's (1990) distinction between education and organizing. Working as educators we're focused on the dynamics of how learning happens and how best to foster that. If learning requires extensive scaffolding, then that's what we need to provide. Working as organizers, by way of contrast, involves trying to counter, usually from a marginalized position, the actions of organizations who don't represent your interests. We have to react speedily and forcefully to decisions, policies, and initiatives designed to blunt antiracism, and sometimes don't have the luxury of time to set up a program of incremental learning.

What follows for the rest of this chapter is a typical sequence of steps that we take as we try to get people who haven't done this before to engage with their whiteness, even as they deny that this work is necessary.

Adjust Your Definition of Success

Before we take an initial step into any room in which we're working we need to do some important internal mental work. Both of us want to do good work and both of us believe passionately in what we're doing. Some part of us would love to think of ourselves as the lone heroes and heroines of pedagogy depicted in movies like *Dead Poets Society* (Touchstone Pictures, 1989*)*, *Dangerous Minds*, (Hollywood Pictures, 1995), and *The Great Debaters* (Harpo Films, 2007). The central characters in these teaching dramas are charismatic individuals who wring transformative changes in their students' lives. We're not immune to these portrayals. Also, the linear progress of increasing perfectionism that's so much a part of white epistemology has its hold on us. Finally, the institutional evaluations and performance appraisals we're subject to invariably measure our effectiveness by how much learning we're prompting or how much people change.

Put all these elements together and it's easy to go into an event designed to help people recognize their whiteness assuming that success will be represented by large numbers of people telling you how the racial blinders have been lifted from their eyes and how they now see whiteness and white supremacy in every corner of their lives. We've both privately yearned for "Kumbaya" moments of racial healing when people put their arms around each other and sing "We Shall Overcome." So before we meet with any group we have to give ourselves a stern talking to and tell ourselves, "That ain't gonna happen." We keep in mind the fourth rule of courageous conversations (Singleton, 2012, 2014)—expect and accept a lack of closure. Anticipating any kind of resolution or consensus is naïve. Fox (2014) asked us to "remember we're human. We don't have to resolve all tension or come to complete understanding. The point is to talk. The process is everything" (p. 75). We agree.

What counts as success for us is leaving a session with some evidence that people are ready to continue a conversation. We expect a lot of confusion, pushback, and some expressions of outright hostility. We anticipate long, awkward, uncomfortable silences, participants crying, some angry outbursts, and to feel like unequipped novices a lot of the time. We tell ourselves that if we're defining "going well" by things adhering to the white epistemological norm of staying calm, keeping things on an even keel, and not letting things "get out of control" through the expression of strong emotions, then we're destined to fail. So we have both tried to reframe what we count as failure and success. We accept there will be periods of noncommunication along the way as people need time to process the starkly different realities they hear from others in a group or from the facilitators. But if, at the end of a session, people are still open to talking further, then for us the event has been an enormous success.

Begin by Getting a Sense of How People Feel About the Event

As we begin a workshop, class, institute, or training session we'll usually conduct an anonymous Sli.do poll (previously Poll Everywhere) on how people feel as they come into the event. We'll include a range of possible responses from "excited" to "fearful," "wary" to "holding my judgment." One quick formulation is as follows.

Question: *Which of the following feelings or emotions are you aware of as you get ready to talk about race?*

Anxious. I'm worried about saying the wrong thing, that I'll be humiliated, or that things will get way too uncomfortable.

Excited. I need to know more about this and look forward to some real talk today.

Resentful. I object to being made to show up for this event. I don't think it's necessary because race is a made-up issue pushed by left-wing groups.

Determined. I know today might be uncomfortable, but this is too important an issue not to take seriously. So I'm going to stick with it.

Confused. I don't really see why we're doing this because I'm not aware of any glaring racism in our institution or community.

People can check as many of these options as they wish and after they're done (we usually allow about a minute) we pull the findings up on the screen in the room so everyone can see the spread of responses to the poll. This gives us a sense of where people are in their readiness for this conversation and allows us to honor the resistance, skepticism, and hostility that exists. Perhaps more importantly, it gives us the chance to address the emotionality of the topic head on and to let participants know that now we're entering a brave space where people will feel strong emotions.

If a majority of participants check the "Resentful" option, then it's probably worth our while to dig deeper into the causes of that resentment. For that eventuality we have a second Sli.do poll in reserve.

Question: *Which of the following options comes closest to your reasons for feeling like today is going to be a waste of your time?*

- Race is a nonissue anymore—we've had a Black president.
- This event is pushing a narrow Black Lives Matter racial agenda.
- This is a discussion for people of color, not for us.
- Whatever I say I'm going to be called a racist—so there's no point in me talking.
- I'm sick of being blamed for things I had no control over, like slavery.
- I'm not a racist—I don't see color.
- Here we go again with the white bashing and white shaming.

Make Sure You Do a Lot of Early Modeling

We both subscribe to the mantra that before you ask anyone to do anything that involves risk or challenge, you need to engage in that same activity yourself and let people see you doing that. Michael's (2015) words resonate for us:

> When I facilitate, I plan for and model self-disclosure for every exercise that I lead. I think about the stories I want to tell ahead of time and practice telling them. I push myself to think of stories that are current so as to model my own ongoing personal struggle and the authentic vulnerability that comes from exposing our current flaws rather than focusing on things we have overcome or learned in the past. (p. 107)

The two of us make sure that we begin an event by talking about what it means for us to be white, how we came to that awareness, and how we constantly forget its significance. Both of us have found that starting with a personal story gives a sense of connectedness and immediacy to any workshop, meeting, or class we're running.

We do acknowledge, however, that using narrative is sometimes an example of white privilege, and that whites can "tell these stories without being viewed as 'angry' or being punished or penalized by engaging in these types of discussions" (Ellington, 2016, p. 215). When Stephen Brookfield discloses a narrative of being race-blind and of struggling to understand his own racism, he is rewarded for being "vulnerable" or "brave." He gains institutional likeability "simply by writing essays or books about racism, by teaching courses about racism at a university, by speaking at plush diversity conferences, or by doing cultural competence or diversity consulting" (Gorski, 2015, p. xiv). As a woman, Mary Hess runs greater risks of having her narrative self-disclosure being seen as overly emotional or an instance of her losing control. But people of color who recount narratives of struggle and mistakes risk being seen as incompetent, overly subjective, and not rigorous enough, "making any apology or admission of vulnerability an impossibility in terms of ongoing credibility" (Okun, 2010, p. 64).

Show How You Value People's Identities

After disclosing some sort of personal story, we then ask people to focus on the nature of identity. Sometimes we'll use a variant of the *I am from* exercise that asks people to respond to various prompts such as *I am from* a place, community, spirituality, class, desire, race, sexuality, or any other indicator you wish to use (Klein, 2019). Another approach is to ask people to tell the story of their names. A third option is to request that people bring in an object that has some significance in defining what's important in their life. If we're with a group for only a short period of time, we'll ask them each to speak the name of someone who is important to them and say why that is so.

The point of these exercises is to show people that (a) who you think you are is important for how you think and act in the world and (b) it's fine to be proud of who you are. Although we both live in a racist world in which whites are systemically advantaged, we don't want to send the message that everyone who is white is inevitably morally compromised or beyond redemption. We talk about the aspects of our white identity that we are proud of, usually our artistic passions or the communities we treasure. Both of us have a healthy skepticism of the automatic privileging of Eurocentric epistemology, but both us also value aspects of that. Although we advocate for holistic health, neither of us wants to be operated on by a surgeon who has not been rigorously trained in her craft or who does not have a detailed knowledge of anatomy. Both of us believe in evidence-based practice. We may sometimes query the procedures used to collect data and the way logic is seen as the province only of elite whites (Bonilla-Silva & Zuberi, 2008). We also often criticize the agendas of those conducting research, the agendas of funding agencies, or the way research is reported and disseminated. But we both believe that the accurate collection of empirical data is crucial to informed decision-making.

This early emphasis on valuing people's identity is intended to avoid people descending quickly into shame and guilt at their whiteness. We want to show that we are not self-loathing haters of anything white. The idea is to affirm that people should be proud of who they are and where they've come from. This is a necessary precursor to them (and us) starting to bring elements of racial identity into the mix.

Address the Process to Be Used

Many resources in antiracist training stress developing group norms or ground rules early on. Our experience is that the extensive time that can be spent doing this does not always have the beneficial effect one would antici-pate. We don't want to discourage you from asking participants how they would like to talk to each other, but if you do that you can expect some pretty standard responses. White groups in particular will emphasize being respect-ful and agreeing to disagree. We find that these suggestions often allow for the expression of classic avoidance behaviors that allow people to stop really coming to grips with race. Being respectful can mean "Don't upset me by suggesting I'm not a good person." Agreeing to disagree can mean "Let me stay with my experience and don't ask me to take yours seriously."

We prefer to introduce the notion of moving into brave spaces (Pawlowski, 2019) in which we're aware that discomfort, intense emotions, and deep feel-ings are bound to arise when we talk about something as raw as racism and white supremacy. If we do suggest ground rules, we will keep them short and quick, so that groups can remember them easily. Singleton's (2014) coura-geous conversations rules are easily remembered—stay focused, stay engaged, expect discomfort, and accept a lack of closure. We have also used some of Visions Inc's (2018–2020) rules such as "OK to disagree, not OK to blame or attack" or "make 'I' statements only." A rule we developed ourselves to use for short periods is the three-person rule—once you've spoken don't speak again until at least three others have contributed.

Provide Shared Video Information That Shows a Different View of the World

After we've modeled our commitment to analyzing our own white identity and shown that we're not out to bash anyone who's white just because of their race, we then start to up the ante. The next step is to provide a view of the world that comes as a shock because it presents a picture of life as being determined *wholly* by one's racial identity. We begin by asking a predominantly white audience to describe the most important conversation they've ever had with their sons. With small groups this can be done verbally and with large groups using a tool such as Backchannel Chat (backchannelchat.com). The responses typically cover a gamut of topics—how to deal with bullying, what it means to be a man, how sex works, the importance of treating women respectfully, what constitutes sporting success, how to deal with failure, and so on. It's pretty rare for any mention of race or whiteness to come up.

Then we show the very brief op-ed documentary from the *New York Times* titled *A Conversation with My Black Son* (Gandbhir & Foster, 2015). Here African American parents describe the talk they all have to give to their sons about how to react when they're stopped by the police. In a short 5-minute burst a white audience is privy to a world in which the racial identity of Blackness is seen as the determining factor in negotiating the external world. The video doesn't engage in white bashing or focus particularly on white racism. It simply states that Black boys in a white world will be stopped by the police solely because of their race. Consequently, responsible and caring parents need to prepare them to manage that eventuality.

Because the whites in the audience who are parents presumably think of themselves as being responsible and caring, this video appeals to a universal instinct of wanting to keep your children safe. We can then briefly comment on how we as white parents never had to prepare our own sons to deal with the police, because we assumed they would never be perceived as threatening or singled out for treatment solely because of their race. This allows us to introduce the concept of white privilege and the invisible knapsack of automatic advantages whites carry around with them (McIntosh, 1988, 1998), one of which is assuming that the police are there to protect you.

Use Scenario Analysis

Now it's time to get the audience more involved. In the past we'd probably have moved to encouraging people to talk directly about their own experiences of race. These days, however, we typically insert an intermediary step of some kind of scenario analysis or brief case study. We'll present a two- or three-paragraph fictional situation in which a central character is taking an action, making a decision, or considering a choice. We ask people to put themselves into the shoes of the central character and to try to re-create what that person is thinking and the assumptions under which they're operating.

The scenario we write is always centered around a racial incident. It might describe a landlord deciding which potential renters to interview based on the sound of applicants' voices over the phone or by consulting their Facebook profiles. It could be a situation to do with hiring or college admissions. A more complex scenario we've used has been one in which a white facilitator establishes a ground rule in which declarations of perceived racism by people of color are always to be trusted by whites (Brookfield, 2013).

The exercise begins with people individually answering the following three questions about the scenario:

- What assumptions is the central character making as she or he acts this way, makes this decision, or considers this choice?
- How could the central character check whether or not these assumptions are valid?
- What's a different perspective on the situation that the central character is not taking account of? This could be an interpretation of what's happening that she or he has not considered and that might come as a surprise to her or him.

We then ask people to share their responses in groups. In this process people will often identify assumptions that come as a surprise to their peers and propose widely varying explanations of what could be happening in the scenario. Because the scenario or case study focuses on a concrete situation, it grounds what might be otherwise abstract discussions of race, identity, and whiteness in terms of specific experiences. It's important to stress at the outset that there is no right or correct answer to any of the questions. Saying this takes a lot of pressure off people's shoulders. Because it is not the workshop participant or student's own reasoning at stake, and because all the attention is on the fictional character's assumptions and interpretations, people are mentally freer to play with notions of race and whiteness than if we had begun with an example from their own lives.

Structure Discussion Protocols

Now it's time to move to the examination of personal experience. This is the point at which we used to start before we had a better understanding of the preparatory steps needed to get people to this point. However, we recognize that even with extensive preparation, talking about what their own whiteness means is still a difficult step for many to take. People don't want to say the wrong thing but don't know what the right thing is. They may feel that because they have lived only in white environments that they have nothing to contribute to a discussion of racial identity (itself a prime marker of whiteness). This may be the first time they've ever talked seriously in a group about race, so it's important to help them into the process.

We've found that it's useful to structure discussions by proposing specific protocols to guide how people talk to each other, but *not* what they say. Our protocols typically focus on hearing from everyone before moving into deeper conversation. We want to encourage careful and attentive listening, and to stop people defining an agenda too early or co-opting a discussion with their own personal concerns. Some of the protocols emphasize the importance of silent processing as much as active speech. Chapter 7 describes a number of these protocols in great detail.

In contrast to our expectation that setting structured protocols might be experienced as artificially constraining or limiting, the feedback we've received overwhelmingly is that it's welcomed. People appreciate knowing what's expected of them and welcome the fact that the exercises we use are designed to ensure no one is left out.

Keep on Top of What's Really Happening

Facilitating any kind of racial dialogue is complex and whites talking about racial identity entails the additional difficulty that you're trying to get people to see as extraordinary something that they have taken for granted. Whiteness is the sea within which people swim and becoming aware of how that whiteness is tied to power and to keeping people of color marginalized is a daunting prospect. In whiteness work the two of us believe that we make the road by walking (Horton & Freire, 1990). In other words, we're constantly changing plans, making adjustments, and introducing new directions based on what we're learning about how the group is experiencing what's happening to them. We may have a rough road map comprising the guidelines we outline in this chapter, but the terrain we're traversing is constantly changing. Sometimes dramatic tectonic shifts happen as a group experiences a major crisis. At other times you discover your map is outdated by a technological innovation, a change in group membership, or an unexpected outside event.

Because each context we work in is different with its own particular history and dynamics, it's important for us to try and keep on top of what's happening so that we can make necessary adjustments along the way. Two tools are especially helpful in this regard. The first is the web tool Backchannel Chat. We open a backchannel chat feed for each session we run so that people can register anonymously any comments, reactions, or criticisms they have as the session is proceeding. We commit to checking this feed every 15 minutes or so and address questions, comments, and issues as they arise. Or if we're needing immediate information on how a session is going, we'll pause and ask people to go to the day's Backchannel Chat feed and let us know what has been most helpful or confusing so far. This tool is especially useful in a one-off event where we only have a group for a limited period of time.

When we're meeting with the same group several times over a longer period, we'll use the Critical Incident Questionnaire (CIQ), a tool Brookfield devised in the early 1990s that is available for free download from his website (www.stephenbrookfield.com). This is a five-item, one-page form that asks participants to note at what moments in a session they were most engaged and most distanced, what actions that anyone took that were most helpful or most confusing, and what surprised them most about the session. The responses are anonymous and the facilitator collects the forms, reads through them, and notes the main themes that arise.

The next time the group gets together the session starts off with leaders presenting the findings from the previous week's CIQ. They note differences in the group's responses, identify problems that are emerging, and address concerns that are voiced. When appropriate they show that they're making adjustments and changes based on the CIQ data. If people say on the forms that they want to avoid controversy and contention and evade talking about race, leaders rejustify why it's important to stay focused on that topic. Ever since we've used this tool, neither of us has had a group that's spiraled out of control or tried to sabotage our efforts without us knowing that this was happening early on. We both believe that forewarned is forearmed and knowing what's developing early on in a group's life allows us to respond better to emerging problems.

I'm White but Don't Call Me Privileged

Before leaving this chapter we want to address one final issue. Many times in exploring whiteness we've heard a heartfelt critique from people who are struggling to survive economically that the notion of white privilege or the term *white supremacy* makes no sense at all to them. They tell us they're from a working-class family, are the first in their family to get a high school diploma, work three jobs to stay afloat, have had to fight to get to college, are deep in debt from loans, struggle to pay bills and arrange transport and childcare, and that nobody's giving them a hand out or leg up.

The two of us were born in working-class communities in Oshkosh, Wisconsin (Hess) and Bootle, Liverpool, UK (Brookfield), so we sympathize with this critique and with the way that foregrounding race sometimes ignores class analysis. At some point in becoming a white antiracist the notion of intersectionality—of how class, gender, sexual orientation, and ability are connected—inevitably comes into play. But in the moment when notions of privilege are soundly rejected by whites struggling to make ends meet, how do we respond?

The first thing we do is to recognize the legitimacy of the critique. We don't try to deflect the reality of people's experiences. We honor the truth-telling people are doing and, when possible, talk about our own history of collecting the dole, being unemployed, and piecing together a wage out of multiple short-term jobs.

Then we say that in the United States there are multiple ways people are excluded from their share of the American dream. If you live in an economically deprived rural or urban neighborhood without decent transport, schools, health care, and jobs, then you're getting the shaft from a system that clearly privileges urban wealth and power. We then point out that being poor is the most crushing blow of all, and that racism and poverty are twin pillars of oppression in the United States.

But then we point out that one's economic position is something that can potentially be changed, but that one's racial identity can't. For example, if there's a sudden oil boom in North Dakota and people of all races get hired at equal rates, you can conclude that race is less of a factor in employment. But when new employees then try to find accommodation in local communities, people of color are likely to face restrictions that whites don't. When whites go to spend their wages in stores, they are not followed around by security in the way commonly experienced by people of color. When whites go out on the town to blow off steam, local police are going to look more benignly on a group of whites playing loud country music in a car and shouting at random passers-by than they are when encountering a group of people of color blasting out hip hop. And if a car is stopped for erratic driving or any other infraction the racial identity of the driver plays a big part in determining how a white police officer reacts to them.

Then we end by reiterating the truth of the economic exploitation of whites and acknowledging that all forms of systemic exclusion need to be addressed. We say we don't want to get into what is often called the "oppression Olympics" where people compete to document the relative devastation experienced by racism, sexism, poverty, homophobia, and so on. We finish by reminding people that for this particular event we're focusing on racial identity, while acknowledging that multiple forms of oppression exist.

Our definition of *white privilege* is that it is the absence of the penalties incurred by those who, because of their skin color or phenotype, are judged to be "less than." Essentially it is "an absence of the consequences of racism. An absence of structural discrimination, an absence of your race being viewed as a problem first and foremost, an absence of 'less likely to succeed because of my race'" (Eddo-Lodge, 2017, p. 86). People of color have a set of assumptions and understandings surrounding them that presume criminality, violence, laziness, and a lack of intelligence on their part that whites, even those who are economically destitute, are not as subject to.

One final point. As the Midwest Critical Whiteness Collective (Lensmire et al., 2013) has pointed out, discussions of privilege sometimes dive deeply into a confessional mode. As the whites in a group carefully enumerate the various manifestations of their privilege, it's easy for them to confuse acknowledging their white identity and admitting to their collusion with racist systems as taking some form of antiracist action. Although we believe that understanding all the unearned privileges we have is as good as any other way to start examining whiteness, we must be wary of equating owning up to one's previously unacknowledged privilege with making substantive change. An antiracist white identity has to be an activist one. Although intrapersonal reflection is a kind of cognitive action, we see the living out of an antiracist impulse as the attempt to dismantle racist structures, systems, policies, and practices.

We wish we could claim that our way of dealing with protestations regarding the existence of privilege always works, but have to acknowledge that it often doesn't. But then, as pointed out early in this chapter, we tell ourselves not to equate something working with people seeing the light in the way we want them to. We admonish ourselves to remember that success is simply keeping the conversation going. That way, if we're still talking about race and racial identity—even if people are objecting to our analysis and saying passionately how we've got it wrong—then we feel we're being successful.

5

USING STORIES TO
UNCOVER RACISM

S tories stick. Stories incite. Stories move. When the two of us think about
our activist involvements, we both immediately remember how an individual or group's story of brutality or violence outraged us so much we
had to get involved. We think of the powerful and galvanizing effect on the
Black Lives Matter movement of stories of Black men being shot in the back
as they ran away, of rounds of bullets from multiple weapons tearing into an
already dead Black body, and of an "I can't breathe" cry being repeated over
and over. On a smaller scale we think of colleagues being fired or marginalized because of their activism. Hearing a dramatic story of how one person's
experience of racism encapsulates the workings of white supremacy touches
our imagination, our feelings, and our emotions and gets us thinking, "What
can we do about this right now?" It gets us on the streets in front of police
stations, governors' mansions, financial institutions, and legislative bodies.

Human beings are "storying" creatures who tell stories to make sense of
their own and others' experiences and to cast a larger narrative arc over our
actions and biographies. A recognition of the mobilizing power of narrative is
at the heart of what Denning (2007) called the secret language of leadership.
By telling a quick story of how one Zambian village instituted malaria pre-
vention by sharing basic information about preventive techniques, Denning
helped persuade the World Bank to change its mission from lending money
to knowledge dissemination. The two of us follow Denning's lead by doing
our best to tell stories from our own practice in workshops and to share
media pieces created by others.

In every society there is always a battle for what comprises the dominant
narrative or story. In the United States, whoever controls the dominant narrative, whoever defines what is seen as the evolution of the country, uses that

power to secure their interests. The official "American" story is of the evolution of a democracy that is ever more expansive and inclusive as historical wrongs are righted and the capitalist system and a free press secure liberty and justice for all. As long as this story stands as historical and empirical truth, efforts to highlight enduring structural racism are hindered and blocked.

However, we believe, like Reinsborough and Canning (2017), that "on issue after issue, the narrative landscape is dramatically shifting, as pressure mounts and fault lines give way. Today, the whole dominant narrative itself seems to be up for popular consideration. It's on" (p. xiii). And nowhere is it more "on" than in the challenge to the official U.S. story of racial progress, civil rights legislation, the first Black presidency, and hence the removal of the last vestiges of slavery and racism. On the one hand, we have the narrative that anti-Black racism has been solved and that white people are now the victims of preferential treatment for people of color. On the other hand, we have the narrative of continued violence legitimized by white supremacy, the fact of permanent white structural advantage, and the reality of an emerging multiracial country.

Although stories are a richly powerful resource for antiracist work, they can also be a double-edged sword. In a world where journalism, science, and other institutionalized forms of knowledge development are under attack, and where what defines authority is how authentic someone sounds, the power of story can be dangerous. As we can see in the broader political landscape, stories that have very little basis in fact—and are even outright lies—can, if told with sufficient force and conviction, cause people to doubt their own experience. Stories scapegoating vulnerable groups as the cause of unemployment and crime become enshrined in policy and embedded in the workings of societal and institutional structures. These stock or official stories need to be challenged by larger, more diverse stories, stories that help to illuminate how systems operate.

Creating a Context for Storytelling

Context matters, and yet we are living in a time of context collapse. It used to take months and even years for urban legends to develop and be circulated. Today, in a nanosecond, bots can disseminate across cyberspace dramatic but entirely fictional stories of welfare fraud, Black on white violence, and murder or rape supposedly committed by illegal immigrants. These become simulacra—versions of simulated reality that become more "real" to people than actual empirical truth. These fake stories are buttressed by all the accoutrements of legitimate reporting such as multiple (fictional) eyewitness

accounts and doctored photos. Powerful and disturbing, these stories raise
fear of the other to chronic levels and create a bifurcated schism around the
fault line of patriotism. Believe these stories and attack mainstream media
and you're considered a patriot. Critique them and demonstrate their obvious falsity and you're labeled an enemy of the people.

So stories are not all benign or helpful. How a story is told, and by
whom, profoundly shapes how it is heard. There are forces at work beyond
whatever setting we are engaged with that are seeking to sow divisiveness,
encourage fear, and promote either/or thinking. So any attempt to do antiracism work by sharing stories of how whites build antiracist identities has to
begin with intentionally creating a shared context for that work.

First, we need to introduce the spaces in which we are gathering.
Antiracist gatherings in the United States typically start by acknowledging
that participants stand on land first inhabited by indigenous people that was
later colonized in an act of genocide by European settlers. It's important to
mention genocide and to acknowledge local battles, lynchings, massacres,
and other atrocities. That simple acknowledgment helps set an epistemological context for approaching race as a socially and politically sculpted
phenomenon. But, as podcasts like *This Land* (crooked.com/podcast-series/
this-land/) make clear, the question of the legality of a hosting institution
claiming to "own" the land on which it's built is seriously suspect, given the
history of broken and disregarded treaties between the U.S. government and
indigenous peoples. In most institutions you'll find some people working
on reparations, debt forgiveness, and free tuition and board for indigenous
students.

After introducing the space on which the workshop is held, taking time
for personal introductions helps invite the complexity of this work into
the room from the very beginning. We have seen the following different
approaches work well:

- *Circle of objects.* People gather in a large circle and each participant
  places an object that has some personal meaning for their identity in
  the middle of the space. Each person is then invited to pick up their
  artifact and talk about why it means something significant for their
  identity. This allows people to talk emotionally and often with great
  pride about their own background or family history. It's an early way
  to break the expectation that whites often have that they are under
  pressure to confess their apparent racism.
- *I Am From.* Here each person composes a personal poem responding
  to structured prompts regarding their identity and then reads their
  poem to the whole group. The "I Am From" poem stresses the positive
  aspects of personal identity and moves past the shaming process of

kicking off a conversation with an admission of guilt from white attendees (Klein, 2019).

- *When I First Became Aware of Race.* Going around the room each participant takes a turn to answer the same question—"When did I first become aware of race?" This allows for the revelation of the inevitable diversity of experience with race that's going to be evident in every group.
- *The Story of My Name.* Participants take their first name, surname, or a nickname and talk about how those names came about. This is often a surprisingly emotional experience (at least to participants) as they recall family struggles or speak with deep love about family members.

Any group comprises a mosaic of diverse experiences so it's important to find a way to invite the rich but hidden resources in the room to come to light. For example, all-white groups sometimes have members who have spouses in mixed-race relationships or who are raising children of color, who can bring depths of understanding to a workshop that may not be immediately apparent unless they are able to introduce themselves at more length.

A typical dynamic that sometimes emerges in a white-dominated workshop is participants playing the "I'm Woker Than You" game. Here, some group members engage in an attempt to show their racial awareness by using the specialist language of critical race theory (Delgado & Stefancic, 2017), quoting academic literature such as Sullivan (2014) and DiAngelo (2018), or by citing history and individuals unfamiliar to many. Group members new to racial work are made to feel inadequate or inexperienced. This is a variant on the disdaining dynamic noted by the European American Collaborative Challenging Whiteness (2010), whereby whites who believe themselves to be racially cognizant communicate contempt and pity for their supposedly unenlightened colleagues.

It's important to be aware of this possible dynamic and to head it off by taking a number of steps. Leaders and facilitators who have extensive experience can emphasize their suspicions of any self-congratulatory instincts they feel whenever they start to tell themselves (and others) how woke they are. The way leaders phrase questions for groups to consider is also important. For example, posing as an opening discussion question "What elements of learned white supremacy do you most struggle with inside yourself?" is very different from starting off by asking, "How do you fight against white supremacy?" Both questions are important but they should be sequenced appropriately. The first question is a better starting question because it implies that all members are on the never-ending journey to become a white antiracist. This kind of formulation can stop workshops kicking off with each participant vying to demonstrate how "right on" and "woke" they are.

Beginning With Ourselves

Our primitive ego brains tend to make sense of the world through bifurcation. We mark people, events, and things as "same" or "different," or "with us" or "against us." This kind of binary thinking is often identified as deriving from the European Enlightenment and its belief in positivism and scientism (Jones & Okun, 2001). Delving deeply into our own histories is a way of realizing the complexity of identity and resisting the false individualism our dominant culture trumpets. Note that we are not resisting individuality; each of us is unique and the specific events, loyalties, loves, and experiences of our lives are what mark us as who we are in a way that is totally distinctive. But we also contain multitudes. We're not contained only in our unique elements, but also defined by all that reaches out in and through us to interdependence, to plurality, to difference as joy.

Mary Hess grew up with stories and practices her family learned through the rough economic times of the depression and farming. These included stories of looking out for each other as neighbors, even those you might be competing with in other contexts. Her mother's early involvement with community theater meant that Hess was frequently drawn into community with people who loved people of the same gender, at a time when that was frowned upon. She also grew up in church spaces, where people lived the belief that humans are gifts of God and that as neighbors we must include even those we experience as enemies. These stories helped her to be more open to hearing the stories of people of color, once she was in spaces that invited those stories.

Stephen Brookfield's parents met while serving in post–World War II occupied Germany, so he grew up with stories of fighting Nazism. His father escorted convoys to Canada, Sweden, and Russia; his mother served in the Women's Royal Navy Service (WRENS); his aunt was a codebreaker; and his godmother was an army nurse in Libya. In these stories Britain was an isolated small island fighting doggedly and alone against the might of the German empire. His narrative of how life should be lived was framed around the idea of never giving in or giving up, a reverence for Churchillian-style leadership (which he later critiqued severely), and the importance of collectively sticking together through the worst of times. Brookfield's embrace of solidarity and collectivism is grounded in these stories as is his own faith in the value of stubborn determination and persistence.

For each of us, it is the combination of our stories—those we mourn for the ignorance that shaped us and those we embrace for the resources they offer—that fuels our work on developing antiracist identity. Stories give us identity and when the two of us introduce ourselves at the start of a workshop, training, or course, we are essentially telling stories that brought us to this work, or that illustrate the need for us to get involved. A story that illustrates a turning point in our lives, or that shows that we still have so much to learn, is a great way to kick off an antiracist conversation. A good story can crystallize relevant dynamics of how racism is enacted, how pushback happens, or how easy it is to "miss" the racial significance of something. If the events described are ones that people can recognize or identify with, then that brings them into meaningful participation much more quickly than a statistical analysis. We can't ask people to share their stories if we haven't first told some of our own in ways that are humble, honest, and deeply conscious of context.

Setting Ground Rules for Storytelling

When asking people to share personal stories, it's a good idea to set some ground rules, or to evolve them with the group. Stories are such personal creations that people can go deep into detail without realizing that others are getting lost. So we need to bring that, and other, tendencies to people's attention. Typical rules we suggest are agreeing to speak only in the first person, practicing openness to multiple perspectives, not interrupting, and not monopolizing the "floor" by taking up all of the available time. We ask group members to take the risk of speaking half-formed ideas and to assume that awkward comments are expressed in the sincere effort to be honest with each other. Singleton's (2012, 2014) four "courageous conversations" ground rules are easily remembered and very adaptable: stay engaged, speak your truth, expect to experience discomfort, and expect and accept a lack of closure.

One agreement that Hess often works with is from the Hypatia Institute (thehypatiagroupinc.com). In simple form it is as follows:

Respect others.
Be open.
Listen actively.
Take risks.
Be accountable.
Q-tip (quit taking things too personally)

Alternatively, she often uses an agreement that began with the Center for Courage and Renewal (n.d.) and has been elaborated upon by the Fund for Theological Exploration (2012, p. 11):

Give and receive welcome.
Be present as fully as possible.

What is offered in the circle is by invitation not demand.

Speak your truth in ways that respect other people's truth.

No fixing, saving, advising, or correcting each other.

Learn to respond to others with honest, open questions.

When the going gets rough, turn to wonder.

Attend to your own inner teacher.

Trust and learn from the silence.

Observe deep confidentiality.

Know that it's possible to leave the circle with whatever it was that you needed when you arrived, and that the seeds planted here can keep growing in the days ahead.

Shared covenants like these are not perfect or panaceas. They are shaped by the identities and experiences of those involved and sometimes represent racial blind spots. For example, emphasizing "respect" risks being interpreted as never challenging a peer or never pointing out the racism embedded in a particular remark or action. We both resonate with the desire to move into the more ambitious "brave" spaces advocated by Pawlowski (2019) and agree with Farber-Robertson (2000) that the goal of honest talk is to "advocate and act on your point of view in such a way as to encourage confrontation and inquiry into it" and cultivate "a high capacity for advocacy coupled with a high capacity for inquiry and vulnerability without feeling threatened" (p. 27).

Starting a workshop by building a shared agreement on how stories will be shared helps create a common context for the group's work. It also gives you as the facilitator a way to do some quick assessment. You can tell a lot from the concerns that people raise as you walk through elements of an agreement and the manner of their participation. Do they speak up frequently and engage, or sit silently neither agreeing nor disagreeing? You can also gauge the degree to which people are already on the same page, or whether you are going to be working with people who are at odds with each other and the goals of the event. And of course, while you're assessing the group, they are assessing you. Are you listening carefully? Do you ask clarifying questions rather than assuming you know what is being said? Are you open to half-formed ideas? Do you gently deflect shaming responses and invite genuine curiosity?

Two common elements often found in group agreements include "no fixing" and "we come as equals." We have learned a lot with and from groups who have struggled with these elements. "No fixing" doesn't mean that we're not to consider solutions or responses, but rather acknowledging that we're not here to set someone else straight. "No fixing" conveys that we're not trying to author a grand solution, but rather to keep learning and build-ing partnerships for the future that draw on each other's wisdom. Indeed, wisdom usually clarifies that no universal fix exists and that contextually shaped, partial responses are the best we can hope for.

Similarly, "we come as equals" might have a nice ring to it and point to the aspiration of shared learning. But does it also help us to be mindful of the ways in which power manifests between us with respect to race, gender, sexuality, ability? There will be some in a group who assert their truth in an unambiguous and forceful way. But what if you and others recognize that truth as racist? If someone insists they have never been racist and that they never see color, we can recognize those as sincerely held beliefs, but we are obligated to point out how those beliefs are often central to a white suprema-cist consciousness. Moral equality does not imply epistemological parity. Just because we come as moral equals doesn't translate into the false equivalency of believing that all views are equally worthy, all experiences equally valuable, and that denying that racism exists is one acceptable view among others.

Shared agreements function like rules of a game. They give us space to try something out, to "play" with ideas in a way that makes it more likely that we can be transformed. We have often used the movie *The Color of Fear* (Wah, 1994) to demonstrate the practices of structured conversation grounded in storytelling. The film records the experience of a racially diverse group of men talking about their racial identities. There are two white men in the group, one of whom has worked on his own racial awareness and one who subscribes to color-blindness. Viewers are drawn into the stories of these two men and through them into the contradictions of white racial identity. Other participants in the film (two are African American, two are Latino, and three have Asian heritages—Japanese and Chinese) model being present to one's own pain at the same time as being committed to structural analysis and building cultures of reconciliation and healing. We have never *not* found this film useful.

The film, which is now available in full on YouTube, shows how shared agreements function. There are several moments in which a participant vio-lates a common discussion agreement such as speaking on behalf of others, interrupting, or refusing to own their feelings. In each instance the group asks that participant to step back and remember what they are committed to. Using this film early in a longer workshop invites people to see the utility of a conversation agreement and models what to do when the agreement is contravened. It shows how to acknowledge the depth of the pain that engag-ing racism evokes, but also the healing and reconciliation that can emerge when that pain is expressed. For white persons in the thrall of white fragility (DiAngelo, 2018) it offers a constructive way through discomfort.

Learning From Our Own Stories

Once covenants and agreements are set, the next step is to work with each person's own life story while building a space in which each story contributes to a larger whole. When we teach longer workshops or classes, we often ask people to respond to an autobiographical set of story prompts in writing or voice ahead of the workshop. When such writing is shared in advance (via Google Drive, a learning management system, or even simply email), there is an opportunity for people to begin to learn a little bit about each other prior to coming to the learning event. A few writing prompts can invite people to ponder their personal racial identity development prior to showing up for conversation.

Hess and her colleague Vivian Jenkins Nelsen often ask people to respond to the following questions:

1. When were you first aware that people were received differently because of assumptions about race? Tell a story or give an example.
2. What advice, rules, and information did your parents or grandparents give you about associating with people whom they assumed were from a different racial space? Give an example or tell a story.
3. What racial words did your parents use or forbid?
4. Who was the most influential person in shaping your racial views as a child? Why?
5. How were people of color portrayed on radio, television, or in films and books when you were a child? Who was your favorite character?
6. Whom did you admire as a teen who was from a different racial/ethnic context than you? Why?
7. How have your views on race changed since you were a child?
8. How do your family members feel about the changes?
9. Which views have remained the same?
10. How have such views about race helped or hindered you in your work life?

These questions can, of course, be framed with respect to other forms of oppression. Here, they help to "till the soil" of preexisting understandings of racialization. By inviting workshop participants to share stories that have shaped their experiences we signal that we are open to and interested in the fullness of their experiences.

In response to these prompts people often write about how the elements of a white racial identity are learned early in life, usually as an implicit acceptance of the universally superior nature of white experience.

When race is foregrounded it is usually depicted as something that Black, brown, native, and other people possess. As people grow older they often encounter other framings of race through popular film and media or in schools and malls. But the normative nature of whiteness which holds that light skin is the norm and every other skin tone is "other" remains at a subterranean level.

To build a collective story for workshop participants we have used the "power flower" exercise (Figure 5.1) that we learned from the Ontario Institute for Studies in Education (n.d.). Here, the petals of a flower in a line drawing diagram are used to explore which elements of identity in a particular setting are perceived as threatening and subsequently marginalized, and which define dominant narratives. Focusing on elements such as native

Figure 5.1. The power flower.

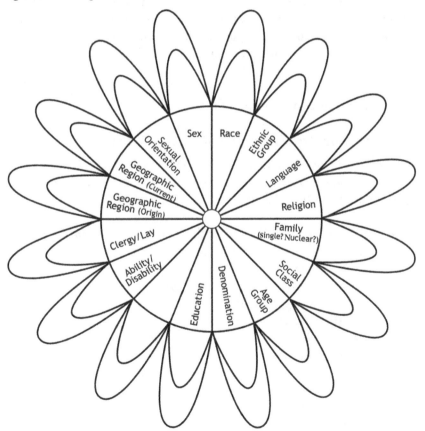

Note. From Arnold et al. (1991). *Educating for a change.* Between the Lines Press. Printed with permission.

language (is yours dominant, or are you a second- or third-language learner in this space?), citizenship status (do you have documents or not?), skin color (is your skin light or dark?) offers ways for group members to recognize how different people are situated in the wider cultural and racial matrix.

Using Digital Media

It is often easier to share a short video that has been thoughtfully produced about a specific element of racialization than it is to simply tell someone about the idea. Video, image, and graphics have an aesthetic impact that hits people viscerally as well as cognitively. Reading accounts of racial discrimination can certainly affect us powerfully, but seeing images of human beings smothered, shot, beaten, insulted, spat on, or demeaned can never be deleted from one's consciousness. When a group watches a video together, they have a shared experience that can then help propel them into deeper conversation. After watching you can just ask a simple open-ended question such as "What emotions or feelings do you have right now?" People can respond on a social media tool like Backchannel Chat, or they can do some quick free writes, or just share what they're feeling verbally. This sometimes helps people go straight to the source of their fear of talking about race.

Stories of White Racial Identity and Color Blindness

Resources that are freely available on the web are tools that workshop participants can return to again and again and share with others. The following are examples of such digital pieces and how we use them:

- Francesca Ramsey's 4-minute video *5 Tips for Being an Ally* explains how privilege operates with a sense of humor and pop culture references (youtu.be/_dg86g-QlM0). Unpacking varied responses to such a piece with respect for all of the responses (even those which you want to challenge) helps shape a space for transformative learning.
- Brené Brown's (2017) response to the white nationalist march at Charlottesville (www.facebook.com/brenebrown/videos/we-need-to-keep-talking-about-charlottesville/1778878652127236/) sets out why white people need to engage white supremacy directly and what it means to hold people accountable. It invites whites to reframe their experience of current events in a way that participates in building an antiracist identity.
- *How Can We Win?* by Kimberly Latrice Jones (2020) is a powerful and emotional expression of how it feels to participate in a 450-year-old

game where the rules are fixed to preserve anti-Blackness (www.youtube. com/watch?v=sb9_qGOa9Go). A useful resource to demonstrate to white groups the "realness" of Black frustration.

- World Trust, an organization focused on creating media to engage social injustice, has a film called *Mirrors of Privilege: Making Whiteness Visible* (world-trust.org/mirrors-of-privilege-making-whiteness-visible/). The film offers interviews with a number of established educators (Peggy McIntosh, Francine Kendall, Tim Wise, and others) that explore different ways in which white privilege hides itself.
- "What It Means to Be American," a short extract from the classic *Color of Fear* documentary (Wah, 1994), in which Victor Lewis succinctly summarizes how being white, being human, and being American are considered synonyms in U.S. culture (www.youtube. com/watch?time_continue=3&v=2nmhAJYxFT4&feature=emb_ logo). This is a useful conversation starter for groups that attempt to keep emotions at bay.
- Trevor Noah's remarkable meditation on the 2020 shooting of George Floyd and the weaponizing of whiteness against an African American birdwatcher in New York's Central Park (www.youtube.com/ watch?v=v4amCfVbA_c&feature=emb_logo). This can be used to illustrate the power of turning questions on their head as he suggests that instead of asking, "Why would people loot?" the real question is "Why *wouldn't* people loot?"
- The Racial Justice Collaborative in Theological Education has collected many videos in an online blog space that is easily searched (rjb.religioused.org/resources/).

Stories Examining Structural Racism

Given the wide range of historical injustices around race, a large number of documentary films exist examining this issue. They are all constructed from archival footage and interviews with participants in the events depicted. A few we have used in predominantly white contexts include the following:

- The California Newsreel series *Race: The Power of an Illusion* (news-reel.org/video/race-the-power-of-an-illusion) lays out the history of the idea of race and shows how that idea came to function within structures such as federal housing support, military GI benefits, and many other government policies.
- *Eyes on the Prize* (a film made in 1987 about the civil rights movement in the United States) (en.wikipedia.org/wiki/Eyes_on_the_Prize).

- *Traces of the Trade: A Story From the Deep North* (a film made by a seminary student in 2008 about tracing her family's involvement in the slave trade in New England) (www.tracesofthetrade.org).
- *Unfinished Business* (a film made in 1986 about Japanese internment in the United States during World War II) (www.farfilm.com/unfinished-business-film/).
- *Dakota 38* (a film made in 2012 about the single largest mass execution in U.S. history, following the U.S.–Dakota conflict) (www.smoothfeather.com/dakota38).
- *A Time for Burning* (a film made in 1966 about the efforts of two Lutheran churches in Nebraska [one white, one Black] to engage racism) (en.wikipedia.org/wiki/A_Time_for_Burning).
- *13th* (named after the 13th Amendment to the U.S. constitution that abolished slavery, this 2016 film examines mass incarceration as a source of social control and economic wealth) (www.netflix.com/title/80091741).

Digital Stories From Current Communities of Color

There has been a true flowering of independent media in the last 2 decades. It is impossible to stay abreast of all that is being created and shared, but some of the videos that have been viewed and shared millions of times include the following:

- Chimamanda Ngozi Adichie's TED talk *The Danger of a Single Story* (www.ted.com/talks/chimamanda_adichie_the_danger_of_a_single_story?language=en).
- The Stylehorse Collective's *We Shall Remain* (youtu.be/Gs0iwY6YjSk).
- The Cleveland City Club features speakers such as Julie Lythcott-Haims, Ta-Nehisi Coates, and Irshad Manji (www.cityclub.org/archives).
- Colorlines.com and RacismReview.org both curate examples from across the web of people working on racial justice.

Working in predominantly white institutions we have found that media created by artists and activists of color bring additional voices into the conversation without fatiguing our colleagues of color who are rightfully tired of assuming the responsibility to teach whites about racism.

Hollywood Movies

We mostly dislike the common narratives of Hollywood films because they almost always reinscribe dominant racial categories, even as they purport to be changing them. They are part of the white savior industrial complex (Aronson, 2017)—the culture industry that produces movies in which big-hearted white teachers fight to lead their BIPOC students to academic success and self-reliance. This is a place in which we must be careful to consider whether the narrative of a film is a "stock" story (one that subtly or not so subtly affirms white supremacy), a story of resistance, or even a powerful counter-story (Bell, 2010).

Over the years many films have been lauded for their empowering antiracist messages. *Crash* (Bob Yari Productions, 2004), *Dangerous Minds* (Hollywood Pictures, 1994), *Cry Freedom* (Universal Pictures, 1987), *Gran Torino* (Double Nickel Entertainment, 2008), *The Help* (DreamWorks, 2011), *Remember the Titans* (Walt Disney Pictures, 2000), *Hidden Figures* (Fox 2000, 2016), and *Green Book* (Participant Media, 2018) are all examples of these. The problem is that these represent people of color as being caught in systems of domination from which they must be rescued by "good" white people. These films are compelling in that they call out to that within us that wants to see people emerge from domination. But the hidden "trick" of these films is to center the experience of a white character, drawing the viewer into once again making whiteness the normative focal point, and subtly nudging viewers toward a view of such liberation as individually produced by a "white savior."

These films can be introduced later in a workshop as opportunities to deconstruct dominant narratives and reaffirm commitments to shared and collective action. We have hosted events such as a viewing of the film *The Help* paired with a panel of people who grew up in situations in which they or their parents were "the help." Such discussions open up a much more complex reality. In this instance, our colleagues Vivian Jenkins Nelsen and Duchess Harris were able to call attention to the utter absence of engagement with the underlying sexual terrorism present in the situations the film portrayed. They spoke from their own experiences, sharing stories from their extended families who had been victimized in just such ostensibly "good white" environments.

There are some rare examples of Hollywood films that depart from this common narrative, centering the experience of a person of color—films such as *She's Gotta Have It* (40 Acres and a Mule, 1986), *Fruitvale Station* (Significant Productions, 2013), *Get Out* (Blumhouse Productions, 2017), *Moonlight* (A24, 2016), and so on—but the Hollywood film industry is still predominantly white and male. However, the emergence of streaming networks such as Netflix, Amazon Prime, AppleTV+, and Hulu have encouraged story arcs like *Dear White People* (Sister Lee Productions, 2017–present) that spread over many hours and allow for more stories produced by filmmakers and activists of color.

Learning Through Shared Stories

It's not enough to consume other people's stories, no matter how helpful they may be. We need to find ways to listen into existence our own and others' stories that acknowledge the trauma white supremacy inflicts as well as illuminating how it's resisted.

One activity we use is the "four corners" exercise in which groups are invited to respond to prompts placed in the four corners of a room. This exercise grew from the work of intergroup dialogue pioneered at the University of Michigan (Dessel & Rogge, 2008). As people move from corner to corner they pivot the standpoint of group members from oppressor to oppressed, depending on the prompt (one placed in each corner of the room):

- Describe a time when oppressive comments or actions were directed to you (based on any aspect of your identity).
- Describe a time when you were a perpetrator of an oppressive act or comments.
- Describe a time when you witnessed an oppressive act and did nothing about it.
- Describe a time when you witnessed an act of oppression and intervened.

Before moving to a particular corner, each small group starts by talking about the fears that members have talking about oppression, discrimination, or race with people who share their racial identity, and then with those who don't share this identity. Facilitators, preferably in a multiracial team, model having this conversation first before inviting a group to spend a few minutes talking about this.

When it's time to go to a corner, small group members spend 15 minutes responding to the particular prompt they find there. When time is up, they move clockwise as a group to the next corner, where they spend 15 minutes responding to a different prompt. After all the groups have visited all the corners, the whole workshop reconvenes for a metareflection in which, among other things, participants discuss the differences between stock, concealed, resistance, and counter-stories (Bell, 2010).

Each of the corners has an identified facilitator who ensures that no one story dominates at that corner and that all get a chance to share. The lead facilitator explains the timing (for example, spending 15 minutes in each corner) and keeps the whole group on track by calling "time" when it's the moment to move clockwise around the room. The corner facilitators of this exercise are instructed as follows:

- Don't interrupt or speak when someone is answering the question.
- Try to avoid spending a lot of time answering individual questions.
- Keep the group on track with time.
- Help people to step out of their comfort zone and let down their guard a bit.

We have found that this exercise invites a range of complex stories and generally helps participants refrain from making snap judgments based on how people shape their appearance. It also invites personal stories that create a more shared context in the workshop.

Creating New Stories Together

A crucial project in combating white supremacy is for people to build antiracist identities across racial differences. To do this we need to create shared stories collaboratively from the ground up.

The Story Circle

In a story circle a group of four people gathers to do four rounds of storytelling. In each round one person tells a story, and the other three listen in a specific way. You can invite people to tell a story that focuses on a specific event or incident, such as the following:

- A moment when you knew you were observing genuinely collective action
- A moment when you watched someone else disrupt racism constructively
- A moment when you knew something was wrong about race but had no language to describe what was happening

The other three group members are assigned different kinds of listening roles, such as the following:

- *Factual listener.* This person listens for the facts or actions of the story.
- *Feelings listener.* This person listens for the feelings expressed or embodied in the story.
- *Values listener.* This person listens for the values embedded in the story.

As the storyteller describes a specific incident or series of events, the other three group members are listening with their particular perspective. When the story is done, they then share with the storyteller what they heard in the story from their listening vantage point.

Once a full round has concluded, the roles rotate one person to the right, and the process is repeated. If you offer people 3 minutes to tell a story, and then roughly 10 minutes for the other three people to share what they heard, you can complete all four rounds in approximately an hour.

Titling a Story

Another exercise we use focuses on a group generating a title together for a particular story. This process does not require a specific number of people per group, although three to five people is probably optimal.

In the titling exercise one person tells a brief story (here any of the prompts from the previous exercise would work, or you could choose a different one), while the other members of the group listen carefully. Once the storyteller is finished, he or she faces away from the other participants and listens as they offer potential titles for the story. After all possible titles are suggested, the storyteller turns back around and chooses one of them, explaining why it appeals to them. If none of the titles "work" for the story-teller, he or she can offer a different title.

Asking the storyteller to turn away from the other group members helps him or her to concentrate on what is being said, rather than focusing on the individuals who are sharing possible titles. Turning away embodies a form of distancing oneself and then coming back into the group. It helps if stories are limited to no more than 3 minutes and a time limit is set on the discussion of titles. If you run this activity with lots of small groups, you can then collect the set of titles from each group and present them as a "table of contents" to the whole workshop that can ignite some purposeful curiosity.

Final Thought

The exercises in storytelling we offer in this chapter all stress the importance of careful listening. The various ground rules we advocate are designed to create a space in which a story can be "held" rather than having the story-teller "be held" by it. Brown (2017) pointed out in the video we referenced earlier that a story can own us or we can own it and write a different ending. When we are open to hearing someone else's story, we are drawn beyond our previous ways of seeing the world. But we have to remain conscious of the danger of uncritically assimilating, and celebrating, all the stories we hear. There are many types of stories that float around us and in which we have been immersed that are designed to keep racism in place. And there are other complicating stories that we have no awareness of.

As Bell (2010) made clear, our stories about race can be stock stories that simply reinscribe white supremacy, or they can be concealed stories that circulate alongside of stock stories but are held within minority communities as sources of strength and pride in identity. We need to move beyond both stock and concealed stories into stories of active resistance, and ultimately to generate counter-stories that

> are deliberately constructed to challenge the stock stories, build on and amplify resistance stories, and offer ways to interrupt the status quo and work for change. Such stories enact continuing critique and resistance to the stock stories and enable new possibilities for inclusive human community. (Bell et al., 2008, pp. 8–9)

6

EMBRACING THE
DISCOMFORT OF RACE TALK

Whites like the two of us know that examining our racial identity, and becoming aware of how that identity means we benefit from a racist system, is inherently discomforting. As we've discussed, whites' journey to increased racial cognizance typically involves denial, shock, shame, guilt, embarrassment, and humiliation. So preparing whites to experience discomfort as they enter the brave space of racial conversations has to be one of the most pressing tasks of anyone trying to help people develop an antiracist white identity. Few want to volunteer for what Tilley and Powick (2015) described as the radical stuff of having their comfortable worldview exploded. The desire to cling to the belief that one is a good white person explains what DiAngelo (2018) called white fragility, whereby the chief concern becomes preserving one's emotional equanimity.

We suspect that the reason that many race-based discussions move quickly into cries from participants to be "respected" by each other is because being treated respectfully is equated with not being upset, not being challenged, and not being called out. When your whole being is focused on preserving your identity and self-concept as a good white person, and your emotional synapses are screaming, "Keep me safe!," then embracing discomfort is completely counterintuitive. Yet, as Stevenson (2014) argued, it is at the moment when you are feeling most threatened that the potential for the greatest learning is often present.

From work on critical thinking (Brookfield, 2012) and transformative learning (Cranton, 2016) in adults, it's clear that disequilibrium and disorientation are often the beginning of the most meaningful learning we do. But the sense that radical shifts are in the offing means that people are understandably reluctant and resist this effort. How can we help whites who believe they are color-blind embrace the discomfort of examining that belief? And if we're leading racial conversations but we have no therapeutic training, how can we guide them through their anger, outrage, sadness, fear, and anxiety?

Modeling the Embrace of Discomfort

Okun (2010) observed that "our culture is terrified of people who feel so deeply, particularly if that feeling occurs in people and in ways that transgress the predictable" (p. 151). When we get close to the pain of racism, the prospect of unleashing strong emotions is enough to cause many of us to want to retreat from any kind of race talk. This is why conversations on how white supremacy has pervaded our lives and shaped our actions

> will always be hard . . . will always be emotional and loaded to various degrees—and if they are not, then you are likely not having the right conversation. Racial oppression should always be an emotional topic to discuss. It should always be anger-inducing. (Oluo, 2018, p. 4)

Alerting people to the prospect of discomfort that awaits is a painful but crucial first step in helping them develop a white antiracist identity.

So as you enter into a new initiative or project focused on becoming antiracist, you need to remind yourself that discomfort itself is a sign of success, not of things gone awry. If people aren't significantly discomforted, then probably not much of importance is happening. This is just as true for ourselves as for those we teach. We need to model embracing our own discomfort in front of those that we work with. We need to remember that when we feel flustered, foolish, embarrassed, or out of control, those are not signs that we're unskilled or have lost the plot but rather an indication that we're fully engaged in difficult work.

When starting off a course, workshop, or training, one thing we suggest is beginning with a statement of what it is that you bring to the work you're doing with them. This summarizes how you've engaged (or not engaged) with race in the past and the way in which you continue to struggle with the difficult task of seeing the white supremacy that you've been immersed in. As an example, here's what coauthor Stephen Brookfield often says:

> *What I bring to this work as a white person is a history of not really noticing race for a large part of my life. I've had the luxury of thinking of race as something that others have, particularly people with Black and brown skin. I also bring to this work a history of being socialized into white supremacy—the idea*

that whites, because of their supposedly superior intelligence and ability to think calmly and objectively, should naturally be in positions of power and authority. It's been hard for me to notice just how much whiteness is the standard against which everything is being measured, because that's just how normality has always been presented to me.

I definitely bring a history of learned anti-Blackness and a fear of Blackness as something violent, unpredictable, threatening, and dangerous. This fear is sedimented in my consciousness, embedded in my synapses, part of my white racial DNA. I don't expect ever to be rid of it, but I can at least be more aware of it and notice when it rears its head in my own actions and in practices and policies I see all around me.

I also bring a sense of urgency that's developed over time that race, especially anti-Blackness, is the biggest unaddressed problem in the United States. So I'm trying to do better in trying to understand how my whiteness automatically privileges and protects me, compared to colleagues and friends of color. I'm trying to learn how to call out racism when I see it, both in interpersonal interactions and in institutional practices. I want to understand the dynamics of being an antiracist white person—for example, learning how I can use my white privilege to say and do things that carry less risk for me as a white person than they would for a colleague of color.

One of my problems I bring to this work is that I feel I've never done enough and that I never get it right. So I have to struggle against the pressure I put on myself of never making a mistake, of always being perfect. I now understand that trying to do race work as a white person can be done in one of two ways—imperfectly or not at all. I know I will say and do the "wrong" things and make a lot of mistakes and that I'll feel uncomfortable a lot of the time. But I also know that that's the nature of the beast and that if I feel comfortable probably not much of consequence is happening.

We also want to stress something we touch on throughout the book regarding the nature of success. As you prepare to teach a class, run a training, conduct a town hall meeting, or lead a task force, remember not to equate success with dramatic, road to Damascus transformations. Whites who are trying to develop an antiracist identity will be confused about how to do this, guilty that they are not making enough progress, and disappointed that they are not immediately viewed by people of color as their allies. The more they understand about the systemic, deep-seated nature of racism, the more they risk becoming demoralized by radical pessimism, by the feeling that as they realize just how pervasive racism is, they are simultaneously robbed of any sense of agency in combating it. "What can little me do against history, power, and culture?" is a question that will inevitably be asked. The answer, of course, is that big changes will come only through movements and collective action, something we will address later in this chapter.

Letting Go of Anxiety

Many readers of this book are probably already deeply into the work of developing an antiracist white identity and developing workshops for students, colleagues, and communities. But if you're doing this for the first time, you'll invariably feel the anxiety rising up within you. What can you do?

A nearly universal response to lessening anxiety involves breathing. Take one or two really deep breaths. Pay attention to your breath, and remind yourself that this work is larger than you are and that you are part of a larger community engaged in a social movement. Learning how to pay attention to your breath has all sorts of other useful dynamics. When you recognize that your breathing has started to speed up and your heart is pounding, try to pause and ask yourself what caused this shift within you.

Breathe—and reach out. No one can do this work alone. Reaching out can simply mean reading something a colleague has written or listening to a song that evokes shared energy for justice. Maybe it's pausing to look at a photograph of a rally you've been to or reading a note of thanks from someone for your efforts. Whatever helps bring to mind that you are part of a larger, collective effort will support the lessening of anxiety.

Confronting Guilt and Shame

Guilt and shame are some of the most powerful and discomforting emotions white people face as they learn how they have benefited from racism and how they've perpetuated that in conscious and unconscious ways. These are appropriate responses and, as Okun (2010) wrote,

> allowing ourselves to feel the guilt and shame can usher in a stage of profound personal transformation, one in which we realize that we participate in racist institutions and a racist culture, that we both benefit from and are deeply harmed by racism, and that we perpetuate racism, even when that is not our intention. (p. 60)

But we do not need to wallow too long in such feelings. Instead, we can experience them as a catalyst for learning and a deeper sense of commitment and purpose. One of the key elements for turning guilt from an incapacitating emotion to an empowering imperative is recognizing that, given the reality of systemic oppression, guilt is shared. Feeling guilt means you're waking up to the ways in which the system has positioned you and granted you benefits you have not earned, while denying such benefits to others. Recognizing that positioning can give you energy for changing the system. This is why it's so important to distinguish between guilt and shame. Guilt is recognition of action you regret; shame is a much more immobilizing feeling that you are yourself, in your very being, somehow wrong. Oppressive systems benefit from people turning their awareness of pain inward, where it can destroy the individual person. Shared pain can lead to shared accountability, and shared action.

In multiracial groups assume that expressions of white guilt and shame will very quickly become irritating to many people of color. Eddo-Lodge (2017) expressed this sentiment most succinctly:

> I don't want white guilt. Neither do I want to see white people wasting precious time profusely apologizing rather than actively doing things. No useful movements for change have ever sprung out of fervent guilt. Instead, get angry. Anger is useful. Use it for good. Support those in the struggle, rather than spending too much time pitying yourself. (p. 221)

In a reflection after a workshop Brookfield had run on teaching race in white spaces, one of the participants, Carmina Maye (2020), wrote the following: "I honestly have been having a hard time being in predominately white classes lately as people in this country realize, *again*, the issues that exist in America for Black people" (p. 2). At one point in a small group discussion Carmina heard a white participant describing her struggles with her own friends and family. Carmina's reaction is telling:

> While she was giving her long spiel on her good work, I couldn't figure out where to place my feelings. I could see it from a mile away; I even prepped myself for it before the class. I prepared for THIS, but I still wasn't ready. Her actions were soooo predictable, well, to me. It was something I knew was bound to happen in a class placed right in the heart of the world grappling with whether or not Black lives matter. But still felt completely uncomfortable, sick. Now, I am not one to dim anyone's light, but all I felt like saying was, "oh, okay. That's cute. You want a cookie?" I couldn't help but think, "this is not something new, why is it new to you? Why are you just now having these conversations?" I do not know this woman and may never have a class with her again; however, I will always remember what she did and how it made me feel. (p. 2)

It's important to note that once we learn how the term *racism* describes systems that construct and enforce white supremacy, and how we are implicated in those systems, the label loses some of its vicious power. This understanding can itself become an entry into deeper work. This is why helping people to think structurally is such a crucial educational project. Our initial intention in any kind of teaching, training, or leadership is to *normalize* racism. By that we mean to help people understand that racism is based in a learned ideology (white supremacy) supported by actions, habits, practices, policies, customs, and institutional functioning that are perceived as normal and unremarkable. We try to stress at the outset of any training or workshop that in a culture permeated with the idea of white superiority, *not* to have learned and practiced racism would be almost imaginable. But before we say this to others, we have to believe it of ourselves.

Both of us know we have elements of racism within us that will never disappear. The most we can hope for is that we are sufficiently aware of them to enable us to limit their influence on our actions. We must try to watch out for the "savior" complex, whereby we view ourselves as having "beaten" the racism lurking inside ourselves and cleansed ourselves of racist inclinations. So as you approach the discomfort of working to teach about antiracism, try to be kind to yourself. Don't expect yourself to be an antiracist superhero who never thinks or does racist things. When you witness racist elements in your actions, tell yourself that this is, of course, completely normal.

Dealing With the "R" Word

A quick glance at commercial media confirms that being called a racist is considered a *very bad thing*—in Oluo's (2018) terms, "the worst thing to happen to anybody anywhere" (p. 213). For those who think of themselves as good, color-blind whites, it's the ultimate insult because it's usually applied to people who do overt violence against people of color, commit blatantly destructive acts, and use hate speech. Kernahan (2019) pointed out that President George W. Bush stated that being called racist by Kanye West was the lowest point of his 8-year term—this in a presidency that contained the 9/11 destruction of the Twin Towers and the death and violence of an unjustified war in Iraq.

In an effort to address the power of the term *racism* head on, we often start out talking in workshops, classes, or trainings about the times when we've heard the comment "You're a racist" directed at us and how initially we rushed to defend ourselves or negate the accusation. Then, we outline a different response we've tried to take of standing in inquiry and wondering in what ways that might be true. We acknowledge how we have benefited from the social construction of race and white structural advantage and how, once we become more open to perceiving the pain of racism, it has moved us into exploring ways to change it.

We also model embracing discomfort in the moment by not glossing over the inevitable contradictions we experience as privileged whites blind to our own white supremacy. For example, Hess remembers a specific workshop in which using the CIQ caused people of color to say that its anonymity meant it was another way for people to enact microaggressions. In the face of this observation Hess paused, breathed deeply, and listened closely to the criticism being offered. In that specific workshop she and her team chose to stop using that tool and picked a different one. Following that workshop, she brought the experience as a "case study" to other colleagues of hers, several of whom are scholars of color who use the form. The upshot of that experience has been that she continues to use the CIQ process, but introduces it with more nuance and context.

Responding to Racist Comments

In a predominantly white space there are bound to be inadvertently racist comments and sentiments expressed. One of the most common situations you'll experience will be hearing someone say something that has racist undertones, but that falls short of being an overt macroaggression. When this happens you need to address it. This is particularly important if the group has members of color.

However, you have to watch out for the tendency to use this as an opportunity to demonstrate your "wokeness." If you're too quick to pounce on these in a way that blames and shames whites for their unwitting racism, this "creates hostility and resentment on the part of many students who feel as if only 'politically correct' comments are permissible" (Sullivan, 2014, p. 52). We both struggle with walking the line between the need to point out racist comments and the need to keep those who are inadvertent racists in the conversation. Sometimes the line between deliberate intent and unwitting ignorance is very clear, but at other times it is almost undetectable.

As a general guide we suggest the following steps:

- Stop the conversation and pause to say something along the lines of "You know there's something about what you just said that's bothering me, so let me just check in about why that is."
- Check your understanding of the person's words with them and ask if you've missed or misinterpreted something.
- Ask the group if anyone else is bothered by the comment.
- Explain why you found the comment troublesome by giving an example of when you've thought or said something similar yourself.

- Frame your interjection by also saying which elements of learned racism you detected in the comment.
- Finish by saying how important it is to get into the habit of interrupting conversations whenever you hear something problematic.

We find Perez's (2018) description of her response to leading a multiracial, all-queer group in which a white man used the "N" word to be helpful. She suggests a series of steps including recommending that the group slow down to address the incident, specifying a time limit to discuss it, emphasizing "I" statements, and checking in when the allotted time is up.

Channeling Collective Anger and Outrage

The social activist Horton (1990) famously maintained that it was important to keep the flame of anger and outrage burning, but not to let it become a fire that consumes you. Anger is a great catalyst, but not an emotion that one can live in for lengthy periods of time. Yet anger and outrage are perfectly rational responses to learning how we have been duped by a system that causes so much suffering. Digital social media latch onto potent emotions like anger and outrage as a way to command our attention. Clicking on "thumbs up" or summoning an "angry face" emoji in a Facebook stream may give us a quick and superficially satisfying way to respond, but it rarely invites collective action.

One important challenge in that dynamic is to find appropriate targets for such anger. Far too many people find themselves led into blaming specific people who perpetuate the system—a president, a senator, a corporate or media tycoon—rather than directing their anger to its root causes. To understand how a racist white person gains enormous power one needs to know how slavery played a central role in shaping the unfettered capitalism that accrued ever-greater wealth to whites at the expense of people of color (Beckert, 2014; Grandin, 2015). Replacing an individual, no matter how satisfying that might be to some, is nowhere analogous to replacing a system.

When we find our own anger arising, we need to be thoughtful about where to direct it. A facilitator who focuses solely on expressing their own anger is walking a dangerous path, given that people come to workshops from multiple settings with different motivations. In a mandatory training on diversity, inclusion, or antiracism your expression of justifiable anger can quickly backfire. You may be seen as proselytizing and demeaning people, blaming audience members for not being "woke" enough (European

American Collaborative Challenging Whiteness, 2010). This is a self-inflicted form of sabotage.

If you begin by expressing anger, we suggest that it be directed at the way your own cultural socialization kept you blind to racial injustice and prevented you from seeing what was really happening around you. Then, point out that anger is best expressed in collective action that seeks to disrupt systems of oppression. One reason why protests, vigils, and other forms of nonviolent civil resistance have proven so effective over the centuries is because they invite people to connect their anger to a greater purpose, one that stretches beyond individual hurt and moves together into action on behalf of all (Chenoweth & Stephan, 2011).

As Parker Palmer (2011) noted, when we stand in the tragic gap between what we dream to be possible and what is currently the case, our hearts will be broken. The key question is whether they will be broken into shards or broken open in larger connection. Embracing discomfort means being willing to be opened up, to be transformed. It requires a form of fierce kindness that refuses to avoid challenges and steps directly into learning that can be catalyzed by strong emotions. Yet it is "kind" because it continues to believe in and be based upon strong respect for and appreciation of our shared humanity.

Creating Spaces to Embrace Discomfort Together

What kinds of spaces support embracing discomfort? These are spaces in which our feelings can be expressed and engaged, spaces in which we can draw on our hearts as well as our heads, what are sometimes called holding spaces, containers for transformation (Eoyang & Holladay, 2013). We have already stressed the importance of starting with some kind of shared agreement or guidelines for how to proceed. Similarly, we have argued for inquiring regularly into how a process is going through the use of Backchannel Chat or the CIQ. These two practices—shared grounding and constant inquiry—form bookends on our practice.

In between the opening and closing of a workshop it is crucial to invite a range of sensory engagement that generates integrated and whole learning. We need to invoke the concept of brave as well as safe space by clearly naming what is to come. People need to be resocialized regarding their expectations of what counts as the norms of conversation. Eurocentric epistemology privileges staying calm and frames expressions of righteous anger as "being disrespectful." Similarly, patriarchy and white supremacy regard crying tears of frustration or sadness as "losing control" or being "too emotional." So we need to prepare people for the strong feelings that will emerge when they study how systems of racism function.

We must also watch out for shaming people for their responses. We must demonstrate how to ask authentic questions and how to respond to questions that arise from ignorance. We need to hold clearly to agreements, so that if someone is consistently violating such principles and refuses to change their behavior, they must be asked to leave a class, meeting, or workshop. For all these tasks we have found several practices to be helpful.

Begin With a Meditative, Grounding, or Prayerful Pause

We like to begin by attending to our bodies and pausing to focus on the task to come by asking everyone to spend a minute or so considering some basic ground rules. Using the courageous conversations model (Singleton, 2012, 2014; Singleton & Linton, 2005) you can ask people to envisage quietly what it would mean to stay engaged, speak their own truth, assume good intent, expect discomfort, and accept a lack of closure. This should be done as a silent reflective pause of about a minute.

Another option is to ask for a minute of calm breathing when people sit up straight, place their hands (palm upward) on their knees, and breathe slowly. This brings people into the moment so they can focus fully on the conversation.

If the event is taking place in a religious setting or a spiritual retreat, you can even use the following prayer that Hess has found helpful in many of the contexts in which she teaches:

> Keep my anger from becoming meanness.
> Keep my sorrow from collapsing into self-pity.
> Keep my heart soft enough to keep breaking.
> Keep my anger turned towards justice, not cruelty.
> Remind me that all of this, every bit of it, is for love.
> Keep me fiercely kind. (Truman, 2018)

Finally, another option is to ask everyone to read a quote that for them captures some important truth about race. Give people a minute or two to sit quietly with the quote and ask them to ponder what the quote means for their own antiracist commitments.

Model Your Own Racial Autobiography

We argue throughout this book for the general importance of teachers, trainers, and leaders modeling how they work to become white antiracists.

There is no more crucial point for this to happen than at the start of an event. If you are a white facilitator leading a group of predominantly white participants in an effort to uncover the white supremacist ideology that lives within us all, then you need to begin by disclosing your own racial autobiography. Talk about times when your own racist instincts have come to the fore, how you have responded when people point out your racism to you, what prompted the realization that you were not the good white you thought yourself to be, and the ways that you struggle right now with the learned white supremacy you keep discovering within yourself.

The best modeling acknowledges your struggle to grapple with an awareness of your collusion with racism, your feelings of shame, and your search for an antiracist positive white identity. Gallman et al. (2010) pointed out that "to grapple implies an emotional, as well as intellectual, struggle" (p. 2), and modeling how emotionally taxing you find examining your whiteness— yet why you must keep doing that—is very reassuring for many people. As a "type A" personality who loves problem-solving, Brookfield likes to talk about how difficult it is for him to keep doing this work knowing that there will be no tidy resolutions or fixes. But then he also talks about how supported he feels when working with other people who share this frustration.

Ensure Your Leadership Is Collaborative and Multiracial

Working as part of a multiracial team means trusting our colleagues to "call us" on behaviors and beliefs that aren't helpful and shows people what it looks like to work collaboratively against racism. A multiracial team that publicly addresses its own racial dynamics provides a model of a productively discomforting conversation that can be replicated. Becoming aware of one's learned white supremacy is an important first step for whites, but it's not enough just to have this knowledge. We need to be able to build a common antiracist cause across multiple racial identities. Certainly there are times when working in a racial affinity group is useful and necessary. But ultimately we cannot get stuck in talking only to those who share our identity, history, and experience.

Stand in Inquiry

As we move forward we need to model standing in inquiry, showing how we constantly seek more information or new experiences. This entails wondering why things are and how they could be, asking good questions, and remaining open to learning. We ponder why we feel a certain way when we hear a story that's new to us. We wonder why we so often feel immediately defensive in the light of new information. We speculate if there could be other elements to a situation of which we are unaware. This models, as Farber-Robertson (2000) suggested, a way to "advocate and act on your point of view in such a way as to encourage confrontation and inquiry into it" (p. 27). Feedback mechanisms like backchannelchat.com or the CIQ process allow participants in a workshop or class to see facilitators standing in open inquiry about their own practice.

Additionally, we can also probe more deeply into typical complaints we hear, such as there being only a few people of color on staff at a particular institution. Ask the complainant to say why they see that as a problem, or what possibilities might arise from having a more varied staff. When someone blames a particular person for this situation, or perhaps condemns the institutional culture of whiteness, ask about the dynamics we might have access to changing. What responsibility do we bear, what actions might we take, that get at the root cause of that problem? Recognizing white privilege and systemic racism is not a "pass" on individual responsibility, but rather a catalyst for discerning what steps one can take to confront it.

Scaffolding Levels of Discomfort

Inviting people into discomfort is easier when a basic trust in the facilitator exists. Okun (2010) believed the foundation of all race-based work is building relationships with people, a theme echoed by many others, including Smith (2019), Cavalieri et al. (2019), and Barnett (2019). Early on, students need "a container, a space, where students know they can bring their questions, their ignorance, their curiosity, their range of feelings without having to fear that they will be blamed and shamed" (Okun, 2010, p. 112).

It's sometimes easier to talk about a dynamic of oppression that parallels race but uses another construct. Yancy (2018b) described how he precedes an analysis of racism by talking about his learned sexism and how hard it is for him to see how deep the ideology of patriarchy is ingrained within him. Similarly, Okun (2010) noted how "our socialization about class does not seem to carry the emotional rage and defensiveness attached to race, at least not until we begin to delve more deeply" (p. 115). Understanding the dynamics of oppression around class and/or gender can prepare people to apply the same analysis to race. We think of this approach in the same way as hamstring stretching before taking a run or vigorous exercise. The intent is to warm up the muscles so that they don't cramp or seize up when more stressful exercise begins. In this case you're warming people up to engage with the intense effort of examining racial oppression and white supremacy.

Build Differentiated Spaces of Response

In any learning space people process in many different ways. Regularly inviting participants to reflect in silence first, to make notes about their own responses to a prompt before entering into a shared discussion, is one simple way to create an altered dynamic. Extemporaneous speech is valued so highly in our culture that silence is often framed as awkward. But periods of deep thinking are necessary in any process involving discomfort. People need time to sit with the discomfort and learn not to seek closure.

We need to learn to sit with discomfort, not to shortchange it, and to be skeptical of attempts to "skip over" it quickly. We have often found that people puzzle over silences in their CIQ responses, and so the next day, in processing the CIQ, we can encourage people to think about and to ask what it might be teaching them. Groups will also typically seek to minimize discomfort by adopting a "let's agree to disagree" policy so that they can move to the next item. If this happens remind people that agreeing to disagree also means considering how to negotiate living with people who have a 180-degree different view of the world.

You should also pay careful attention to the kinds of discussion prompts you use. Are your story and discussion prompts focused on specific events, dilemmas, or problems but open-ended enough to create room for multiple responses? Do they invite honest engagement or the opposite, an assumed answer (Vogt et al., 2003)?

A useful practice that incorporates multiple forms of conversation is snowballing. Here you invite people to start by thinking on their own about a question and making some notes concerning their response. You then ask each person to share that with another person for a short period of time. Each pair is then invited to join another pair to speak about the questions and themes that arise. After a time, each quartet shares ideas with another to form an octet. The sharing progressively increases as octets become ensembles (groups of 16), and ensembles become orchestras (groups of 32). This exercise incorporates everyone's participation but in a way that includes varying dynamics of individual introspection, intimate sharing with another, small group discussion, and large group conversation.

Beliefs and Behaviors

One of the best ways to help people embrace discomfort is the "beliefs and behaviors" exercise. Here people examine examples of constructive and destructive beliefs and behaviors that appear regularly in communication among differing racial groups. The exercise starts with a list of beliefs and behaviors common in groups of white people that can hinder communication with people of color. This is followed by a list for groups of people of color that can hinder communication with white people. After working through such lists, we then turn to a list of beliefs and behaviors that can *help* intercultural communication. We generally do this exercise within small groups, with lots of room to explore and question the lists. They are a catalyst for discussion, not a prescription.

The following example is from work that Hess does with her colleague Vivian Jenkins Nelsen, in the Twin Cities of Minnesota:

Beliefs of white people that hinder intercultural relationships

- Racism is not a problem.
- "Reverse racism" is a problem.
- Color-blindness is the best diversity strategy.
- Color/culture is unimportant in interpersonal relations.
- White culture is superior.
- Liberal white people are not racist.
- All people of color are alike.
- People of color must be micromanaged or watched.
- People of color are oversensitive.
- People of color try to "use" white people.
- People of color always welcome and appreciate inclusion in white society.
- People of color like familiarity by white people.
- People of color are accepted into college because of affirmative action.
- People of color can't achieve academically or in business.
- People of color need lower standards to achieve academically.

Beliefs of people of color that hinder intercultural relationships

- All white people are intentional racists.
- White people are united in their attitudes toward people of color.
- Whites cannot and will not change except by force.
- The best diversity strategy is to "be nice."
- Whites are trying to "use" people of color.
- White people have all the power.
- All white people will let you down in the "crunch."
- All white people are alike.
- People of color have no racial prejudices.

These are examples of *beliefs* that make relationship hard. By the same token, there are *behaviors* that hinder relationship, as shown in the list that Hess and Jenkins Nelsen use:

Behaviors of white people that hinder intercultural relationships

- Resisting change until confrontations are inevitable
- Playing by white rules

- Associating only with "safe" people of color
- Expressing acceptance and friendship too quickly/easily
- Acting superior
- Offering help where it is not needed or wanted
- Only discussing behaviors of people of color
- Talking about, not to, people of color
- Associating only with white people
- Interrupting people of color when they speak
- Testing the competence of people of color and not white people
- Insisting that one is not prejudiced
- Relating "my best friend is a person of color" stories to prove one is prejudice free
- Telling racist jokes

Behaviors of people of color that hinder intercultural relationships

- Using avoidance as the only way to relate to white people
- Using confrontation as the only way to relate to white people
- Giving answers one thinks whites want to hear
- Ignoring the history, lifestyles, and contributions of other groups of color
- Telling people off too early and harshly
- Making snap judgments too early in relationships
- Associating only with one's race
- Rejecting honest expressions of acceptance and friendship
- Failing to keep commitments and offering no explanation
- Not expressing honest feelings

It is, of course, unhelpful to focus only on things that hinder relationships. We also need to reflect on beliefs and behaviors that can help these develop. So, again, being clear that these lists are situated very specifically in the Twin Cities of Minnesota, Hess and Jenkins Nelsen offer the following ideas or beliefs that can be helpful in developing good relationships:

Beliefs of white people that help intercultural relationships

- White people need to know and value the ethnic heritage/culture of Asian, Indian, Latino, African American, and other cultures.
- White people need to know and value their own ethnic heritage/culture.
- White people can't fully understand what it means to be a person of color.
- Interdependence is needed between people of color and white people.

- Color is a real difference, but not the basis on which to determine friendships or neighbors.
- There are more similarities than differences between cultures.
- People of color have standards of excellence.
- Anger is a legitimate response to racism.
- Openness is healthy.
- I may be part of the problem.

Beliefs of people of color that help intercultural relationships
- Some white people are committed antiracists.
- White people can change biased beliefs and behaviors.
- Interdependence is needed between people of color and white people.
- Color is a real difference but not the basis on which to determine friendships or neighbors.
- There are more similarities than differences between cultures.
- Openness is healthy.
- I may be part of the problem.

Again, specific to context, the following ideas or behaviors can be helpful:

Behaviors of white people that help intercultural relationships
- Expressing feelings openly and directly
- Assisting other white people to understand racism and privilege
- Supporting ideas/actions of people of color
- Demonstrating an interest in learning about cultures of people of color
- Working through difficult conversations
- Taking risks, being the first to confront problems
- Examining one's own motives, prejudices, and covert racism
- Accepting the leadership of people of color
- Treating people of color as individuals
- Meeting people of color halfway
- Walking your talk

Behaviors of people of color that help intercultural relationships
- Respecting another's point of view
- Acting powerfully, not defensively
- Taking risks, being the first to confront problems
- Working through difficult conversations
- Expressing feelings openly, directly, and in a timely way
- Examining one's own motives and prejudices
- Walking your talk

- Treating all people as individuals
- Showing pride in one's heritage
- Meeting others halfway

This exercise invites learners to reflect on the default assumptions they carry but have never been aware of, let alone engaged. It allows people to think about their beliefs and behaviors without directly shaming anyone, because the feelings they instigate are considered at one step removed. The difficult emotions that arise can be "held" rather than overwhelming people, because they are being described as the water in which we swim, and about which we can be curious.

Engage Visual, Dramatic, and Musical Senses

Inviting participants to use visual, dramatic, and musical senses can also be very helpful in getting them to embrace discomfort. For example, the world café model for discussion (www.theworldcafe.com) has people draw pictures and share words on large pieces of newsprint paper and then move among tables to view what others have drawn or written. Embodying gestures through the theater of the oppressed (Boal, 1979) can be a very effective way to engage discomfort constructively. Traditional barriers between audience and participants break down as people intervene to change the way that dramatized situations of oppression in their specific settings unfold.

Another simple process is to bring in a short piece of popular music that expresses some element of challenge around race and invite the group to listen to the song and then draw or write words in response. Some of the songs we have used in the past for groups of predominantly white people include the following:

- "Grassy Narrows, Home to Me," N'We Jinan Artists (youtu.be/EgaYz8YWsO8)
- "Skin Deep," Playing for Change version (youtu.be/OtU9xCbVY6I)
- "This Is America," Childish Gambino (youtu.be/VYOjWnS4cMY)
- "Ella's Song," Sweet Honey in the Rock (www.youtube.com/watch?v=1tG1dNJh2rw)
- "Where Is the Love," Black Eyed Peas (youtu.be/YsRMoWYGLNA)
- "White Privilege," Macklemore and Ryan Lewis (youtu.be/Y_rl4ZGdy34)
- "Most People Are Good," Luke Bryan (youtu.be/e6EGQFJLl04)
- "One," Birdtalker (youtu.be/Odlw8WdsZS8)

There is so much available online that the key here is choosing a piece that resonates with your group. The idea is not to "solve" the problem of race in music but rather to invite your participants into a deeper engagement with both heart and mind.

Using this kind of music models a respect for and awareness of the creative strength, powerful beauty, and compassionate invitation offered by people who have been hurt by these systems. Whites doing antiracist work can easily fall into the trap of seeing people at the sharp end of racism as only victims, rather than as strong and creative resisters. Sharing recorded pieces by people of color offers strong contrasts to dominant representations and invites in those voices without burdening those in the group with this responsibility. Similarly, using music created specifically by white people to resist racism offers an invitation to those whites present.

Use Case Studies to Invite People Into Discomfort

Case studies are a rich resource in which whites can practice how to lean into antiracism work. They invite people into a concrete situation in which they imagine and role-play possible responses in the midst of discomfort. Diane Gillespie (2003) has written with conviction of the pedagogical utility of using case studies to teach about white privilege. We often present a vignette in which a white instructor presents to a group an antiracist ground rule of never trying to talk people of color out of their experience of racism. Participants are asked to state the different assumptions they think the instructor is operating under in this study, how she or he could check them out, and what different interpretations could be made of this ground rule.

A film we mentioned in chapter 5, *A Time for Burning* (Quest Productions/ Avernus Productions, 1966), has long been used in a variety of universities across the United States as a case study to explore the dynamics of racism. This 1960s documentary follows two Lutheran churches—one white, one black—as they struggle to respond to the race riots of the time. Although old, this is still so vivid in its evocation of racism that it offers whites ways to think concretely about what to do as they grow more aware of racial oppression.

The Pluralism Project, hosted by Harvard University, explores religious diversity and, in a world characterized by Islamophobia, also engages racism (pluralism.org/casestudy/). The project's case story about Somali taxi drivers and the Minneapolis airport includes newspaper stories, people's testimonies, and many other rich details for wading into the complexity of a collective response to racism.

The recent "hashtag syllabus" movement—for example, #StandingRock-Syllabus, #FergusonSyllabus, and so on—is a particularly resource-rich place to find case studies. RacismReview, an online blog/resource site, has collected a number of such syllabuses (www.racismreview.com/blog/hashtag-syllabus-project/).

The pedagogical goal of case studies is to help participants think through the various possibilities of action present in a given situation. Each potential action can be explored for its utility, its awareness of structural and systemic realities, and how it ignites and sustains collective responses. This gives people necessary practice in trying out strategies we want them to employ.

Engage Discomfort in the Larger Sphere

Bryan Stevenson (2019) reminded us that injustice prevails where hopelessness persists. Moving beyond numbness or denial requires finding hope in the midst of discomfort. But it can be difficult to sustain hope if only anguish, rage, and the inability to conceive of successful change exists. So we need to develop the hope that resides in, and is nourished by, collective forms of resistance and action. After all, workshops and classes are only moments in an ongoing journey to develop an antiracist white identity. Helping participants find ways to connect to resources and forms of resistance in a larger community of antiracist activism is crucial.

No person should leave one of your antiracism classes or workshops without clear ways to continue to grow. Many whites live and work in contexts that are deeply isolated due to the structural and systemic racism of segregated housing and education. They may never have thought about how to begin a relationship with people of color. So we try never to enter a workshop without having a list of local resources, both people and organizations, with whom people can connect.

Hess often teaches in distributed online formats at her school where students come from multiple states across the United States and sometimes abroad. She begins by asking her students to learn about the demographics of their settings and requires that they seek this information not through anecdotal experience—which for white people is often ignorant of reality—but through using sociological tools and databases.

She has found that local churches who are connected to denominations with antiracism policies can be a starting place for finding partners in this work. Although Martin Luther King Jr. once remarked that Sunday mornings are the most segregated hour of the week, it's also true that the national offices of such churches are building networks that help local communities to challenge racism, as shown in the following examples:

Evangelical Lutheran Church of America (www.elca.org/Resources/
Racial-Justice)
United Church of Christ (www.ucc.org/justice_racism)
Presbyterian Church USA (facing-racism.pcusa.org)
Episcopal Church USA (www.episcopalchurch.org/racial-
reconciliation/resources)
U.S. Roman Catholic Conference of Bishops (www.usccb.org/issues-
and-action/human-life-and-dignity/racism/)

Similarly, many communities have YWCAs that focus on doing antiracism
work (standagainstracism.org), and many local foundations are also beginning to fund "courageous conversations" and other frameworks in which
racism is engaged. Public schools can also be a rich context in which to
develop relationships across various differences.

There are also numerous resources online that provide ways to connect
in community. Sharing resources in your local community—starting a book
reading group, watching a movie together, joining in a cultural event—can be
enhanced by drawing on these online networks, as in the following examples:

RacismReview (www.racismreview.com/blog/)
Colorlines (www.colorlines.com)
TeachingTolerance (www.tolerance.org)
Demos (www.demos.org/about)
Equal Justice Initiative (eji.org)
Color of Change (colorofchange.org)

Our best advice here is to "stand in inquiry" and to seek out spaces in
which people of differing racial identities are already active. Joining in
collective witness and action together is a powerful place from which to
begin relationship.

Final Thought

We offer a few summary words of advice:

- Find ways to enter into situations with which you are not familiar,
  and learn how to be at peace with that lack of familiarity.
- Learn practices that rely on solidarity and lengthen the timeline for
  change—when we act as if everything has to be fixed tomorrow,
  despair is inevitable.
- Recognize that societal resistance to the work of antiracism becomes
  most vicious when that work is becoming most effective.

- Build trusted relationships with several close colleagues/friends with whom you can test your reactions.
- Find your hope, and then build practices that help you to resist despair and fear into your daily awareness and your work, whatever it is. As examples we offer the work of poet and essayist Audre Lorde—for example, *Sister Outsider* (1984), and the work of organizational theorist Margaret Wheatley—for example, *Perseverance* (2010).

Discomfort—however you name it—can be a powerful catalyst for transformation and a strong resource for learning. It is a feeling to be embraced and engaged rather than something to be avoided or denied.

7

RUNNING "REAL"
DISCUSSIONS AROUND RACE

The most profound moments in the journey of becoming a white antiracist often come in conversation with others. Books, films, and digital stories can all be powerful triggers, but when other people ask us challenging questions, or give us very different perspectives on situations we thought we understood, change begins. At its core becoming a white antiracist happens dialogically. Unless we're in deep and authentic conversation with critical friends to explore our core assumptions about race, movement toward this identity is hampered. It's so easy to float through life believing oneself to be an ally, a good white person, a moral being. Staying within our racially homogeneous bubbles, there is often little inclination or opportunity to be shocked into thinking about race in a different way.

A meaningful discussion in which we contemplate a fundamentally different reality is an important moment of productive dissonance. Seeing yourself as structurally racist when previously you regarded yourself as free of bias and prejudice spurs you to significant reappraisals of how racism is embedded in your frameworks of analysis and behaviors. When we are told that our view of the world is fundamentally distorted by racial misconceptions, or that we have completely missed taking account of the experience of large swathes of the population, we are forced to take account of this new reality. Our first instinct may be to deny this and try to push such a discomforting perspective away. But, like Wile E. Coyote constantly returning to chase after the roadrunner, the memory of that conversation nags at us. The disequilibrium that an intense, sometimes painful, conversation induces cannot be endured. Sooner or later we have to make sense of what we heard and felt, usually in the company of others.

However, despite our conviction about the importance of dialogue, we've both been part of racial discussions that went way off topic, allowed for the unchallenged exposition of bigotry, and spent far too much time debating whether or not racism is real. We've seen discussions quickly degenerate into name calling, accusations of racism, or total silence. Both of us have been guilty of not stepping up as quickly as we should to call something out, even though we know that the worst thing a white facilitator can do in the eyes of people of color is to let a racist comment go unchallenged.

All discussions run the risk of going off track but this is particularly the case with race-based talk. Before people will risk participating in race conversations, they need to know that those leading them in this venture have planned carefully and thoughtfully for such talk. They need to know that leaders won't skirt around difficult issues and that they'll keep the discussion focused on race. They want to be sure that people won't be allowed to dominate unfairly and that everyone gets an equal chance to participate. This chapter reviews different discussion exercises that we have found achieve these purposes and keep people engaged in moving into an antiracist identity and practice.

Structuring Racial Discussions

The longer we conduct discussions around race, privilege, or white supremacy, the more we believe that we need to exercise our power as teachers, facilitators, and leaders to set protocols for discussion participation and to intervene when these are being disregarded. We never prescribe where a discussion will end. But we are quite happy to establish structures that guide *how* people talk to each other.

If we *don't* do this, one of several things will probably happen. Perhaps the discussion will remain distanced from a real engagement with race as people deploy all the mechanisms of white fragility (DiAngelo, 2018) to avoid examining their own collusion in, or enactment of, white supremacy. Alternately, people will be frozen in fear of saying the wrong thing and anxious about being called racist. That means they'll stay silent. And then there's the ever-present danger of egomaniacs running riot and trying to convert everyone else to their agenda unless something is in place to prevent this happening. So a priority for leaders of race-based conversations is to find ways to invite everyone to participate in a manner that feels comfortable for people.

One particular dynamic we strive to avoid is spending too much time discussing whether or not systemic racism is real. On the one hand, we want to dignify each person's experience and we understand how important it is for them to be able to speak in their own authentic voice. On the other hand, we know how easy it is to spend a disproportionate amount of time trying to convince them that racism exists. If we're in charge of a session where people have volunteered to learn about racism, we usually insist on a ground rule that we will *not* debate whether or not we live in a racist society, but instead accept this as incontrovertible fact.

Alternatively, if participants have been mandated to attend our event, we assume that there'll be a lot of skepticism around. So we make sure to allow for the early expression of frustration, disbelief, and resentment. We'll say that everyone has a right to believe what their experience teaches them, but then say we're going to present a view of race and racism that will be very different from that which they hold. We'll do a lot of autobiographical disclosure concerning our own continuing enactment of racism and we'll present contrary narrative and testimony, often in digital form. We ask skeptical participants to play for a short time what Peter Elbow (1986) called the believing game—to think, speak, and act for a little while as if they believed that racism is real and pervasive and to consider what that would mean for their own lives and actions.

Whenever we introduce a specific protocol or ground rule, we lay out for participants what it's designed to achieve and how it operates. Of course, groups sometimes rebel against our rationales and declare them to be unnecessary. This happens less in courses and professional development workshops than it does in community meetings, but participants can still sabotage protocols by misapplying them, skipping steps, or not following directions.

Despite these problems we still believe that the protocols described in the following paragraphs have a good chance of stopping conversations prematurely spiraling out of control or allowing participants to evade the subject. Clear protocols can encourage contributions, equalize participation, acknowledge different learning styles or expressive modes, and keep domineering members or confident extroverts in check. Applying protocols that surface and privilege unacknowledged or excluded perspectives and experiences encourages people to stay in conversation longer than when discussions are unstructured and white supremacy is implicitly running the show.

Backchannel Chat

Early in discussions of race, social media can be used to ensure that the widest possible array of perspectives is surfaced. Having everyone participate by posting something anonymously to a social media site stops a discussion moving to a premature consensus that expresses the merits of a color-blind ideology. It also means that everyone has the same chance to have their voice heard. Under the protection of anonymity people are freed up to say things that otherwise they would be too fearful to risk mentioning in speech.

One tool we've used a lot is backchannelchat.com. We've mentioned this a couple of times already in this book, but here we want to explain why we think this is such an important tool. Backchannel Chat is an open access platform that facilitators, leaders, and teachers can use to create a forum on which people can post comments anonymously. Before a workshop, class, or meeting, the leader or teacher logs into backchannelchat.com and creates a web page on the theme of the session. As they do this they are assigned a code that, once entered, will allow anyone to access the forum.

When everyone is gathered together for the training, class, meeting, or workshop, participants are told to go to backchannelchat.com and create an ID. We ask that they use only numbers and that no names be used. People are also provided with the access code that allows them to view the page created for that day. They can then post comments, questions, or reactions anonymously. We use this tool in discussions in three ways.

To Get a Quick and Early Sense of What People Are Thinking

One of the things we might do is pose an initial question before the discussion begins and give participants 1 or 2 minutes to post their response to the forum. Questions we use might be the following:

- *What does white supremacy mean to you?*
  This question surfaces participants' understanding of this term and helps you gauge their reactions to what for some will be intimidating terminology. People's responses give you good information on how ready they are to examine their own experiences and thinking. It also helps you decide how much time you need to spend modeling your engagement with your own racism.
- *What's the most recent example of racism you've witnessed or enacted?*
  Responses to this question help you determine how people understand racism. If people describe mostly individual acts of bias and prejudice, then you know it will take a while to get them to the point of examining institutional and systemic racism. However, if most of the examples provided are of policies, structural inequities, and disproportionate access to education, health care, and legal aid, then you can feel much more confident diving into systemic factors. This question can also give you a sense of how ready a group is to move

into looking at their own collusion in, and enactment of, racism. If the majority of examples are of acts committed by others, that tells you it will take some time to ease people into turning the spotlight on their own actions. But if there's a preponderance of responses detailing participants own personal actions then you can move quickly into asking for personal disclosure.

- *What's an example of an antiracist action you've witnessed or enacted?*
  The same comments made regarding the preceding question apply to this one as well.

- *What are the components of an antiracist identity?*
  Answers to this question are pretty revealing in that they often indicate the widespread existence of a color-blind perspective. If the responses equate antiracism with treating everybody the same and not seeing color, that tells us something valuable about the audience. If, however, people say that being antiracist means committing to collective action against structural inequity, then we know we're dealing with a more sophisticated group.

After posing one of these questions to the group we give people up to 2 minutes to think about their response and then post it onto the backchannelchat.com page created for the session. When the 2 minutes is up, we show the feed on whatever screen is in the room and look at it as a group. The screen is full of anonymously posted responses that represent a wide diversity of perspectives.

The response rate is so high in this activity that within a 2-minute period we often hear from 70 to 80% of participants—a much higher percentage than would have been the case if we'd posed the question verbally and taken spoken responses. This is an opportunity for everyone to say whatever is on their mind in a way that, because of its anonymity, feels relatively safe. Nobody can dominate by shouting or speaking at great length.

This tool also surfaces the different perspectives in the room, thereby preventing a rush to consensus or "safe" middle ground. The questions posed previously are all extremely complex and the responses to them represent multiple experiences. So early on everybody is confronted with a complicated range of different ways of thinking about the topic. As the group reviews the Backchannel Chat feed, we point out the wide variety of viewpoints and cluster comments into broad themes. With groups less used to talking about race the clusters often prioritize the color-blind perspective. More experienced groups may sometimes present themselves as allies. This gives us an early opportunity to identify dominant elements of white identity and to problematize the notion of allyship.

We also look for single comments that stand alone and point out that these may represent the most important contributions, because they identify issues, problems, or viewpoints that the majority often misses, ignores, or omits from consideration. By focusing on a singular experience we have the chance to counter dominant ideological narratives of racial progress or to point out that one person's expression of allyship is another person's experience of being co-opted, colonized, or talked down to. If there are comments about the event being an example of politically correct white bashing, we take those as an opportunity to address honestly and publicly the resistance we know is usually in the room. We talk about how we ourselves push back against the idea that we have elements of racism embedded within us and we reference the weariness and trepidation we feel as we enter race-based conversations. We don't want to hector participants who feel racial discussion is unnecessary, and we want to acknowledge their sincere conviction that they are moral, fair-minded people. But through our self-disclosure we also want to interrupt and challenge these ideas and reaffirm why we believe this work is so crucial.

This tool allows us to point out that multiple worlds are in the same room. Habermas (1990) maintained that maturity begins when we cease to universalize our own experiences, and if people are to think critically about race, it's essential that they're exposed to multiple realities. We want to shake up any sense people have that there's a settled consensus, or similarity of experience, around race.

For newcomers to racial discussion the spread of responses revealed on Backchannel Chat may be overwhelming, particularly if they're looking for a series of simple steps to take in becoming antiracist. We try to defuse this sense of being inundated by complexity by commenting on our own sense of confusion at yet again being confronted by the intricacies of race.

To Provide a Pause as We Go Deeper Into a Topic

Discussions of race often follow a familiar path of beginning with clear expressions of antiracist intent, followed by periods in which the complexity of the task is gradually revealed. As the layers of an antiracist commitment are peeled away, new questions inevitably arise. For example, avowals of allyship in multiracial groups often lead into discussions of what true alliances look like and what benefits whites get from being able to declare their solidarity with the struggles of people of color. As the power dynamics of allyship come to the fore, facilitators can pose a pertinent question such as "What should white allies expect to lose?" or "What constitutes an act of inauthentic or false alliance?"

Asking people to respond to these questions via Backchannel Chat allows time to pause and ponder extremely complex issues. One of the problems of speech-based discussion is that participants often feel an implicit pressure to say something quickly, as silence is experienced as embarrassing or awkward. Under the pressure to talk people can blurt out things that don't represent what they're trying to say, or the first thing that comes into their heads, and be met with strongly negative and hurtful reactions. Struggling for mutual comprehension around race is going to be a flawed and stressful process, and in that endeavor we will keep saying imperfect things. So pausing regularly to ruminate over tough issues is an essential dynamic in discussions. Using Backchannel Chat to help people quietly ponder and then post initial reactions to difficult questions can help move discussions deeper and deeper. After a quick survey of group members' postings, the conversation can then probe the most provocative comments and note what has been missed so far.

To Gather Comments, Questions, and Reactions

Discussions are often mercurial, changing direction constantly as new ideas are introduced and new questions raised. Sometimes it takes so long to formulate a relevant question that by the time you've worked out what you want to ask the discussion has moved on. Or maybe you're bothered by an assertion but can't immediately pinpoint what it is that is so troubling. Perhaps you want to affirm something someone else has said, or extend their comments with an illustration, but before you have a chance to do this a new contribution has taken the conversation elsewhere.

Backchannel Chat gives participants the chance to register questions, comments, and reactions in their own time, even as the spoken discussion veers off in new directions. As the person leading the event you can check the feed about every 15 minutes and then address issues that have been raised and respond to observations posted. You'll also be able to assess how well you're connecting with a group. If there's a major disconnect between what you think you're doing and how the group is responding to your actions, this will show up on the Backchannel feed. That allows you publicly to address miscommunication, gaps in understanding, or mistakes you've made.

Circle of Voices

Circle of voices is a small group discussion protocol that we use several times at the outset of our time with a group. It is designed to accomplish three specific things:

- To give everyone in the room a chance to participate by hearing their opinion spoken without anyone interrupting them
- To make sure that participants hear the widest range of perspectives on a topic before deciding what to focus on
- To socialize people early on into the idea that listening carefully to what others are saying is the most important habit to learn in discussion

Given that people sometimes come to race-based discussions with fears and anxieties about being shouted down, or not being heard at all, it's important to introduce early on a protocol that insists on a fair hearing for everyone's viewpoint. It's also crucial that people actually listen to what others are saying. There's no way that common ground can be found, or that meaningful communication will happen, if people are there only to broadcast views they deem to be self-evident and impervious to challenge. When we introduce the circle of voices exercise, we lay out the three reasons outlined in the preceding list for using the protocol. We stress that its purpose is to give everyone a fair shake and to make sure that all perspectives in the room are expressed and heard.

Circle of voices begins with a period of mandatory silence. You pose a question to the group and ask for everyone to stay quiet for 2 minutes as they write down some initial thoughts or responses to the question. Once the 2 minutes are up you call time and ask groups of five to form.

Each group then engages in two distinct rounds of conversation. In the first round each member of the group shares for about 60 seconds what they were thinking about or wrote down during the initial 2-minute period of silent thinking time. The ground rule here is that no interruptions are allowed as each person speaks. Even if extroverts want to jump in and support a speaker by encouraging them or telling them why their comment is so great, this is disallowed. Participants must listen quietly to each person's contribution.

This "no interruptions" rule ensures that everyone in the room hears her or his unbroken voice in the air at least once during the class session. The longer that introverts stay silent, the harder it is for them to speak. So if you want to hear from everybody, it's essential that you engineer an early opportunity for that to happen, even if only in small groups. The "no interruptions" rule is also designed to stop an early consensus from emerging. Because everyone begins by sharing an unfiltered response to the question, people hear all the perspectives that are held in the group.

Depending on the number of groups in the room the facilitator's role here is to watch out for (a) anyone who takes an inordinate amount of time to make their initial comments and (b) anyone who contravenes the "no interruptions" rule. If you see either of these things happening, you go over to the group concerned and remind members of these ground rules. In racial discussions emotions are high and convictions are strongly held, so you will need to exercise leadership here. People will find it hard to listen for a minute uninterruptedly if they feel untruths, stereotypes, and bigotry are being expressed. They'll naturally want to jump in and point out the error of someone's ways. But if you're interested in any kind of communication developing, you need to use your authority to insist on the "no interruptions" rule. Hearing inconvenient truths is often the beginning of critical thinking.

Once everyone has spoken their initial uninterrupted response to the question, the second round of open conversation begins. Now anyone can speak in any order and interruptions are fine. However, a new ground rule applies in this second round regarding what people can talk about. Basically, participants can only comment on what another person said in the first round. This can include asking questions about someone's initial contribution, commenting on something that resonated, disagreeing with a comment, or indicating how a first round contribution opened up a new line of thinking. But whatever comments are made in this second round of open conversation, they have to link directly and explicitly to something someone said in the first round.

This rule is deliberately designed to socialize participants into acquiring the habits of careful listening and attentive responding. Knowing that you can only speak about what someone else said in the opening round of sharing forces you to listen closely to people's initial contributions.

Some race-based questions we typically ask during the circle of voices exercise are the following:

- *What images or actions come to your mind when you hear the term* racism?
  This would be a question we'd pose at the start of a session with people who probably hadn't spent much time thinking about race. The idea would be to get a sense of where everyone is in their understanding. However, we've also used this question with relatively advanced groups composed of people experienced in discussing this issue.
- *What is the most important point for you in Yancy's "Letter to White America"?*
  This kind of question would be used when members had studied some specific material before the discussion. The responses help us understand how people are prioritizing elements of this content and provides a sense of which aspects resonate most with them.

- *What would be an example of white supremacy that you've witnessed or enacted in your everyday life?*
  This question is designed to delve more deeply into participants' lives. We often use the "witnessed or enacted" phrasing because it gives group members the chance to decide how much they wish to reveal. Answering the "witness" part allows people to put some limits on their personal disclosures; responding to the "enacted" prompt invites them into direct sharing.

In online classes, trainings, and workshops you can debrief the circle of voice discussions by asking participants to post to the Backchannel Chat feed some of the questions and issues that arose in their groups. Everyone can then see what all the groups discussed and you can choose the most provocative or insightful posts to be the focus of large group conversation.

Chalk Talk: A Visual Discussion

Academics are word people. At scholarly conference sessions, PowerPoint presentations are sometimes stuffed full of direct quotes in a font that's so small it's hard to read from more than a few feet away. Don't assume that people gathered to discuss race work share this preference for language and texts. Do assume that you need to build in plenty of graphics, slides, and videos for people who think and process visually.

The chalk talk exercise, developed by Hilton Smith (2009) of the Foxfire Fund, is a great way to construct a visual representation of the different ways group members think about race. It also allows you to hear from a lot of people in a very short period of time. We use it mostly to unearth the concerns of people—a class, a workshop, an organization, a community—before building a plan for change. A chalk talk dialogue can be an excellent way to kick off a session on how to detect and combat racism, or the steps needed to develop a more diverse, inclusive environment.

For those uncomfortable with English as their second language, or those who are unused to speaking up in public settings, chalk talk provides a chance to express opinions or convey experiences without worrying about choosing the correct words or saying the wrong thing. The chance to use images instead of words frees up participants to communicate in quite dramatic ways. In antiracist courses and workshops people draw images of a heart stabbed by a dagger and dripping tears, or a body broken in two, that will touch people deeply and stop them in their tracks.

The process begins with the leader or teacher writing a question in the center of a large black- or whiteboard and circling it. Markers or chalk sticks are placed by the board and, once the question is posted, everyone is invited to come and stand by the board to participate in the activity. The facilitator explains that for about 5 minutes people should post responses to the question on the board that can be written or drawn. The only ground rule is that people should stay silent. Staying quiet allows participants to think about their responses to the question and to process the information going up on the board.

As well as responding to the original question, people are encouraged to post new questions and also respond to what's going up on the board. They are asked to look for postings on different parts of the board that seem to connect in some way. When they see such connections, they are told to draw a line connecting the postings and to write a brief remark along that line about why these two images or comments seem to be similar. We ask that they follow the same process—draw a connecting line with a few words of explanation along the line—when they see two images or comments that appear to be contradictory, or that represent significantly different perspectives.

Several people usually start drawing or writing immediately on different parts of the board. As the facilitator you can also participate by drawing lines connecting images, writing questions, and adding your own comments. After 5 or 6 minutes there's often a lull in posting, or the board has become so full that there's no more space for people to write or draw anything else. You then announce that the silent part of the activity is over and ask people to stand back, view the whole board, and start looking for common clusters of responses.

When it comes time to debrief you can begin pointing out that the different handwriting or drawing styles on the board signify that lots of people have participated. In 5 minutes or so, you typically secure input from 60 to 70% of people who will have posted a comment, drawn an image, or created a line connecting points together. If, in a similar 5-minute period, you had posed a question verbally to the whole group and then asked them to speak their responses, you would have heard from maybe three or four people and felt compelled to earn your wages by responding in some way to each comment.

The first time you try chalk talk with a group you can do the initial debrief yourself. Keep participants standing by the blackboard and look first for comments or images that generate the most lines in and out. Explain that because these have generated the most dialogue, they probably represent issues for further discussion. But look also for outliers—images and comments that stand alone and generate no lines. Point out that these could represent important blind spots or omissions and therefore need to be considered. The second time you run a chalk talk dialogue you can ask participants to do the debriefing themselves.

The final stage in the exercise is to invite everyone to take pictures of the dialogue on their laptops, smartphones, tablets, or other handheld devices. This is particularly important when you run a chalk talk exercise at the outset of a new unit of study or as the first activity in a community dialogue. Photographing or videoing the board allows the group to return to this dialogue over the coming weeks as they go deeper into the topic.

Here are two questions we have used as the focus for chalk talk dialogues based around race:

- *When have you witnessed, experienced, or enacted a racial microaggression?* This question offers participants multiple frames for posting on the board. Those who have been on the receiving end of such aggressions can share how that felt, whereas others can indicate when they've observed them. The term *enacted* invites those with a degree of self-awareness to share times they've committed them. This question has been very helpful in generating dialogues that clarify the subtle, slippery nature of such acts.
- *What does inclusion look, sound, or feel like?*
  "Look, sound, or feel like" is a common formulation for a chalk talk dialogue. It is designed to free up people's creativity by encouraging them to draw images that represent feelings and sounds. Interesting variants on this format are the following:
  What does privilege look, sound, or feel like?
  What does systemic racism look, sound, or feel like?
  What does an antiracist environment look, sound, or feel like?

Although we typically use chalk talk early in a group's time together to communicate the different agendas and experiences that group members hold surrounding race, we have also used it in a more summative way. Sometimes it's instructive to pose the same question you used in an opening session of a course, workshop, or training as the final activity a group conducts. Comparing the two graphics presented can indicate how far a group has grown. For example, if you pose the question *What does an antiracist environment look, sound, or feel like?* as a bookend to a group's time together, some very clear differences usually emerge. In the first visual there will be multiple comments about institutional conduct, personal behavior, and organizational policy. The emphasis is all on actions "out there" in the world. In the summative graphic the postings usually include more references to the importance of people rooting out racism in themselves.

Chalk talk is a way of jump-starting a discussion of race. The common clusters and points of contradiction or divergence will suggest opening themes, problems, or questions that the group can then consider at greater length. Or perhaps outlier images and words that stand alone and don't attract any comments or connecting lines can be a beginning point for conversation. These may alert group members to the presence of racial groupthink and the ways in which white supremacist conditioning causes certain perspectives to be ignored or marginalized.

Circular Response

Discussing race is an evolving process. Early on you want to get people to stop universalizing their own racial experience and to realize that fundamentally different racial realities exist in the same group. To understand that the mental frame through which you view the world is one that presents whiteness as equivalent to normality is an enormous first step. But as people start to examine how a color-blind ideology allows them to ignore the reality of systemic racism, the conversation will deepen and complexify. Simple black/white binaries will be replaced by an emphasis on intersectionality, on the ways that class, gender, sexuality, and other factors complicate our understanding of how some people are marginalized in different ways.

We believe that as discussion progresses we need tools and protocols sequenced to fit the different stages of a group's evolving life together. In the case of the circular response protocol, we would never use this early on in a group's history but instead hold it in reserve until we're past the midpoint of our allotted time together.

Developed by adult educator Eduard Lindeman (1926), this exercise shares the circular format of circle of voices but is significantly more complex. Its intent is threefold.

- First, it underscores the importance of careful listening. We are struck by Sara Lawrence-Lightfoot's (2000) assertion that the most fundamental way you show respect to another person is by letting them see how carefully and intently you listen to what they're saying. In this protocol participants clearly demonstrate how they strive to hear each other.
- Second, it stresses how good discussion is organic and cumulative. When the protocol is followed correctly, the contributions of individuals are built upon and extended by other members of the group.
- Third, it helps groups focus in more deeply on exploring one or two facets of a problem, rather than being diverted by multiple considerations.

The process begins with the facilitator, or the group itself, posing a common question. People form themselves in circles of 10 to 12 members. They are silent until one person decides to start off the conversation by giving an initial response to the question posed. In this first round of conversation people are asked to keep their comments to a maximum of 2 minutes and not to interrupt each other, no matter how enthusiastic they are about a contribution or how much they want to ask questions about it.

But there is an important caveat to how the conversation proceeds in this first round. After the first person has finished speaking, the person to their left goes next. After taking the time silently to process the initial speaker's comments, the second person must start by building on, or responding to, the first speaker's comments. This response does not have to be an endorsement or paraphrase of the opening contribution. The second speaker can raise a criticism, express a disagreement, extend the first comment in an unpredictable way, or simply say she or he finds it difficult to come up with a response. In this last case people say something about their source of difficulty—maybe the first speaker used unaccustomed language or was talking about unfamiliar experiences.

The third speaker then has up to 2 minutes of uninterrupted airtime to build on or respond to the second speaker's comments, and the process continues around the circle until everyone has spoken. The facilitator can be a part of the group but she or he should not be the first to speak. Whenever the leader does speak, it's important for them to pause and think for a while before talking. Leaders should model taking the time to show that they're striving to listen carefully and doing their best to build on the previous speaker's comments.

During this first conversational phase of the protocol, anxiety is usually high as people wait for their turn, hoping and praying the person before them says something they can understand and respond to. We notice speakers leaning in to follow what people do with their comments and how those frame subsequent contributions. Once everyone has spoken in the first round, the group then moves into completely open conversation with no ground rules, time limits, or order of speech. People can introduce completely new topics, express support or disagreement, extend previous contributions, or raise questions about something someone else said in the first round.

To do circular response well you have to listen carefully. After all, if you don't attend closely to the person before you, then your opportunity to respond appropriately to their comments is significantly reduced. Where race is concerned, paying careful attention to an unfamiliar perspective is particularly important because people often bring such entrenched worldviews to this topic. The ground rule disallowing interruptions in the first round of talk means people have to attend to experiences, opinions, and stories very different from their own. As the first round of discussion progresses, one or two issues often seem to keep surfacing, albeit with different interpretive frames. That means that when people move into the open discussion phase, they're more primed to see complexities and contradictions. This is very helpful when considering a multilayered topic like race.

Some typical questions used for this protocol are the following:

- *What are the most powerful blinders to whites seeing their own racism?*
  By the time we introduce circular response the group has got to know each other fairly well, so a potentially threatening or probing question like this is more possible than at earlier stages of the group's existence. The complexity of the question seems to suit the first round of the protocol, because people often wait and think for some time about their response to the previous speaker's comment on this topic.
- *What's the best way to open someone else's eyes to a different racial perspective?*
  We like to use action-oriented questions in circular response discussions because these typically occur after people have spent a considerable time becoming acquainted with the building blocks of racial cognizance (white supremacy, white privilege, microaggressions, aversive racism, interest convergence, and so on). By then lots of stories have been shared and experiences analyzed. So when we get around to doing this protocol, people are usually ready to focus on taking action.
- *How do we build an antiracist environment?*
  This question is worded to help people focus on realizing the need for solidarity, alliances, and networking in any social change effort. Although making an individual stand is important, we want people to shift their frame toward recognizing the crucial dynamic of collective mobilization. Organizations and institutions are far more likely to integrate antiracist policies, structures, and practices when people collectively commit to holding them accountable.

Bohmian Dialogue

The longest discussion protocol we use is Bohmian dialogue. Named after theoretical physicist David Bohm (1996), this process builds on his attempt to create an open forum to explore intractable problems. The purpose is to build an organic conversation in which participants collectively create meaning by recognizing connections and commonalities and by building on each other's ideas as freely as possible. The activity is designed for large groups of around 40 people, but we have also used it with groups of 15, 20, or 25. Bohm recommended spending up to 2 hours in this dialogue, but we have used it for shorter, 45-minute periods.

The first stage in a Bohmian dialogue is for people to study some common resource. When an academic class is engaged in the process, you can ask students to read or view some pertinent material beforehand. Perhaps we'll assign Christine Sleeter's (2016) and Robin DiAngelo's (2016) autobiographical reflections on how they became aware of their white identities. In organizational or community settings we don't know who will show up so we usually begin the process with everybody viewing some relevant video. One of our favorites is a *New York Times* "op doc," *A Conversation With My Black Son* (Gandbhir & Foster, 2015), in which Black parents recount how they prepare their sons to be pulled over and racially profiled by the police and the different ways they advise them to respond to this event. Another is the "What It Means to Be American" excerpt from the *Color of Fear* documentary (Wah, 1994). Here a Black man (Victor) expresses his pain, anger, and frustration in response to a white man (David) who has told him to just be American (Lewis, 2013). A third is Jones's (2020) *How Can We Win?* video, shot after the 2020 Minneapolis police murder of George Floyd.

After the videos are over, the group forms the chairs into one large circle and you explain how the process works and what the conversation is for. The two of us say that there are three primary reasons we're doing this.

- To understand the different experiences of race and racism that are in the room as a way of identifying and developing points of common connection
- To build on the intersections we discover to explore steps we can take to combat racism and develop an antiracist identity
- To develop some collective thinking about how we can best make common cause against white supremacy

We remind people that because these are incredibly difficult projects, we need to listen carefully and intently to each other and spend a lot of time processing the meaning that others' contributions have for us. We predict that there will necessarily be long periods of silence in the room as people digest and mull over what others have just said. We urge participants to try to be comfortable with the room being quiet and insist that this is an essential part of the process.

Then it's time to explain the specific ground rules that structure Bohmian dialogue.

- There are no winners or losers here so don't try to overpower or diminish contributions you dislike or take issue with.
- This is not a debate so try to refrain from creating binary opposites ("He's racist but she's antiracist"; "That's liberating but this is oppressive").
- Don't try to convince or persuade; the point is to understand and connect where we can.
- Only one person speaks at a time.
- Speak only when you have something to say or when you have a response that's prompted by another person's remarks.
- Be comfortable with long silences.
- If it helps you focus, feel free to close your eyes or look at the floor.
- Expect radically different opinions and perspectives but express them in just that way, as different "takes" on an issue.
- Focus on identifying common ground and how to build on this.

We also clarify our own role in the dialogue. We let people know that we'll be both contributor and umpire. If people start to get into a debate, try to convince or rebut each other, or declare another contribution to be wrong, our job is to step in and remind them of the point of the exercise. We are trying to understand the alterity of racial experience and to find points of common connection that can prompt action, not to blame people for their wrong opinions.

Some questions suited to this activity include the following:

- *What would it take for us to trust each other?*
  This question is suited to multiracial groups that include whites whom you feel are too quick to declare themselves allies and assume that, having made this declaration, they will be welcomed and trusted by people of color.
- *What stops us realizing our common potential?*
  This question works well with groups that are getting frustrated with their inability to progress as fast as they'd like in some kind of antiracist work. In groups like this it's easy for people to slip into race-based blaming and commit all kinds of unwitting microaggressions.
- *What do we miss or misunderstand about how racism works?*
  Here you're trying to challenge a group to go deeper into analyzing the workings of racism. We use this question if we feel the group is

slipping into thinking that just by citing the clear existence of racism and the injuries it inflicts, people will be convinced to give up racist ideas and practices. Our hope is that the visceral and emotionally sedimented nature of white supremacy will be revealed.

- *How do we build common cause?*

  This question is project-focused and one that appeals to many people. It is hopeful and oriented to the future. Of course once people start responding to it the complexities of how people define common cause, let alone how this is realized, quickly come to the fore.

Appreciative Pause

This final activity is used as a coda to intensive discussions on race. One of the behaviors most absent in discussions is that of people giving appreciation for the contributions others have made to their learning. So after a race-based discussion, particularly one that has been tense, fraught, and emotional (in other words, after pretty much every discussion on race!) we find it's helpful to practice the appreciative pause. This is a brief period during which *only* expressions of appreciation are allowed. Appreciations are publicly spoken (in small or large groups) for questions posed that suggest a whole new line of thinking, comments that clarify something that up to then was confusing, connections that were made between ideas or contributions, risks that people took in opening themselves up to the group, and examples that were provided that increased understanding of a difficult concept. People also identify tonal contributions, referencing the honesty, supportiveness, and empathy demonstrated by peers.

A Final Observation

We want to end this chapter by reasserting something we have already stated. You shouldn't go into a discussion on race with an overinflated sense of what is possible. Unfortunately, institutions often situate racial discussions as moments of "healing." This "healing" framing underscores the idea that a successful discussion is one where reconciliation and goodwill emerge, with people exiting the room holding hands and expressing solidarity with each other.

In our experience group members never end a discussion feeling healthy, whole, and without pain. Instead, they leave with a range of complex feelings. Some depart vowing never to touch this topic again. Others exit feeling confused and shaken. Some leave feeling that for the first time they have participated in honest talk about this topic. Others are angry or deflated as they realize the depth of misunderstanding revealed and the work ahead that's necessary to get people to listen carefully to each other. But many will leave feeling an itch of necessary discomfort that needs to be scratched. Scratching that itch is what will bring them back into conversation at a later date.

8

GETTING PEOPLE TO
THINK STRUCTURALLY
ABOUT RACE

How does racism endure? How does the insane notion that whole groups of people are less than fully human because of a different phenotype or level of melanin in their skin come to be accepted as conventional wisdom, as common sense? Genetically there is far more that unites than divides us and the DNA of white Europeans and Black Africans differs in no significantly discernible way. So what causes large swathes of the white population to ascribe innately lower levels of intelligence and personality traits such as a propensity for violent criminality to Black and brown people? And what stops communities of color from rising up in revolution?

The short answer is the paramilitary power of the state. Police departments around the country have become militarized in terms of their vehicles and armaments. White police officers can cite that they fear for their life as a justifiable reason for shooting dead any Black person who they feel in some way is acting erratically. After all, under white supremacy, erratic behavior by people of color is viewed as one small step away from the volatility and violence ascribed to Black bodies.

The long answer to why this acceptability remains unchanged lies embedded in the tradition of critical theory (Brookfield, 2004), which ascribes the mass acceptance of enduring inequality to ideological manipulation. Put simply, if you can get people to see the world in a certain way, then they will keep themselves in line. You won't need to bring military force onto the streets to control people's behavior thereby ensuring that an insane system stays in place because people will do that themselves. If most people think that whites and men should be in control of making the major decisions on how resources should be allocated, because whiteness and masculinity are equated with calm reasoning and the use of logic and objectivity unsullied by emotion or passion, then, as Traister (2018) observed, white patriarchy runs the show.

The Ideology of Individualism

Individualism as a dominant ideology in the United States comprises a set of beliefs and practices that help deflect challenges to a blatantly unequal system. It comprises two core beliefs. The first is that everyone exists on a roughly level playing field and that anyone can make what they want of their life by dint of their own perseverance and hard work. When parents tell their children that they can be anything they want to be, this seems an optimistic and motivational message. It encourages children to imagine alternative futures and inspires their dreams. Anyone can lift themselves up by their bootstraps and soar out into the world as a confident leader or dynamic entrepreneur. Capitalism as an idea is founded on the belief that free enterprise allows any individual who is smart, hardworking, and dynamic to become economically successful.

The second core belief is that we are in control of our individual destinies, captains of each of our souls. What we make of our lives is deemed to be a result of the personal decisions we take at the significant turning points we all experience in life. The feelings, instincts, and intuitions that govern our actions are believed to be unique to us alone. Together they constitute our particular identity, the one that maneuvers through the terrain of an individual life. At some deep level we see ourselves as disconnected from the settings, locations, and people that surround us and engaged in taking on the sole responsibility for creating our life.

This individualist emphasis is an enduring, deeply rooted, and extremely powerful element of the American psyche, particularly for whites. It's bound up with notions of personal expression, the flag, freedom of speech, and Lady Liberty waving in generations of hopeful immigrants and giving them the chance to make better lives for themselves. Archetypal figures such as the cowboy, the frontier settler, even the venture capitalist embody the notion that anyone can be president or the CEO of a global corporation.

Of course this is a *white* lie in that life chances are irrevocably tied to racial identity. So if you are white, then it's very well documented that the chances that you will be able to aspire to and create wealth are higher (Lipsitz, 2018). The myth of individualism uses Black exceptionalism—the political successes of individuals of color from President Obama, Condi Rice, and Colin Powell to millionaire sports figures such as LeBron James or Kobe

Bryant and mogul media entertainers like Sean Combs, Kanye West, and Beyoncé—to prove its truth. "Look at all these successful Black politicians, media moguls, and billionaire sports stars—they prove that anyone can be wildly successful irrespective of their race!"

Individualism and Racism

But perhaps the most pernicious effect of the ideology of individualism is to present racism as a matter of personal choice. If each of us is really in charge of charting our own course, planning and realizing our own destiny, then individually we can decide whether or not to be racist. Racism thus becomes a wholly personal choice, something that white people decide to opt into, or reject, on a day-by-day basis. When racism is perceived as a series of individual judgments and actions—today I was racist but yesterday I was not—then combating racism becomes seen as a matter of personal fortitude. Whites can resolve to be on high alert for their own enactment of racial microaggressions, can vow to monitor their implicit biases, and strive to cut out racist jokes, tropes, and stereotypes. Viewed this way, whites can convince themselves that real progress is being made, one person at a time.

We don't want to dismiss these individual kinds of efforts as naïve. The two of us take them very seriously and try to work on ourselves in the ways just described. But we're also aware that seeing antiracism as a personal choice obscures the systemic nature of the phenomenon. In reality, individual acts of racism are the personal enactments of structural reality. White supremacy as an ideology ensures the continuing dominance of one racial group by portraying its exercise of control as an uncontestable empirical truth. Individualism as an ideology obscures that fact by perpetrating the idea that where one ends up in life is all down to personal fortitude, grit, or luck.

In this perspective the fact that whites end up in positions of power and authority is not the result of systemic oppression, but just the way things shake out. It's seen as almost a matter of chance that those who constantly reap the material benefits of capitalism are mostly white. Individualist ideology means that the continuing disenfranchisement and marginalization of people of color is not understood as linked to school district funding mechanisms, the specific design of intelligence tests, or redlining housing policies. The disproportionate levels of infant mortality or poor health care among communities of color is disconnected from the fact that members of poor communities (which are composed disproportionately of people of color) piece together employment from multiple part-time jobs, none of which carry health benefits.

Doing antiracist work on your own learned biases and stereotypes without paying attention to the way that the power of rich white elites remains undisturbed ultimately plays into the hands of white supremacy. As Crass (2015) observed, "We can't think our way out of the problem of white privilege by being really aware white people" (p. 16). Focusing exclusively on individual consciousness raising poses no real danger to white supremacy. In particular, middle-class whites (like the two of us have become) can convince themselves that personal reflection and introspection is the important thing we can do—"start with yourself!" At some level, of course, this is true. Looking at your own history and socialization can be a significant entry point to activist engagement. And publicly modeling your own disclosure of how you have peeled back the layers to realize what racist instincts you've internalized is a crucial first step as you start to encourage other whites to explore how to become antiracist.

But if all that happens is that you feel you have a better understanding of yourself, then racism endures. True activism happens when all people of different racial identities realize their common interest in organizing and fighting for the basic necessities of a fulfilled life—stable employment, a safe community, decent wages, access to affordable health care, clean water, and education for all. The greatest threat to white supremacy is when people start to perceive that their lot in life is not the result of individual accidents or the vicissitudes of fate and that they all want the same things. Once people realize that, then they start to build alliances across racial groups, develop mass social movements, and create political parties that truly represent the desires of so-called "ordinary" people. Understanding that stoking racial divisions among poor whites and BIPOC folks is a tactic to prevent a mass movement for economic and environmental justice from developing means that people will start to combine in a common project to get their piece of the American pie. That puts white supremacy on the defensive.

It's also true that when people start to see racism as structural and systemic, when they understand that biases, microaggressions, and racist stereotypes are *learned* rather than originating in individual psyches, there is less embarrassment to owning up to them. Thinking structurally should be the theoretical north star that guides activism, the framework that "consistently explains patterns of injustice" (Love, 2020, p. 132) and gives us "language to fight, knowledge to stand on, and a humbling reality of what intersectional justice is up against" (p. 132). The logical outcome of structural thinking is that instead of whites blaming people of color for taking jobs, using affirmative action to get college places, and becoming welfare kings and queens, both whites and BIPOC folks realize that the common enemy is the white supremacist economic structure.

When whites understand that a white supremacist view of the world is embedded in institutions and systems, when learning racism is seen as a normal part of enculturation and socialization, then it becomes easier for people to talk about how it's manifested in their own lives. In their analysis of the roots of implicit bias, Daumeyer et al. (2017) argued that "a model of implicit bias that situates its expression on situational factors, then, should be more acceptable to individuals" (p. 258). We have both observed this to be true. Seeing bias and advantage as structurally created helps decrease the white fatigue that Flynn (2015) described whereby whites, even if they are committed to antiracism, feel personal responsibility, guilt, and shame when race takes center stage in classes, workshops, or meetings.

If racism is understood as a structural phenomenon, the focus is placed on *systems* of exclusion and acculturation. This is why the two of us often say that to grow up in a racist world and *not* to have learned racist conditioning would be very strange. We try to normalize racism by presenting it not as a shameful personal moral defect but as a natural outcome of living every day in white supremacist systems and structures.

An antiracist identity must focus on understanding racism as structural and systemic, and on a commitment to taking collective action to change those structures and systems. Working on your own racist habits, inclinations, and biases is important and necessary, but it's only the beginning of the journey to become a white antiracist. We must move from the individual to the systemic, from the personal to the collective. We must help build movements, commit to institutional and community initiatives that address inequity, and focus on changing policies and political parties. People come and go but structures and systems endure unless some collective effort disrupts them. In short, we need to think structurally, not individually.

Locating Structural Inequity in Groups: The Privilege Walk

People embedded in individualist ideology and unused to thinking structurally will usually not react well to beginning with a critical theory analysis. In contrast, engaging them in an experiential activity that confronts them with how uncomfortable structural realities are part and parcel of their daily lives and personal experiences will likely be more successful. One such activity is the privilege walk. Based on McIntosh's (1988) initial idea of whiteness as a knapsack of privileges, this exercise demonstrates physically the structural inequities based on race, class, and gender that exist in a group.

The process begins with everybody standing in a straight line across a large room. In response to a series of prompts people take a step forward or backward (or stay in place) depending on their responses. Typical prompts include the following:

> If you studied the culture of your ancestors in school, take one step forward.
>
> If one of your parents was fired from their job, take one step back.
>
> If your parents owned the house you grew up in, take one step forward.
>
> If you believe the police are there to help you when you're having difficulty, take one step forward.
>
> If you've ever been the subject of racial abuse directed at you, take one step back.
>
> If you rely on public transportation to get around, take one step back.

As people move backward or forward in response to these prompts, a geography of the classroom quickly emerges in which people of color, women, and LGBTQI folks are mostly situated toward the back. This demonstrates how racial and other identities touch participants' lives in a real-time training, class session, or meeting. It's a very effective way to illustrate a big abstract idea like structural inequity. The exercise shows how what seem like the idiosyncratic events of people's personal lives are actually determined by an inbuilt structural advantage enjoyed by whites.

As a group observes its white members, and particularly its white men, moving forward or standing in place as others move toward the back of the room, leaders and trainers can use that stark physical reality to begin a consideration of structural racism. The fact of structural inequality is, quite literally, embodied in the space where people are gathered. You can then follow up by introducing research that underscores how access to wealth, health care, higher paying jobs, and education matches the pattern of how participants were located in the room (Flynn et al., 2017; Roediger & Esch, 2012; Saito, 2020; Wilkerson, 2020).

Beginning With Story: The Brain Fart

We like to start work on thinking structurally with some kind of narrative or story that people can personally relate to and then work backward from this particular event to help them see how specific actions are structurally framed. The following is an example of a story that Stephen Brookfield uses to lead participants into structural thinking.

I was running what I thought was an effective student discussion one day in a university class that was overwhelmingly white and mostly female. I considered the discussion as successful because it seemed that everybody was participating in roughly equal measure.

About 30 minutes into the class I raised a particular issue and asked everyone to contribute their thinking on the topic. A couple of students hesitantly ventured their initial thoughts and I practiced my usual waiting time until eventually everyone had spoken. The contributions were focused and thoughtful and I was pleased by the way the students had brought a variety of perspectives to the issue.

I began summarizing the main themes that I thought had emerged from the comments and started to differentiate the contradictory views that I felt had been expressed.

Suddenly a white woman participant, Jenn, raised her hand.

"Excuse me, we haven't heard from Mia," she said.

Mia was a young Asian American woman and the thought that I had overlooked her was immediately embarrassing to me.

"I'm really sorry about that, Mia," I said. "I don't know how that happened. My apologies, I don't know how I missed you. Can we hear from you what you're thinking about?"

Mia made her contribution and shortly afterward we took a midclass break.

I was still bothered and feeling embarrassed by my not noticing that Mia hadn't spoken and as I brewed up some tea in my office I started to go over what had just happened.

It became obvious to me almost immediately that this was a classic example of a microaggression. Microaggressions occur when members of the dominant culture act unwittingly in ways that diminish, demean, and marginalize members of minority groups. These actions are so subtle that the receivers are often left wondering, "Did that really happen?" They ask themselves, "Am I making too much of something? Am I imagining this?"

When challenged, those committing microaggressions usually respond by saying the person identifying the aggression is being too sensitive, making a mountain out of a molehill, or just misunderstanding what was said or meant. Members of the dominant culture often jump in to excuse and explain away the aggression, saying that it was a slip of the tongue, came out the wrong way, and that no harm was meant. This is often accompanied by character witness testimonials of how the aggressor doesn't have a racist bone in their body, is a good person, and cares for all people.

The class resumed after break and I began by speaking about what had happened when I had overlooked Mia.

"I want to thank Jenn for bringing to my attention the fact that I completely overlooked Mia in class. What you've just witnessed is a classic example of a racial microaggression. I had no intent to exclude Mia from the discussion and no awareness of that happening. Yet when I thanked you all for contributing

and began to summarize your comments I completely overlooked a woman of color. Microaggressions are the small acts of exclusion that whites often enact against people of color. They're not deliberate or intentional and they happen with no wish to harm someone else. But that's what happened when I went into my summary without noticing that Mia hadn't spoken."

Almost immediately the only white male member of the group, John, spoke up.

"You know, Dr. Brookfield, I think you're being way too hard on yourself. You just had a forgetful moment. Not every action has to do with race. Sometimes you're just tired. You just had a brain fart. I don't think you should blame yourself. If we take this to the extreme we're never going to be able to do or say anything without being thought of as racist."

I thought it was beautifully ironic that John's response captured the dynamic of microaggressions whereby members of the dominant culture jump in to save others who they feel are being unjustly accused. I, not Mia, had been the one to name my own microaggression, and yet John had felt compelled to jump in and save me from myself.

I told John that he had just exemplified how whites try to excuse other whites who are called out on their microaggressions.

John was offended by my comments. "Well, it's obvious I can't say anything in this course without being called a racist!" he exclaimed. "This is clearly not a safe space for me so I'm just going to shut up."

Just then Mia spoke up.

"This is not the first time this has happened to me," she said, her voice quavering. "In every class I've been in at this institution I feel I've been systematically ignored. It's like people don't see me or think I'm in the room."

Coding the Story

We hand out the story to people so everyone has a written record and ask them to spend 5 minutes carefully reading it and then to answer three questions on their own:

- What events or actions in the story demonstrate the presence of white supremacy as both an ideology or set of practices?
- How is the specific location of the story affected by wider structures, systems, and forces?
- Whose interests inside and outside the specific location of the story are served or harmed by what's described?

After completing their private responses, people then share them in small groups. The whole workshop, class, or meeting then reconvenes and we hear what people have talked about.

Here's how the discussion of "The Brain Fart" might go.

What Events or Actions in the Story Demonstrate the Presence of White Supremacy as Both an Ideology or Set of Practices?

Because the story is about a racial microaggression, it's pretty predictable that people will point out how Brookfield's forgetting to include Mia is an example of white supremacy in action, because it represents a typically white blindness to the effect of one's actions. They'll also acknowledge that Jenn's interruption represented a challenge to white supremacy.

John's intervention to excuse and save Brookfield is almost always cited as an example of white supremacy in play. By excusing Brookfield's overlooking of Mia, John is saying that race had little significance in the situation and that this was a one-off event and not any form of systemic exclusion. John's announcing that he now doesn't feel safe in the course and that he's going to withdraw from subsequent conversations is also cited as an example of white fragility (DiAngelo, 2018), the privilege of whites being able to choose when they wish to engage with race.

How Is the Specific Location of the Story Affected by Wider Structures, Systems, and Forces?

The story takes place in a specific classroom and it's easy to assume that this constitutes a more or less self-contained universe. But in the small groups participants often start to dig deeper.

The College

The first point of analysis is usually the college. People ask about the college's mission statement and the degree to which the class itself exemplifies or contradicts that statement. They want to know how the college is funded and the health of student enrollments. Like many private institutions, it is tuition-driven so an overarching concern is to attract the maximum number of students.

We ask people to ponder what influence, if any, that concern might have on the conduct of the class. Has Brookfield created a problem by making a white male student decide he doesn't wish to participate any more in the course? Could this lead to him dropping out and the subsequent loss of his tuition revenue? What will be the financial consequences of Brookfield's naming and teaching about microaggressions? If communities of color become aware of this work, would it cause more students of color to apply to the university? Or would this work be opposed by alumni as too radical and not in keeping with the university's traditions and identity?

We'll then go deeper and ask participants to consider how institutional identities and priorities are defined. This brings levers and influences behind the scenes such as the board of trustees into play. People often think that power in colleges resides in the senior leadership team comprised of the president, provost, and dean's council. In fact, the body ultimately responsible for setting policy, defining goals, and assessing compliance with the mission is the board of trustees.

Knowing this we urge people to go to the college's website and look up the composition of the board. What kind of occupations or interests are represented in the board's membership? Typically, board members are recruited who can ensure the financial stability of the college by attracting possible donors. Hence, many of them hold prominent positions as CEOs or CFOs in major corporations, banks, and investment firms. We suggest that participants employ online search engines to find out about the racial mix of the board and ask what it means for the direction of the university to be set and monitored by a group composed of mostly white business representatives.

The Program or Department

Sometimes we suggest to participants that the analysis could be taken to an ever more local level, that of the particular department or program offering the course. To what degree are the individuals who make up this unit committed to uncovering and challenging racism? Given that the first stage in employee performance appraisals is situated at the department and program level, what implications will this kind of teaching have for those instructors up for reappointment, third-year review, tenure, or promotion? What criteria are used to assess teachers? Are they assessed for the extent to which they make students feel productively uncomfortable? Is assessment connected to student evaluations of teaching? If so, who designs the forms used and what specific items do they contain?

Student evaluation of teaching forms often measure things such as a teacher's clarity of explanations, the frequency and depth of feedback provided, and an instructor's openness to questions. It's rare to find a form that probes the degree to which students were discomforted, troubled, or deeply challenged. We ask people to consider what the criteria for instructor assessment and the items on evaluation forms tell us about the wider forces at work.

This brings us to the "students as customers" orientation of so many nonprofit institutions that ironically find themselves operating with a for-profit capitalist logic of needing to attract the largest amount possible of paying customers. We may also get into the problematic nature of assigning numerical scores to teachers' performance. Given what we know about the complexity of teaching and learning, especially when it involves questions of racial identity, how can the merits of pedagogic work be accurately represented by assigning a score on a Likert scale of 1 to 5?

Whose Interests Inside and Outside the Specific Location of the Story Are Served or Harmed by the Events Described?

Here we're asking participants to shift their frame of analysis from someone who is listening to a description of local events to someone who is considering asymmetries of power. In terms of the specific events of the story, people often say that it's obvious that Mia's interests are served because she got the opportunity to contribute and that John's interests are harmed because he felt Brookfield had silenced him.

When this analysis is expressed, we usually ask participants to go back and read the story again. We explain that we want them to think about the framing of this story within a system of white supremacy and we emphasize that, like all dominant ideologies, white supremacy is designed to be self-sustaining. In other words, it's set up to keep white power and white normativity in place and viewed as the natural state of things. White supremacy protects itself by appearing to be unremarkable, a form of common sense. For us this suggests a reading of the story that's directly opposite to the one just described.

Sometimes the reminder of the construct of white supremacy means that people now talk about Mia and John in different ways. Mia becomes seen as someone who has a history of being silenced by omission. People quote the fact that she tells the class that being overlooked is her typical experience at the university and now present the story as one that illustrates the continuing power of white supremacy.

John's situation is now seen as more complicated. Although people still argue that he has been harmed by Brookfield's intervention and they acknowledge his feeling that he is now in an unsafe environment, his decision to remove himself from the discussion is now sometimes positioned as an act of white privilege. John is privileged because he can simply turn away from the reality of race and choose not to think about what it means to live in a racist world. He has been granted the option of denying reality without much harm accruing to him. This, of course, is directly opposite to the experience of people of color who are robbed of the choice of ignoring the realities of racism and white supremacy.

Doing a Power Analysis

Another way to teach structural thinking is to ask people to conduct a power analysis of a story. Here the intent is to make them aware of how power dynamics are embedded in specific events. Although the 'Brain Fart' story focuses on one class in one institution at one particular moment, the interactions described are shaped by wider asymmetries of power.

To help students do this we give a brief typology of three different kinds of power. We discuss what these terms mean and give examples of them in action.

- *Repressive power.* Power used to constrain options, limit freedom, or maintain the status quo. This could be as simple as a supervisor telling someone not to make trouble by bringing up a contentious issue, or as explosive as paramilitary forces or civilian militias beating up or killing protesters on the street.
- *Emancipatory power.* Power experienced as motivating or galvanizing that fuels activism and the desire for change. This could be a supervisor asking an employee, "How can I help you do your best work?" to Black Lives Matter activists mobilizing people quickly for a day of protest immediately after a police killing.
- *Disciplinary power.* Power that someone exerts on themselves to make sure they stay in line. This is derived from Foucault's (1980) work in which the impulse to engage in self-censorship and self-monitoring is posited as the chief way that social control is exercised. A common example is when you argue for more institutional diversity and inclusion so as not to be regarded as too radical or threatening, when really you would prefer to be asking about how to name white supremacy and institutional racism.

We then ask the participants to do two things.

1. Go through each kind of power and say when you think each is being exercised in the story. Do this initially on your own.
2. Try to identify what wider systems, structures, and ideologies support the exercise of each kind of power. Again, this is done initially by people on their own.

After participants have answered these questions privately, they work in small groups of five to identify and compile the various responses. We then reconvene the whole group and ask each team to present what they've found.

Repressive Power

Brookfield is usually identified as the chief enactor of repressive power. This is because people see his overlooking of Mia as an example of how systems embody white normativity and patriarchy. As the instructor Brookfield has the weight of institutional authority behind his actions. That means it takes an act of courage by Jenn to stand up to him and point out his disregarding of a woman of color. Until he was called on his assumption that everyone had participated in the discussion, he believed he was acting in a democratic and inclusive manner.

John is also sometimes cited as exercising repressive power because he has removed himself from any further discussion of racial issues. On the face of it, this seems like a withdrawing or giving up of power because he will not be rationalizing Brookfield's conduct or explaining it away as a benevolent, momentary error. However, in removing himself from the conversation, he is denying other students the chance to learn how he experiences and enacts white supremacy. After all, the experts on how white supremacy and patriarchy are learned and internalized are white people. By not contributing to future discussions, John is blocking other students' opportunity to understand better how dominant ideologies influence whites' behavior.

Emancipatory Power

Because she spoke up to address Brookfield's overlooking of Mia, Jenn is typically cited as the chief enactor of emancipatory power. Her intervention caused Stephen to ask Mia to express her opinion on the matter at hand. It also prompted him to reflect on the incident during the break and to come back and initiate a conversation on microaggressions.

Sometimes people get into a deep conversation about the problematic notion of a white person "liberating" a person of color and the colonial legacy that embodies. Was it condescending of Jenn to intervene, thereby robbing Mia of the chance to speak up for herself? Did it perpetuate the "savior" mentality, whereby whites take on the responsibility to liberate people of color from oppression? Or was Jenn using her white privilege in a responsible way to bring the exercise of white supremacy to the attention of a powerful white male? After all, she could make the challenge to Brookfield's authority without the risk of being accused of playing the race card, whereas Brookfield could have dismissed Mia as seeing a racial motive where none existed.

Disciplinary Power

Disciplinary power is power exercised by someone on himself or herself, to ensure they keep their conduct within acceptable parameters and norms. In this instance Mia is usually identified as the enactor of disciplinary power. She has learned to stay quiet when she is overlooked or ignored, either because she has learned that's how the world works or because she has suffered the consequences of speaking up for herself. Maybe her peers have told her that challenging a white professor for sins of omission will bring punishment down on her. Possibly her elders have instilled in her a cultural reverence of authority and told her it is disrespectful to criticize a teacher. It could also be that her complaints in the past have been dismissed or not believed. Perhaps she is just exhausted from having to confront all the microaggressions and institutional racism she has experienced.

As people talk about Mia's choice to remain silent, the very notion of choice becomes examined. When you know you will be dismissed or punished for an action, what kind of free choice really exists? Participants ponder whether staying silent was a conscious decision on Mia's part, informed by her past experience of criticizing authority, or whether it was a deeply internalized response that she little awareness of. Perhaps this represents the way she had been taught to move through her life.

The discussion then branches into different directions. Sometimes people focus on how elements of Asian American culture and the Confucian tradition instill a notion of good conduct as listening respectfully to elders and automatically attributing wisdom to their actions and decisions. If we talk about Mia needing to stay silent to survive, then we are back to acknowledging the influence of patriarchy and white supremacy. If the discussion goes in this latter direction, we might then ask participants to research the racial and gender composition of influential bodies such as Congress, the presidency, the military, multinational banking, the judiciary, and corporate CEOs. Female participants tend to bring numerous examples of being systematically marginalized or ignored in the male-dominated institutions or organizations where they have worked.

Ideology Critique

In ideology critique you take a practice that has been designed to be helpful and empowering and examine it for the ways people in an organization, movement, or community experience it differently. The intent is to invert our normal thinking about the apparently obvious benefits and common-sense logic of institutional ways of functioning, such as introducing a new performance appraisal system. In ideology critique people examine how such practices are structured to preserve hierarchies of power. The process alerts participants to blind spots in their own decision-making and helps organizations understand better how their inbuilt routines regularly exclude certain voices and perspectives.

Facilitators start by presenting an action intended to promote effectiveness or realize the organization's mission statement. Participants are then asked to do the following on their own:

- Describe the practice and attribute meaning and significance to it in terms of the accepted, dominant view. What do the powers that be say that it's intended to achieve? What's the reasoning used to justify its utility?
- Examine that dominant view for internal inconsistencies, paradoxes, and contradictions.
- Identify what's omitted from the dominant view. What are its structured silences and absences? What views, perspectives, and experiences are unrepresented in the dominant framing of the practice or action? Why do you think these are not represented?
- Decide who most benefits from the dominant practice and who is most disadvantaged by it.
- Consider how the practice could be reinvented to be fairer and more inclusive.

After answering these questions privately, people are then put into small groups to share their responses. The exercise ends with the whole workshop, meeting, training, or class convening to hear from everyone.

An Ideology Critique Example: Diversifying the Curriculum

A case we often use is a practice we have seen on many campuses. Faced with the realization that demographic changes mean that students entering higher education will come from more and more diverse racial groups, colleges and universities have attempted to broaden their core curriculum to include more authors of color and to introduce modules dealing with race. The institution then announces this broadening of curriculum as evidence of their responsiveness to communities of color and their commitment to diversity.

Describe the Practice and Attribute Meaning and Significance to It in Terms of the Accepted, Dominant View—What Is It Intended to Achieve and What's the Reasoning Used to Justify Its Utility?
Colleges and universities want to demonstrate that they are nonracist and inclusive so as to attract students from diverse racial backgrounds. They believe that if they include more authors of color, this will make white students more racially aware and help students of color feel that their lives and experiences are represented and valued on campus. This will lead to

lower attrition rates for students of color and help white students develop an appreciation for the contributions of scholars of color. As a result, the campus climate will become friendlier and more welcoming for students of color, and white students will be helped to develop an antiracist identity.

Examine That View for Internal Inconsistencies, Paradoxes, and Contradictions

One possible inconsistency concerns the way that authors of color and modules are positioned. If students see them as add-ons rather than comprising a permanently altered center, then this initiative will be seen as a temporary Band-Aid covering a far deeper structural and cultural problem. Also, if the curriculum is presented as a smorgasbord whereby students can pick and choose which authors to read and which modules to study, we could quickly end up with students of color volunteering to study authors of color and race-based topics, while white students stick with the Eurocentric canon. This will potentially resegregate the curriculum.

There is also the possible contradiction that whereas the curriculum is emphasizing difference and divergence, the teaching methods and assessment rubrics remain unaltered. So although this curricular reform is meant to celebrate different ways of experiencing the world, it is taught in ways that privilege text over oral communication and words over images. Traditions of oral storytelling and collectivity prized by some cultures may well not be reflected in how students' learning is evaluated. Sharing ideas might be interpreted as plagiarism and there will be no opportunity to present group, rather than individually completed, assignments.

Finally, who will teach these new courses? Asking instructors who have little knowledge or training in this area to do this can backfire horribly, leaving students of color feeling exposed and unprotected. Without experience in leading contentious discussions, teachers could end up doing more harm than good by not challenging the racist views of some white students.

Identify What Is Being Omitted From the Dominant View

What are its structured silences and absences? What views, perspectives, and experiences are unrepresented in the practice or action? Why do you think these have been missed? Much will depend on who designs these curricular changes. If a mostly white committee chooses the authors of color to be studied and designs the modules dealing with race, then the authentic experiences of people of color may be missing, particularly the expression of righteous anger and strong criticism of white supremacy. A white view of which authors of color are acceptable and how units dealing with race should be framed can lead to the exclusion of radical scholarship that challenges the foundations of the academy and calls out white supremacy.

The reason why radical scholarship and contentious modules are not included is to protect the interests of the white members of the institution. They wish to demonstrate their multicultural commitment without being called to personal account.

Decide Who Benefits From the Dominant Practice and Who Is Most Disadvantaged by It

If "softer" authors of color are chosen, if race-based modules are designed to celebrate individual diversity rather than delve into structural racism, and if students can choose from a smorgasbord of options (thus allowing white students to omit reading radical authors of color or studying racism), those who benefit from this practice are whites. Members of the board of trustees and the senior leadership team can issue news announcements that highlight the curricular changes as evidence of their racial responsiveness. Faculty who teach these kinds of courses can escape examining their own personal learned racism or naming the racist policies of the institution. If enrollments increase and attrition decreases, then the board of trustees can claim to be managing the institution's financials prudently.

Most disadvantaged are the students of color that this institutional effort is officially designed to serve. They will have been served a false bill of goods and will experience a counterfeit antiracist effort, one that looks as though it's tackling the problem seriously but in fact is designed to keep things exactly the same.

If, however, the authors of color chosen directly address systemic racism and if the new race-based modules focus on how white supremacy is learned and disseminated as representing a commonsense, obvious way of interpreting the world, then the interests of people of color are served. And if word gets out and about in communities of color that the university is serious about tackling racism, then the institution will benefit by attracting increased numbers of applicants of color and producing testimonials from alumni that speak to its genuine antiracist identity.

How Could the Practice/Action Be Reinvented to Be Fairer and More Inclusive?

One possibility is to make sure that there is a high representation of students and faculty of color on committees charged with designing and implementing any curricular changes. This will help prevent the diversification project from becoming a showcase meant to deflect criticism and reject any serious institutional reappraisal. Another option might be to invite members of communities of color that the institution serves to suggest topics that would be at the center of the new race-based modules. These individuals could also serve on an oversight committee charged with making sure the institution sticks to its commitment to combat racism. Ensuring a built-in mechanism to monitor how the initiative is going, and sharing those results with the whole community, is an important account-ability mechanism.

Thinking Structurally in Community

Thinking structurally is a complex and difficult process that does not happen overnight. It qualifies as an authentic example of transformative learning as defined by Mezirow (1991) and, as such, is primarily a social learning pro-cess. The cognitive moves involved in thinking structurally entail shedding as much as possible the individualist ideology that is so embedded in American culture. It requires stepping back from the minutiae of one's life and seeing them not just as personally determined but as reflecting wider social trends and the interplay of economic and political forces.

This is what the mid-20th-century theorist C. Wright Mills (1959) called cultivating the sociological imagination, the effort to understand that private troubles such as getting divorced or being fired are always connected to public issues such as the destruction of local economies and the growth of monopoly capitalism. If you work for a small business in a rural town and a giant Walmart is constructed that takes your customers, this may result in your being laid off, inducing money troubles and triggering a loss of self-worth. All these events can create a spiral resulting in divorce, drug use, and maybe self-harm.

Making a paradigmatic leap to viewing the world structurally and developing a sociological imagination is a process that takes time. It usually happens incrementally and involves multiple movements forward that are then quickly followed by regressions to earlier ways of thinking. Crucial to this journey is a community of peers who are also trying to think structurally about the way that systems and ideologies shape what feel like individual decisions.

In empirical studies of how adults learn to view the world in a fundamen-tally altered way, it appears that a community of inquirers is crucial (Taylor & Cranton & Associates, 2012). This community is what Boyd (2014) called a container, a resting place in which people can, in the company of others on a similar quest, test out new understandings and experiment with new identi-ties. As with all forms of critical thinking (Brookfield, 2012), learning to think structurally happens best when it's experienced as a social learning process. People discover assumptions and new perspectives most meaningfully when peers brings them to their attention. This is why thinking structurally needs to be located in a learning community composed of others struggling to comprehend the world this way.

This finding is hardly surprising if we consider how difficult it is to learn about our assumptions and worldviews simply by deciding we will do some deep self-examination. Even if we complete a sustained period of self-reflection and do daily journaling on race (Kendi, 2020) we'll need to discuss what we're thinking and writing with others on a similar journey. Becoming aware of the mental frames that determine how we understand our experiences is a puzzling and contradictory task. Very few of us can get very far doing this on our own. No matter how much we may think we have an accurate sense of ourselves, we are stymied by the fact that we're using our own interpretive filters to become aware of our own interpretive filters! This is the equivalent of a dog trying to catch its tail, or of trying to see the back of your head while looking in the bathroom mirror. To become aware of structural and systemic factors we need to find friends, colleagues, and peers who reflect back to us a stark and differently highlighted picture of who we are and what we do.

Final Comment

Thinking structurally is a crucial cognitive move in becoming a white anti-racist. Moving away from an individualist ideology means coming to understand our own learned racism not as an inherent moral flaw but as a very predictable result of growing up subject to quietly effective white supremacist conditioning. When we see our own racist acts and inclinations as structurally determined, this helps us move past an extended fixation on guilt and shame. It's easy to spend all your time obsessed with your past sins and embarrassed and mortified by the casual racism you've enacted. This is a dead end. Thinking structurally lifts you out of that extended fixation on your flaws and moves you more quickly to activism.

A structural perspective emphasizes the humanly created nature of white supremacy. Anything that has been created by humans can be dismantled and replaced by them. Of course, doing this will be a long and difficult process that will require collective effort. Antiracist training that focuses on changing individual behavior so one is less influenced by implicit biases and racial stereotypes is an important starting point. But real, substantive change will only come when structures, systems, and policies are fundamentally altered or replaced and that will only happen if people work together in political parties and social movements. So for us, thinking structurally is the mental kick-starter to collective action.

9

USING *YOUR* POWER
TO EMPOWER WHITE
ANTIRACISM

Working to create an antiracist identity means you constantly intersect with power. There's the psychological power of the internal pushback you'll feel as your "good white" identity keeps kicking in and telling you that you're one of the "good" ones, you're not really a racist, and so therefore you don't really need to do this work. There's the power of the resistance you'll meet from those you live and work with who tell you this is not a "real" issue, that we live in a postracial world, and that all this white bashing you seem to be engaged in is just political correctness gone mad. And, of course, you'll most definitely feel institutional power opposing any substantive work.

Institutions love to declare their commitment to inclusion, diversity, and equity, but they also frequently shy away from a serious engagement with white supremacy (Brookfield, 2018). They will spend money on banners, on photo shoots for publicity brochures that include faces of color, and on rebranding themselves as committed to becoming antiracist. The minority of people of color at the institution will find their faces plastered on institutional websites and billboards in a gallery of images that comprises a nicely balanced rainbow coalition of African, Asian, Latinx, and indigenous faces.

The institution will also play representational politics and employ more bodies of color. There will usually be a high-profile appointment of a person of color to the leadership team, probably as chief diversity officer or senior vice president for diversity. But the fact that no other high-level leader is a person of color makes it harder for the individual concerned to develop the network of personal relationships that whites enjoy.

143

All these steps will be accompanied by a vigorous program of workshops and training sessions designed to bring an awareness of race to the forefront. But workshops are oasis moments in institutional life, a temporary reality you enter before returning to the mainstream. Participating in one-off, short-term activities means the likelihood of a sustained and significant change in behavior is low. For example, a study of nurses attending a communication skills workshop found that without subsequent clinical supervision very little transfer of these skills into patient settings occurred (Heaven et al., 2006).

To institutions, however, announcing an upcoming series of diversity workshops looks like something purposeful and significant is happening and that a deliberate, sustained effort is being made to address the problem of racism. Workshops and training are public, visible, and bounded events and can be presented as clear evidence that the institution is responding conscientiously and seriously to the need to combat racism. But without addressing the ideology of white supremacy and attempting to uncover its presence at all levels of institutional functioning, members of minority racial groups find themselves negotiating what they perceive to be a hostile and unfriendly environment.

Parachuting a few bodies of color into a mostly white environment means it's easier to keep difficult questions of racism and white supremacy at bay. Yet the real experts on how white supremacy as an ideology is learned and deeply internalized are whites. People like the two of us are the learners and enactors of this ideology; we know how it frames daily actions, interpretations, and decisions. So instead of always turning to the only person of color in the senior leadership team, the white members need to be examining the way that whiteness as the unquestioned norm and standard of legitimacy can be identified and challenged. We have never seen true leadership from the top on this issue, where those white power holders with the most to lose accept Yancy's (2015) invitation to address publicly the nature of their own learned racism and to disclose how that structures the decisions they make as they move through a white world.

Trying to change how systems work, challenging policies that are in place, or urging that employees be rewarded for antiracist work and institutional criticism usually ensures that repressive power will come down on your head quickly and strongly. But there is another kind of power we want to examine in this chapter, a positive experience of power that shakes things up and gets things moving. This is the power embedded in *em-power-ment*. To feel empowered is to feel a collective surge of energy that runs through a relationship, group, community, or movement. To feel empowered is to know that individually and collectively you possess the skills and knowledge necessary to change a situation. There's a sense of agency, hope, and possibility in the air as people deliberate, strategize, and divide their labor to push things forward.

In this chapter we want to explore how those of us working to help whites create an antiracist identity can use our positions of authority and leadership—whether these are institutionally recognized or not—to move people to embrace the challenge of working actively and constantly against racism. Readers who are in institutionally mandated positions as teachers, leaders, trainers, and staff and professional developers have the power of whatever institutional credibility they have been granted by their employer. Readers working in community, movement, or congregational settings have the power of their experience and their history of a demonstrable commitment to the cause of antiracism. In all these situations people look to their facilitators and leaders to set a certain tone, to create the conditions for conversation, to guide them in the examination of issues, and to provide them with whatever advice, tools, or techniques will help them move an antiracist effort along.

Being Authoritative

In an interesting dialogue in their talking book on *A Pedagogy for Liberation* Shor and Freire (1987) discussed the difference between being authoritarian and being authoritative. It's one of the most profound discussions we've ever read for understanding our own practice as educators and leaders and it's one we still reference today. Put simply, Shor and Freire drew a distinction between being authoritarian, which is the seemingly arbitrary or haphazard issuing of directions with no opportunity for critique or negotiation, and being authoritative.

The root of being authoritative comes from being perceived as credible, competent, and experienced. People need to know they are being led by someone qualified to do the work. They want someone with whom they can identify, but who is clearly experienced and competent—someone who has the required skills and who has been around the block a few times. When that person gives them directions, they want to feel that those are grounded in a rationale designed to develop particular skills or dispositions. Shor and Freire argued that people look for leaders and teachers to exercise necessary authority—that is, to give of their experience, share necessary advice and helpful insights, and guide the less knowledgeable in complex learning.

In the case of becoming a white antiracist, being authoritative means working from a position of experience in which you demonstrate how the struggle you have personally engaged in to uncover your own learned racism informs the way you help others to become aware of white supremacy. It means explaining your actions clearly and providing a rationale for them that's grounded in your understanding of where people are in their own antiracist journey. And it means seeking critique of, and reactions to, your own practices, choices, and decisions.

We believe authoritative leadership in antiracism is exercised in a continuous loop of formative evaluation. You take action, seek anonymous responses to that action, and then publicly report comments, reactions, and critiques of what you're doing. You model being critically reflective about your practice by negotiating and changing how you go about this work based on people's responses. You point out things that you've missed, blind spots you've uncovered, and perspectives you've omitted. When your assumptions about what will help people learn are inaccurate, you acknowledge that and try to develop new assumptions that are more valid. When warranted, you are ready to change what you do and work in an altered way to get people to move in antiracist directions.

But sometimes you have to justify why, even in the face of critiques and negative reactions, you won't budge. After all, asking whites who think of themselves as good people to confront their own learned racism will inevitably induce a lot of resistance and pushback. Sometimes you just need to stand firm in the face of bewilderment or outright hostility because you're convinced of the value of your work. But if you're going to stick to your agenda, you need to justify why you are seemingly being inflexible. You need to show you're striving to understand and honor the reasons why people don't think they need to develop an antiracist identity, even as you insist on your own belief that it's the right thing to do.

In the rest of this chapter we seek to examine a number of discrete tasks, all of which we feel constitute an appropriate use of one's positional power and necessary authority when developing an antiracist identity. We both believe that the "how" of practice—the way in which you lead, teach, facilitate, and organize—is just as important as the "what" of practice. You can sincerely believe you're doing the crucial work of helping people create an antiracist identity for themselves, yet sabotage your effectiveness by forcing the pace, ignoring criticism, and dismissing resistance as uninformed. People won't feel as if their agency is being developed under these conditions. On the contrary, they'll feel manipulated and disregarded. So it's important that you exercise any power you possess in ways that are experienced as empowering.

Clarifying Your Rationale

Moving into an antiracist identity is not something that many whites feel is important to do. Caught in the web of unexamined whiteness they will say that the world is basically fair, that race is not that significant a factor in a meritocracy, and that they treat everyone the same, regardless of skin color or phenotype. In a required course or mandatory training people will be there to comply with institutional requirements. Consequently, their bodies may be present but their minds will definitely be elsewhere. You can expect a range of emotions from apathy to outright hostility.

At the outset, then, you'll need to establish why the session is worth people showing up for. As we've already emphasized, we feel that starting with a powerful narrative is the way to go. Ideally, this will be a story from someone with whom audience members can identify. This could be you as the leader or facilitator, or a white colleague who felt no need to address race until something dramatic happened to smash her or his white worldview to pieces. Personal disclosure can then be followed by testimony from people of color regarding the ways they negotiate the organization. If you don't have anyone available on a particular day, video testimony can be incredibly powerful. Remember to link whatever you're doing to the mission statement of the institution so that no one can dismiss the event as your pet project or advancing a personal agenda.

As teacher, leader, or organizer you need to be as transparent as possible about why you're taking the actions you are. Explain why you're doing things in a particular way so that people can see that there's a thoughtfulness informing your choices. Whenever possible link your explanation to a personal experience to show people you've learned from, and are building on, past events. Making an appropriate autobiographical disclosure about the way a certain situation shaped your thinking around a particular antiracist dynamic gives a confidence-inducing sense that you've been around the block a few times. If people feel you know what you're doing, then they're more likely to believe you when you tell them that it's possible for them to develop an antiracist white identity.

Seeking Feedback and Critique

Helping people develop an antiracist identity is one of the most complex tasks you could ever undertake. For that reason alone, any work in this area should be subject to continuous formative evaluation. You need to keep on top of what's going on so that you can make adjustments when necessary. The more you inquire into how people are experiencing some kind of teaching, training, professional development, or activism, the more you became aware of all kinds of undercurrents and tensions that will take you by surprise. You'll probably find that people are reading all kinds of meaning and significance into your words and actions that you hadn't intended. You'll discover what people appreciate about how you work and what you do that sometimes gets in the way of their learning. As you discover these things you can make constant calibrations to how you're nurturing an antiracist identity.

Even more importantly, perhaps, creating a reflective feedback loop whereby you get information from people on how they're reacting to a process and then reporting out to the community how you're responding to that data models a trust-building sense of openness. There will inevitably be times in this work where you'll say or do something that others will view as racist. Depending on the context, people may be unwilling to voice that criticism publicly. However, if there is some way of collecting data anonymously and people trust that there is no way they can be identified, then they are much more likely to say what's really on their minds.

Backchannel Chat

We commend two particular techniques for getting valid anonymous data, both of which have already been mentioned. The first is Backchannel Chat (backchannelchat.com). Here you create a web page where people log on and give anonymous real-time commentary on what they see happening during a class, training, or meeting. As the event proceeds, participants give reactions to what's happening, ask questions about the content being discussed or about the facilitators' actions, and offer criticisms. If you check the feed every 15 minutes or so you can respond to concerns as they emerge, correct misunderstandings, and model self-critique. This allows you not only to clarify your rationale but also to model an openness to discomfort.

In the middle of events we have been told via backchannelchat.com that we are bashing whites, ignoring people of color, shutting down participants, and so on. When we see comments like this, we can delve deeper and ask why people view examining white racial identity as white bashing or why we focus on whiteness so much when most people feel racism is a problem experienced by people of color. We can deal right then and there in the moment with criticisms that we are abusing our power by talking too much or not bringing everyone into the conversation. If such a critique emerges, we can make immediate changes and try out different protocols that broaden participation.

CIQ

Another tool we both rely on is the CIQ. To recap, the CIQ is a one-page sheet that records how people are experiencing an event by asking the following five questions:

> At what moment today were you most engaged as a learner?
> At what moment today were you most disengaged as a learner?
> What action that anyone in the room took was most helpful to you?
> What action that anyone in the room took was most puzzling to you?
> What surprised you most about today?

The first two questions focus on particular moments, and the third and fourth inquire about specific actions. These questions are phrased so as to elicit the most concrete data we can. The final question on surprises is the most open-ended.

We hand the form out about 5 minutes before the end of whatever class, training, or meeting we are running and ask people *not* to put their names on the forms. We explain that these forms are anonymous so that people will be completely honest with us in their responses. We commit to reading all the responses and starting the next meeting or workshop with a report on what people said.

Once the event is finished we read through the forms and start to code the responses. If a particular action, topic, moment, or activity is mentioned by at least 10% of participants, then it makes it into our report. We also reserve the right to mention individual comments that no one else echoes if we feel these identify an interesting dynamic or surface an ignored perspective.

When the group next reconvenes we start the session by reporting out the main themes from the CIQ comments on our last time together. We strive to be nondefensive in reporting criticisms of our actions and constantly point out how different people experience the same things very differently. If there is strong pushback we acknowledge that and discuss how we're going to respond. Sometimes we adjust what we're doing in response to feedback, and at other times we explain why we want to stick to our plan.

Usually there's a wide range of responses provided and that allows us to talk about the different experiences and perceptions of race in the room. For example, at a recent workshop Brookfield was running a "Trump 2020" comment was posted to the Backchannel Chat feed for the day. He stopped the class to call this to people's attention and said that it was a clear example of trolling—of posting a deliberately inflammatory comment unconnected to the topic being discussed in order to produce emotional responses and derail an event. In particular, he pointed out the chilling effect that comment could have on people of color. No one took responsibility but others then posted on the Backchannel feed that it was just a joke. That then allowed Brookfield to do a quick teaching on the nature of microaggressions, particularly the tendency of people trying to "save" the enactor of an aggression by explaining it away, in this case as an example of benign humor.

In the CIQ responses to the day several people picked out that interaction to comment on. Some participants wrote that Brookfield was too heavy-handed and intimidating in his scolding the author for what they believed was just meant as a humorous comment. Others wrote that they appreciated Brookfield addressing the comment head on as it was made and observed that to leave it hanging there without being called out would have left them feeling unsafe. He was then able to use that example of how comments that to some seem inconsequential are full of significance to others.

One thing we have both learned from CIQ feedback is that we need to exercise our authority to call out racist comments and actions as they occur. Most whites will claim to be nonracist, but those claims will often be met with amusement and cynicism by people of color who have witnessed those same people committing any number of microaggressions. The two of us know that as white practitioners we are being watched and judged by people of color as to our commitment to antiracist practice. If a casual racist joke is made, a stereotype invoked, or an online "Trump 2020" posting left unaddressed, the people of color in any group we work with will conclude that we are not to be trusted. We agree with Kay's (2018) observation that when instructors and leaders ignore "a blatantly hovering question" (p. 57) that is prompted by something problematic someone has said, group members will feel that "real talk" has disappeared and that they're participating in an inauthentic discussion where the leader is not ready to move into a brave space.

Of course, given their past interactions with whites, BIPOC folks may conclude that anyway. But if you intervene immediately to call out racist remarks or trolling, and if you address the hovering question that is in everyone's minds but not yet spoken, you stand a much better chance of being taken seriously than if you let these things go by, hoping they won't be noticed. They *will* be noticed by people of color and your credibility will plunge if you don't immediately call them out.

Setting Necessary Boundaries

Setting necessary boundaries is for us an empowering use of authority. In any situation in which someone is designated as the teacher, convener, facilitator, leader, or trainer, people will look to that person to set the direction the group is going and to help establish norms for interaction.

Don't Debate Whether Racism Really Exists

One of the most important decisions concerns debating the existence of racism. When we open up conversations with whites on developing an antiracist identity, we know there is always an early danger of us going down the rabbit hole of debating whether or not racism really exists. If this gets out of control, then the majority of the time a group has available can easily be spent on this question and addressing how to challenge racism never really gets proper attention.

In situations where people are attending of their own volition we often start by declaring a ground rule that we will not spend any time on debating the existence of widespread and persistent racism in the United States. We say that the way this racism is expressed varies enormously and that we understand that people have different experiences with it. But we let the group know in advance that we will intervene to move discussion along if we get into an extended discussion of whether or not pervasive racism is real. To us this seems a perfectly justifiable use of our authority in groups gathered to learn about how to combat racism.

Making the same declaration in other groups where people are required to attend a course, workshop, or training to raise their awareness of racism is much more problematic. Some whites sincerely believe that we live in a postracial world. If we start off a class, training, or workshop by effectively denying the validity of their experience, then we have dug a deep hole for ourselves right at the outset. No one likes to be told at the start of an event that their view of the world is wrong, particularly if they sense that they will be viewed as racist if they continue to hold onto their truth.

In this situation we advise the following. Begin by administering a Sli.do poll (https://www.sli.do), or ask people to locate themselves on the "Mood Meter" app developed by Marc Brackett at Yale University's Center for Emotional Intelligence (Brackett, 2019). On Sli.do people are invited to respond anonymously to the question "How do you feel as you enter this event?" The multiple-choice answers you provide range from "Anxious" to "Excited," but one of the options we provide is "Resentful—I object to being made to show up for this event. I don't think it's necessary because race is a made-up issue pushed by left-wing groups."

The mood meter is a quadrant divided into four colors (red, yellow, green, and blue), each of which represents a distinctive cluster of emotions (anger, enthusiasm, restfulness, and disengaged). Ask people to register on Backchannel Chat which color conveys their mood, or to pick out a particular word on the chart that most closely describes how they feel.

People log into the Sli.do poll or convey their mood meter readings on Backchannel Chat and the results are projected onto a screen so everyone can see the responses. We do this mostly to gauge where the audience is in respect to a readiness to engage with race, but we also want to acknowledge the fact that there are people in the room who feel that they are at the opposite end of the spectrum from us on this issue. So as we discuss the different ways people respond to these tools, we make sure to acknowledge that we understand that some people believe that the event they're attending is a giant waste of time.

Then we'll state our basic assumption that we live in a world characterized by widespread and persistent racism and we'll do our best to reaffirm why we believe this to be a major problem. We acknowledge that there are those in the room who believe us to be wrong and say that we hope they will be open to changing their minds if they find our evidence convincing. But we admit that this may well not happen and that people have a right to their own opinion. We ask those who feel this way not to interfere with the efforts of those willing to engage with the workshop activities.

Sometimes we declare "boredom rights," an idea we got from Shor (1997), and say that if someone reaches a point of being utterly bored by what's going on, they have permission to take a 10-minute break to go and get coffee, go outside to clear their head, and so on. We'll also do an early "methodological belief" exercise (Elbow, 1986), asking participants to spend 5 minutes role-playing that they believe pervasive racism is a major problem in the United States. As they do this we ask them to consider what it would mean for them in their workplaces and daily lives if that were indeed the case.

Depersonalizing Racism

Racism is such a raw topic that white people will often feel personally threatened by any attempt to get them to talk about it. They will feel as if they are being accused of being racist, of acting in an inhuman way, and may feel they are expected to admit their guilt and shame. This is why we spend a lot of time early on depersonalizing the topic. By that we mean explaining that racism is a set of learned ideas and behaviors that are embedded in the institutions and culture in which we live and that become internalized as we grow up. We emphasize that racism is *not* an essential character trait, but that it is learned, often unconsciously, from our surroundings and reinforced by peers, family, media, and so on.

One ground rule we declare at the outset is to ban the practice of saying "You're racist" or describing someone's actions as "That's racist." Someone who has a comment like that directed at them will either drop out of any future conversation or vigorously deny what they perceive as a charge levied against their own humanity. Early on we will try to model brief conversations that demonstrate how people can call out racism without condemning someone as racist and thus driving them into a hostile and defensive shell. One of us gives an example of an action, choice, or decision we've taken in the past and the other tries to point out how white supremacy is evident in the selected example. In these conversations we'll say things such as "There's how learned white supremacy shapes your thinking"; "That's a powerful example of racist conditioning"; or "I hear some white supremacist influence in that comment."

Alternatively, we'll describe a situation we're aware of and point out the ways that unacknowledged whiteness and the white racial frame (Feagin, 2013) cause us to act in ways that we feel are completely unproblematic. For example, we'll describe how we've often begun a workshop, meeting, or class by introducing ourselves by our first names and asking participants to call us either Mary or Stephen. Our intent has been to break down artificial distinctions and establish a relaxed and casual atmosphere.

We then point out how, over the years, we came to realize that this was an example of white normativity. For us, a college education and an academic career were both within our sphere of what was considered normal. When whites like us say "Call me Mary" or "Call me Stephen" we can make that request without our credibility being called into play. But leaders of color who make that same request say they risk losing some of the necessary authority they need to do their job.

We then point out how many colleagues of color prefer to be addressed in a way that incorporates a reference to their status as doctor or professor. This is because (a) their racial identity constitutes a question mark concerning their credibility, so referencing their title helps remind others of their right to do their work, and (b) because they want to signify a pride in the struggles they have endured to come to the point of expertise they occupy. So something as simple as how you introduce yourself as you kick off a meeting is imbued with racial considerations.

Creating Productive Dissonance

Whites who are caught in a white racial frame, who don't regard whiteness as a racial identity, and who think that their lives can be lived without ever dealing substantially with race will not typically decide to engage with racial topics unless something jolts them out of their settled worldview. This is where teachers, leaders, and trainers need to exercise their power to confront people with a situation, perspective, or piece of knowledge that requires some kind of response from them.

One of the most effective ways to create a moment of disequilibrium is for a facilitator or convener to disclose some of the most shocking racist thoughts or actions he or she has experienced. Audience members at a professional development event, training activity, or community meeting not unreasonably anticipate that those in charge are well developed in their ability to purge racist thoughts from their own consciousness. So when white leaders disclose how racism persists in their own lives, how they stereotype people, or how they feel an instinctive discomfort or even fear when around people of color, this can be very powerful. Hearing whites in charge of antiracist training talk about the way that their learned racism persists in influencing their daily interactions comes as a shock.

This kind of disclosure challenges the comforting perception that there is a clear developmental trajectory in how whites move to becoming antiracist. People will often show up for workshops on antiracism expecting to learn how to be nonracist. Whites can't be nonracist if that means expunging racial thoughts from their mind. However, they can be *antiracist*, which involves recognizing that although you have learned racism within you, it's possible to be more aware of that part of your identity and to gather with others to change racist structures and systems. Becoming a white antiracist does not mean expunging racist learnings from your consciousness so that you reach a point of never feeling, thinking, or acting in racist ways. You never reach a stage as a white person of saying to yourself, "That's it, I'm finally free of racism and from this point on will work only in wholly positive ways." The best you can hope for is to become better at detecting the racist impulses and instincts that keep popping up as you move through the day, and to reframe your choices, decisions, and actions to be as antiracist as possible.

Hearing the experts in charge of antiracist teaching and training discuss this publicly helps derail the train of unrealistic expectations that people are on as they move into antiracist work. On the one hand, it can be disappointing at the outset to hear that racist thoughts and actions will always be part of white consciousness. On the other hand, when leaders and instructors who are deemed to be expert kick off an event by talking about the way they've noticed racism in themselves that week, or even that day, this stops people thinking that by taking a course, workshop, or training they will somehow be nonracist at the end.

Professional development can be helpful and we don't want to dissuade anyone from organizing or participating in this activity. But in the grand scheme of things it's only a small part of the picture. You become an antiracist institution by embedding a desire to recognize and challenge racism in every institutional process, policy, and action. Hiring policies, reward systems for staff and faculty, admissions procedures, the composition of boards of trustees, formats of evaluating learning—all these must place recognizing and challenging racism at their center.

Leveraging White Privilege

Race work, like everything else in life, happens on an uneven playing field. Because both of us are white, we are aware that we can say and do things that would sometimes be difficult for colleagues of color. Our whiteness means that when we bring up issues connected to race we're usually not accused of playing the race card. We're never seen as advancing an agenda based on our racial identity. After all, in the white environments we move through we're not usually seen as having a racial identity, and people are often perplexed as to why we would bring race up at all. Criticisms we face usually focus on charges of our being left wing or liberal, politically correct, self-loathing whites consumed with an unnecessary guilt for, and shame about, actions that happened long ago.

In white environments our whiteness gives us a shield of apparent camaraderie when we stand up and announce that an antiracist event is beginning. Other whites don't tense up and start worrying about saying the right or wrong things in our presence to the degree they do when a person of color is in the role of expert at a class, workshop, or meeting. There's an initial ease with our bodies being in the room, a sense of familiarity based on the fact that we look and sound like others who are there. We are automatically seen as part of the club.

All these things mean that we have a unique opportunity to act in ways that would carry greater risks were we people of color. The defensive shields of fear, suspicion, and embarrassment that would be in place if we had a different racial identity are not in place. That means there's an initial openness to hearing whatever we wish to say. When we introduce whiteness we can pretty much guarantee that we'll be met with bemusement as to why we're even bringing up the issue of race. And, as we've already pointed out, when we encounter outright hostility, it's usually because people feel they have been forced to attend an event that they see as unnecessary. In their minds the civil rights movement righted the historical wrongs of slavery several decades ago.

One way in which we use our privilege of being seen as a fully paid-up member of the whiteness club is to focus relentlessly on the fact that whiteness is rarely addressed in institutional efforts to combat racism. We have consulted with numerous predominantly white organizations and seen the same script repeat itself over and over again. An institution is shaken by a hate crime, or mandated by state or federal law to undertake diversity training, and various workshops, mandatory bias initiatives, and professional development opportunities are instituted to make the organization more culturally sensitive. The focus of these events is on supporting the various members of color who already work at the institution and on making the environment appear more friendly to those thinking BIPOC folk considering joining it.

What gets missed entirely is what it means for the institution to be overwhelmingly white. Diversity efforts can easily be conducted with the focus only on the needs and circumstances of people of color. Yet ask those same people what would make the institution feel more friendly to them and the most common answer you get is for the institution to conduct a serious examination of what it means to be white. The "problem" of race is whites' inability to recognize that they have a racial identity and that the world is organized to support the white supremacist idea that it's best for whites to be in control of decisions and resources because they are inherently more stable, rational, and organized.

As whites we can exercise our power in white environments to insist that our colleagues examine what it means to have a white racial identity. When we push to examine what an organization's fundamental whiteness means, it's received in a different way than if colleagues of color were making the same demand. They would be seen as pushing a racialized agenda. We are seen as asking legitimate, if rather puzzling, questions. When we find ourselves in settings where a small number of colleagues of color are constantly required to speak to issues of diversity, inclusion, and racism, our role as whites is to push, push, and push again to ensure that answering the question of what it means to be a *white* institution is at the center of any discussion. We can bring up the concept of white supremacist ideology in a way that carries less risk for us. We can urge white leaders of the institution to talk publicly about how their own white racial identity frames how they see the world. In public settings we can point out how an espoused commitment to combating racism is undermined by certain hiring and firing decisions. For example, if those who publicly hold the organization to the fire in terms of how they live up to their antiracist declarations are the same people who are marginalized or pushed out, then others will conclude that antiracist initiatives are just public relations window dressing.

Asserting Identity Pride

As we have already mentioned, focusing on whiteness, white racial identity, and how white superiority is learned is often perceived by some whites as white bashing. It's as if by just mentioning the notion of white identity, you're automatically seen as trying to induce shame, guilt, and remorse for slavery. To resistant whites, announcing a discussion of what it means to be white signals that they should get ready to apologize for their racial identity or engage in some kind of confessional self-abasement. And when a workshop begins with the facilitator asking each white person to get up and say, "I am a racist," you can bet that most whites will interpret that as an attack on their core identity.

So one thing white antiracist leaders, educators, and trainers can do is demonstrate that being white is not a crime and that people should not feel embarrassed about who they are. Leaders can introduce themselves by talking about key formative experiences in their lives; how their family, community, and region shaped how they are; and the passions they developed as children and how those carried into adulthood. Neither of us is ashamed of who we are. Both of us feel proud of our backgrounds, roots, loyalties, and passions. Yet at the same time we also know we both carry the virus of learned racism within us. We don't feel this marks us as being beyond the ethical pale or somehow less than a full person. We don't feel our whiteness means we are by definition morally compromised. But we know also that the world will be a better place if whites like us make a concerted effort to uncover our learned racist habits and instincts and seek to limit their influence on our actions.

There is no contradiction between being proud of who you are and where you are from and knowing that you have grown up unaware of how your whiteness advantaged you. It's not as if you were born racist with a white supremacist consciousness already fully shaped in the womb. Racism is learned as you move through the world and absorb the information you are given. In a racist culture it's normal to harbor racist thoughts and not even be aware that that's what's going on. Similarly, it's possible to think of yourself as a "good white" person (Sullivan, 2014) who treats everyone the same and believes a level playing field exists in life for people of color, without ever considering the fact that they may have a completely different experience of your community or organization. This does not make you a bad person— just someone who has not thought much about the centrality of race in the United States.

As we talk proudly about our experiences and invite others to do the same, our intent is to create a starting point to move whites into a more difficult conversation. We reserve a space at the beginning of workshops or trainings to talk specifically about the development of our own white identity. We want to show that we try always to be moral, loving people, but that sometimes we're caught in a particular way of seeing the world. After talking extensively about our own blind spots around race and how we learned a sort of structured blindness, we'll describe the events that led us to look at the world differently. And we'll talk about the kinds of learning we're still doing around the nature of whiteness.

One of the things we've noticed in race-based conversations, and something we have undoubtedly done ourselves, is to talk in a disparaging way of those white colleagues whom we regard as "un-woke." The European American Collaborative Challenging Whiteness (2010) identified this practice as disdaining and warned that if we communicate this attitude to white colleagues, then we're probably dead in the water as far as securing any real engagement on their part. So it's important that we talk publicly about our past and present struggles trying to see the sea of whiteness in which we swim and to understand how that presents itself as the normal state of affairs, simply the way the world works. We present ourselves as people struggling to understand how we have internalized racist beliefs and how we have acted in ways that support white power structures without us being aware of that fact. Once again, publicly modeling your own struggle with uncovering and challenging how your own white identity secures your complicity in white supremacy is a necessary precursor to asking anyone else to do this.

One final point on this issue. Many readers will have friends or family members who are explicitly racist. That doesn't mean you should stop loving them or communicating with them. No one should have to cut deeply personal ties with friends and family because of differing levels of racial awareness. When racism lives at home it's difficult and distressing to call out a good friend or family member and we both admit that sometimes for the sake of peace we have let racist stereotyping and joking go unchallenged at Thanksgiving dinners, birthday celebrations, and so on. Our best tactic is not to pounce on such comments and label them as racist. Instead, we'll say something like "I remember when I thought that and I'd probably still be thinking that way if it hadn't been for . . ." We'll then conclude the sentence by talking about an experience we've had that gave us a different perspective. Maybe it'll be something somebody said to us, maybe it's a video or film we saw, or maybe it's something we read. We know we're not going to change someone's heart and mind over a Thanksgiving feast, but at least we can draw on our own autobiographies to talk about how we've questioned our own sense of white superiority.

Ultimately, however, it's important to conserve your energy to change those who are at least potentially teachable and reachable. Crass (2015) described how he came to realize that constantly trying to persuade his right-wing Grandpa to become antiracist was setting himself up for failure and a misuse of his time and energy. Eventually, instead of debating him every Thanksgiving, Crass "tried to use humor to disarm him and then put out ideas about white privilege and racism—not to convince him—but to engage other people in my family who routinely remained silent in those conversations" (p. 17). In Crass's view, "often we focus a lot of energy on jackasses and trolls; meanwhile, the people who are closer to us politically, but don't know how to get involved, are ignored" (p. 18).

Crass urged, and we concur, that our attention should be on those white people in our communities, organizations, classrooms, and institutions who are listening in to conversations but currently not contributing any-thing to them. This could well be because they don't yet know what to think about race. For them, there has never been a need to come to a viewpoint on race matters, because questions around racial identity or an investigation of their passive support of white supremacy have never been part of their consciousness. Building trustful relationships with them, and showing curiosity about their experiences, is the starting point for intro-ducing an awareness of what it means to be white into the conversation. And then, of course, begins the real work of helping them think through how they might change their individual actions to be in solidarity with others engaged in collective change.

10

SHARING THE POWERFUL HISTORY OF ANTIRACIST WORK

In the midst of a racial crisis, say the aftermath of a police shooting of an unarmed person of color in response to an infraction that for a white person would have prompted nothing more than a talking-to, it's easy to become solely focused in the moment. We are so outraged, so desperate for some kind of racial equity, that all we want is justice *now*! But, although we have one eye on the future, we need always to keep one eye on the past. This is important for three reasons.

First, when whites disconnect themselves from the past history of systemic and structural racism, and in particular the crucial role that collective organizing and action plays in redressing racial imbalances, this means that it's easier to limit their antiracist efforts to interpersonal interactions with friends and colleagues. This is, of course, important and necessary work. But engaging racism in our daily interactions is just the start of becoming a white antiracist. A far tougher task is to uncover how the foundational power of white supremacy has shaped this nation's culture, policies, and institutional history. When it comes either to reinforcing or disrupting systemic and structural forms of racism, the narratives we share about our shared past, or the way we refuse to see this past as collectively created, are crucial.

Second, recalling past achievements informs our antiracist practices today. When we analyze the ways in which movements for racial equality are successful in enlisting large numbers of whites in support, or when we study the tactics of violent or nonviolent resistance, and the differing responses to them in particular contexts, we learn some useful lessons. Researching how traditional media can be involved to get a message out, or to show life-changing images that inspire widespread protest, helps us learn the best ways to engender widespread support. These days any movement for racial justice knows that managing traditional and social media is an important element when pressing for substantive change.

Third, a knowledge of the history of resistance to white supremacy helps us realize that any change is a long haul, a long march while we keep our eyes on the prize ahead. It's a series of battles in which there are gains and losses, two steps forward and one step back, a zigzagging and crab-like movement toward incremental progress. An historical consciousness keeps defeatism in check as you realize the many triumphs, but also the numerous setbacks, that people have endured for centuries.

Finally, whites who may be newly committed to an antiracist identity need to know they have ancestors, that there's a documented history of whites becoming involved in fighting for racial justice they need to be aware of. When you know something about the ways whites in different eras and different contexts have organized to fight racism and to support the struggles of people of color, you realize that you are far from the first to engage in this project. In fact, you have exemplars and models you can look to and learn from.

Crass (2015) described his conversation with two white teenage boys who told him that "until I talked about the tradition of white antiracist activists, including men like William Lloyd Garrison, Carl Braden, David Gilbert, Scott Winn, and James Haslam, they didn't know they had role models to inspire who they could become" (p. 168). White men are so vilified as the apex of white supremacist hate that it is startling for many males to learn that a different conception of white masculinity is possible. That historically in the South African apartheid struggle white activists like Joe Slovo and his wife Ruth First (Wieder, 2013) fought for majority Black rule. That white activists like Andrew Goodman and Michael Schwerner were murdered alongside Black activist James Earl Chaney as they worked in 1964 to get African Americans to register to vote in Mississippi. And that the Tennessee activist think tank at the heart of the civil rights movement—the Highlander Folk School—was founded by white men and led by Horton (Horton, 1990; Preskill, 2021).

So in this chapter we want to look at the power of history to illuminate possibilities for action. Any antiracist initiative should involve teaching people the spoken and written histories of resistance of those who organized, fought, and died for their pursuit of humanity. Becoming a white antiracist certainly involves being aware of the power of white supremacy to legitimize the marginalization and oppression of people of color. But the history of ignored, unknown, and suppressed efforts by all kinds of groups to fight back can be liberating and inspirational (Loewen, 2003). As Davis and Wiener's (2020) history of Los Angeles during the 1960s shows, behind the stock accounts of rioters and lootings that portray minority communities as violent and animalistic are stories of coordinated mass protests by pupils in LA high schools and the health and education organizing efforts by groups such as the Black Panthers and Organization Us. These are stories of hope that can provide lessons and templates for contemporary action.

As we finished this book President Trump announced his 1776 commission to promote patriotic education in order to counter the assertion "holding that America is a wicked and racist nation" (WhiteHouse.gov. 2020, para. 14). There could hardly be a starker example of the contested nature of what counts as a country's "official" historical narrative. Consider the question of what constitutes the history of the United States. Is it the story of immigrants who established a country on the principles of freedom and liberty? Is it the history of refugees fleeing oppression in home countries? Is it a chronicle of the way colonial powers enslaved Africans and murdered and forced Native peoples off their lands in order to build and control wealth?

All of these narratives have some truth in them, but none of them tells the "whole truth" on their own. Loewen (2018) demonstrated how the bifurcation of our dominant national narrative into an either/or story told by winners about losers is pervasive in school settings. Removing statues of slave owners and conquistadors from public spaces and rebranding public buildings named after racists and bigots who advocated genocide represent an attempt to broaden this narrative to include histories that have been ignored and actively suppressed. We can't make steps toward a whole community of justice and peace until we assemble a reconstituted narrative of the history of this country that represents the shared experiences of all.

Serene Jones's (2016) powerful essay in *Time Magazine* argues that until we in the United States are able to tell our national story with deep awareness of its pain and brokenness as well as its joys and gifts, we will never be able to heal the spiritual hurt that persists so strongly in and around us. We need, she wrote, a national story that weaves harm, failure, violence, and tragedy into the official, stock story of progress, goodness, and realizing the humanity of all. One part of developing an antiracist white identity is to learn the multiracial histories that have been kept from us of those who resisted forms of oppression and offered us hope. We need the history of indigenous, First Nations peoples (Dunbar-Ortiz, 2015; Resendez, 2016), of the Latinx community (Ortiz, 2018), and of the history of white supremacy as an idea (Jensen, 2004; Kendi, 2017). And when we think about using history as an antiracist tool, it's helpful to think in terms of three necessary dynamics: *igniting* interest in these histories, *curating* appropriate materials to support curiosity-driven exploration, and helping people *practice* the skills of engaging history critically and collectively. Ignite, curate, practice.

Igniting Interest

What does it mean to "ignite interest" in the history of antiracism? In the midst of the current widespread polarization that exists in the United States and around the globe we need to find ways to bring people into a state of curiosity about the stories with which they are not yet familiar. Denying, concealing, and rewriting history are all ways to normalize a current state of affairs. So in a time when white supremacy has been legitimized, we need to support our students, workshop participants, colleagues, and fellow activists in being curious about the past. We need to initiate a conversation about what constitutes an authentic record of events, and how we judge that particular accounts are authoritative.

Context

An important part of what history offers is context, and this is especially crucial given that we are living in a time of what anthropologist Michael Wesch (2008) has called significant "context collapse." Context collapse is a very common dynamic in the midst of digitally mediated spaces where bits and pieces of information and extracts of stories are lifted up and floated on a vast sea of media messages absent most of their context. These decontextualized scraps of information are extracted from their milieu and used as the basis for drawing conclusions and taking action based on very limited understanding.

A very first step in building shared context is finding ways to be curious together, and to share with each other what our interest draws us to learn. Yet much of the schooling and resourcing that surrounds white people omits large parts of the white supremacist context and focuses attention very narrowly. As classroom teachers and workshop leaders we need to ignite curiosity about stories that have been concealed, as well as stories that share moments of resistance.

Timeline Exercises

One practical way to ignite interest is to start with the many online resources that offer examples of historic moments in the social construction of race and racism. Ask your students, participants, or colleagues to read through a timeline you share and pick out an event they've never heard about. Examples could be the 1919 massacre in Elaine, Arkansas; the 1920 Duluth lynching; the Battle of Blair Mountain or Tulsa massacre in 1921; or the Edmund Pettis Bridge beatings of 1965. People then discuss the event in a small group to see who, if anyone, in the group has any knowledge about it. Participants then seek further information about the event, perhaps starting in the workshop by going online and consulting a carefully curated set of resources (see the following subsections). As they explore and learn about their event, they ask the following questions about it:

- Who is telling us about this event?
- What is the context in which it occurred, and what is the context in which I am learning about it?
- How might other people understand the history around this event differently than I do?
- Why have I been kept in ignorance of this event?
- How does learning about this event change my understanding of history more generally?
- Are there values, lifestyles, and points of view represented in, or omitted from, this event that I can learn from?

After participants have identified the event, worked to further discover what can be known about it, and answered these questions, the next step is to create a representation of the event that speaks to their new understanding and that's accessible to their fellow workshop or class participants. We have had people create short videos, develop websites, create paintings, write poems, and so on. Creating some kind of representation that shares details of an event you have begun to learn about increases self-efficacy and means you exercise creative agency as you construct your way of sharing knowledge. We have found timeline resources such as those noted in the following short descriptions to work particularly well for this exercise.

Facing History and Ourselves
www.facinghistory.org/resource-library?search=timeline
This nonprofit organization has been working for decades to confront prejudices of various kinds. Begun in the late 1970s as a resource teaching the history of the Holocaust, it soon expanded to engage multiple challenges of injustice. It is now a global organization with thousands of educational resources. The link points directly to a huge variety of timeline examples and pedagogical tools.

PBS: Race, the Power of an Illusion
www.pbs.org/race/000_About/002_03-godeeper.htm
    (also more generally: www.racepowerofanillusion.org)
This link points to a specific set of timelines that were created as educational resources to accompany the PBS/California Newsreel series Race, the Power of an Illusion. We have mentioned this documentary series before, and here

we point specifically to their comprehensive timelines. It is rare to have a workshop participant who is familiar with everything on these timelines; thus, they are great catalysts for curiosity.

Densho
densho.org
Densho is a nonprofit organization that is focused on collecting oral histories, documents, and other artifacts from the internment of Japanese Americans during World War II. Their timeline is particularly pertinent in the current context of the United States.

A Very Different Asian American Timeline
aatimeline.com
This timeline offers rich and substantial dates and descriptions of Asian American communities in the United States.

Latinx History
www.pbs.org/latino-americans/en/timeline/
This is a timeline created by WETA and funded through public media grants in the United States. It is specifically focused on Latinx history.

History of Antiracism Movements
www.racialequitytools.org/fundamentals/history-of-racism-and-movements/overview-and-timeline1
Racial Equity Tools is an organization devoted to supporting people focused on racial equity. It offers myriad resources for doing this work, and the timeline noted here is focused very specifically on the history of movements confronting racism.

Historical Timeline of Race Relations
www.womenoftheelca.org/wp-content/uploads/2017/06/Timeline.pdf
This timeline is not quite as comprehensive as some already mentioned, but because it was written and published within the Evangelical Lutheran Church in America it holds a specific kind of authority in that religious community and is an example of a religious community's effort to ignite historical curiosity.

Transatlantic Slave Trade in Two Minutes
www.openculture.com/2016/06/the-atlantic-slave-trade-visualized-in-two-minutes.html

This short video visualization is a compelling history of the slave trade, traced via the various ships and companies engaged in it. The video pointed to here is accompanied by a vast array of resources exploring that history.

Smithsonian National Museum of African American History and Culture
www.smithsonianmag.com/history/158-resources-understanding-systemic-racism-america-180975029/
A collection of 158 links to videos, podcasts, websites, and articles chronicling the history of anti-Black violence and inequality in the United States.

Curating Information

After igniting curiosity, you need to curate appropriate and authoritative materials that can draw your participants ever more deeply into the complexity of the history of race and racism. Careful curation of resources is especially critical in the midst of context collapse, because this can stand against the dominant political practices of "dog whistles" and "gaslighting" that drive and encourage white supremacy and white nationalism. A dog whistle is a way of talking about something, a kind of coded language, that is immediately understood in one way by a particular in-group of people, but which means something entirely else for anyone outside of that group. For decades in the United States, for instance, politicians supporting white supremacy have talked about problems in "urban areas," by which they signal to white voters that they mean people of color. Ian Haney Lopez (2014) was particularly eloquent here, in his analysis of the ways in which "coded racial appeals carefully manipulate hostility towards non-whites" (p. ix).

Gaslighting is the way in which stories are told with the intent of sowing doubt and confusion in groups that have been minoritized. When you are subject to gaslighting, you start to question your own reality and begin to ask yourself, "Am I imagining this history of oppression?" or "Could I be wrong about all this?" When history is written only from a dominant viewpoint and told within a white racial frame (Feagin, 2013), the treatment of race is presented from the perspective of those who benefit from it. Not surprisingly, the stock stories that comprise the history of racist ideas (Kendi, 2017) rule out of order any countervailing or refuting evidence. Gaslighting is a process that effectively silences any confronting questions before they are even voiced.

The enactment of microaggressions (Sue, 2010) often contains a strong element of gaslighting. As people of color bring examples of microassaults and microinvalidations to the attention of those perpetrating them, they are often met with responses such as "Oh, you're just imagining that" or "They were just being forgetful; they didn't mean anything by it." In multiracial groups the white members will often jump in to save each other. We have both seen this dynamic many times. A white person will be confronted with a microaggression they committed and others will try to explain it away as a moment of forgetfulness, an innocent mistake with no evil intent. Not surprisingly, those on the receiving end of these microaggressions then start to doubt themselves and wonder if they're seeing racism where it didn't exist, just being paranoid, or becoming unnecessarily oversensitive.

Understanding how dog whistling and gaslighting function is very difficult unless you are in authentic dialogue with people and groups who are being hurt by these kinds of deliberate, ideologically driven historical narratives. A supportive group of people who are experiencing the same kinds of dismissal as you feel subject to helps you keep an accurate sense of what is really happening. Having people clarify and validate your narrative means that you see you aren't crazy or delusional, that you aren't imagining things, and that you haven't forgotten history. So one part of developing an antiracist white identity is being aware of the local history of microaggressions within your work unit or community, and striving to call these out as they are committed by you and others.

Building shared context through engaging more complex historical accounts of racism is important if we want to ground racial dialogues in a full and accurate understanding of reality. It is never enough simply to offer evidence of racism and racialized systems—no matter how thoroughly researched and substantial that evidence is—unless you can also build a shared context in which those accounts are granted credibility and authority. Historical accounts that draw from a more complex set of standpoints are crucial in this process and we are fortunate that there has been a plethora of richly researched and compelling histories published in the last decade. These histories make the depth and intricacy of racism more clear and incorporate multiple perspectives around race. Yet many white people refuse to engage, let alone accept, these accounts, because they arise in contexts to which these white people do not grant authority.

For example, as we were writing this chapter the National Economic Council director, Larry Kudlow, told reporters that he didn't believe that systemic racism existed in the United States, thus refusing to accept what historians, political scientists, economists, and others have demonstrated. He doesn't have to accept this evidence because in his context—at the apex of power in the White House—he grants credibility to, and accepts authority from, only like-minded figures. He is surrounded by powerful people who agree with him. Similarly, the U.S. Office of Management and Budget directed federal agencies to stop any training efforts that used critical race theory, cited white privilege, or suggested that the United States is inherently racist.

But there are also examples at very basic grassroots levels. The violence following the murder of George Floyd appeared very differently to white people in the suburbs of Minneapolis, who believe that police are only and ever fair enforcers of the law, than it did to people who live in south Minneapolis and are familiar with the decades-long struggle to reform the Third Precinct of the Minneapolis Police Department. Whites living in the suburbs who decry lawlessness and violence have no personal experience with which to contradict their assumptions about law enforcement. Because they share no context with people who do have such experience, they refuse to listen to anyone outside of their frame of reference. We are essentially inhabiting differing realities when we are unable to have a shared context. Confronting the narrowness and oppressive dynamics of these realities is crucial if we are to transform polarization and dismantle racism.

When you are seeking to build shared context that takes seriously our very different experiences of race, you have to attend to which sources the group you are working with finds authoritative. What are the underlying assumptions that are prevalent in your learners? Jones and Okun (2001) have written an outline of the constituent elements of what they call "white supremacy culture," for example, but their essay names so many practices grounded in Eurocentric epistemology that if you are working with academic faculty, it's likely not the first place you want to start. A *New York Times* series called the 1619 Project describes U.S. history as beginning when the first enslaved Africans were brought to North America. If you are working with a group of people who have come to view the *New York Times* as "fake news," this is not information that will be read, let alone taken as authoritative.

Finding the deep assumptions that your group holds and that are also understood and engaged by historians who write the history of racialization is where you need to begin. If your group is in higher education, then thoughtful histories written by acclaimed scholars are a great resource. Some of these are Anderson's *White Rage* (2016), Ignatiev's *How the Irish Became White* (1995), Loewen's *Lies My Teacher Told Me* (2018), Haney Lopez's *White by Law* (2006), Dunbar-Ortiz's *An Indigenous People's History of the United States* (2015), Wilkerson's *Warmth of Other Suns* (2010), Ortiz's *An African American and Latinx History of the United States* (2018), and Zinn's *A People's History of the United States* (2017). If your group is deeply immersed in a religious context, then finding common ground in biblical or koranic texts, and the historians who engage them, could be a place to begin from.

The challenge here is to find a person or resource that embodies authority and credibility for your group and that has conducted a deeper analysis of racism in your context. Once you've ignited curiosity about a specific event that people have never heard of, or a legal framework that has had enormously painful results, then you put resources in front of them that invite a more complex and grounded take on that event or framework. Historical accounts are a powerful way, for instance, to help people see that race is a social construction rather than a biological reality. Simply telling people that race is a social construction generally doesn't convince them. However, walking them through the set of legal decisions in the United States, for example, which at first declared that people of Mexican descent were white, then were not white, and then again were white, can be convincing.

What sources are generally authoritative for your group? What is authentic for your group? Where do they generally get the information on which they will act? Once you have gleaned the current sources they are attending to, you can work to broaden, deepen, and complexify the stories in which they are immersed. You can work from a place that acknowledges that you understand their context and their starting points.

Finding materials within a specific authority framework is more or less challenging depending on what the framework is. What follows are some general categories worth exploring, with just a few examples of the many fine resources available. We are constantly seeking resources that support the building of shared context with a focus on this work.

Documentaries on History and Race

Two documentaries that have worked particularly well in the contexts in which we work are the following: *Race: The Power of an Illusion* (www.racepowerofanillusion.org/) and *Traces of the Trade* (www.tracesofthetrade.org).

Newspaper Resources on Race and History

New York Times: 1619 Project
www.nytimes.com/interactive/2019/08/14/magazine/1619-america-slavery
.html

USA Today: 1619 Project
www.usatoday.com/in-depth/opinion/2019/08/21/slavery-america-behind-
usa-todays-1619-series-black-history/2032393001

USA Today: Visualization of Slavery History
www.usatoday.com/pages/interactives/1619-african-slavery-history-maps-
routes-interactive-graphic/

More Generally From the Pulitzer Center
pulitzercenter.org/builder/lesson/reading-guide-quotes-key-terms-and-questions-26504

Museums Engaging Racial Histories

Museums are a wonderful place to bring people because they have trained educators and rich materials. Entering a physical space together can be very powerful for a group—it builds shared context with an immediacy that is difficult to deny. There are wonderful museums all over but here are a few that have particularly good websites associated with them.

Canadian Museum for Human Rights
humanrights.ca

Legacy Museum and National Memorial
museumandmemorial.eji.org

National Japanese American Historical Society
www.njahs.org

National Museum of African American History and Culture
nmaahc.si.edu

National Museum of the American Indian
americanindian.si.edu

United States Holocaust Memorial Museum
www.ushmm.org

Peer-Reviewed Articles on Race and History

If you are working in a context with people for whom peer-reviewed publishing matters, you can ask your library to put together a collection of articles for workshop participants to engage. There are simply too many for us to note here!

Podcasts on Race

Scene on Radio
www.sceneonradio.org/seeing-white/
Produced at the Center for Documentary Studies at Duke University, this podcast explores the historical construction of white supremacy and the meaning of whiteness.

Seeing Race
speakingofrace.ua.edu/
This University of Alabama series focuses on the supposedly scientific deline-
ation of races in global contexts, including India, Central and South America,
and Europe.

Race in America
podcasts.apple.com/us/podcast/race-in-america-audio/id962890939
Although not specifically historically inclined, this wide-ranging series from
the University of California explores how racism emerges in a number of
public policy, media, and community organizing contexts.

Published Books on Race and History and Bibliography Sites With Specific Emphases

www.ala.org/rt/emiert/usefullinks/links
A librarian will be very helpful in locating books and articles as they will
understand the context in which you are working likely better than you do.
It is worth remembering that the American Library Association has had a
very long commitment to engaging race and racism over the decades and has
continued to offer substantial bibliographic resources. There are also bibliography sites with specific foci, such as the following:

Racial Justice Bibliography
rjb.religioused.org
This site is curated by a group of theological educators, most of whom are
working in Christian contexts.

Racial Equity Bibliography
www.racialequityinstitute.com/bibliography
This site is curated by a group of antiracist educators in North Carolina, and
their bibliography offers a framework that is well situated in that context.

Memes and Racial History

People for whom memes are a primary authority will need help to build
a bigger context if they are to respond to your invitation into more complex engagement. One way to do that is to ask them to create their own
memes. Participants are then put into a position of seeing how memes
work on slyly implied humor, that itself requires some shared context.
A site like Know Your Memes (knowyourmeme.com) can help, as can basic

media education resources (such as ww2.kqed.org/education/2019/03/14/
to-meme-or-not-to-meme-using-memes-to-teach-media-literacy-skills/).

A meme like "Pepe the Frog" that is so deeply implicated in current
white nationalist organizing can be used as an example of how context frames
meaning. The meme did not start out as racist in its original incarnation in
the *Boy's Club* comic series. As its creator Matt Furie (2016) has observed,
the image of a frog was a blank slate on which people inscribed multiple
meanings. It was only in the 2016 presidential campaign that the far right
attempted to co-opt the popular image and use it in anti-Semitic and racist
ways. Now one of the strongest associations of the meme is with white nationalist ideology. See Aleabouni (2018), Hobbs (2019), Knobel and Lankshear
(2007), and Yoon (2016) for articles that help with engaging memes and in
going deeper into racial issues.

Social Media and Racial Histories

Social media increasingly hold compelling forms of authority for people from
diverse contexts. Facebook, Instagram, Snapchat, Twitter, TikTok, and so on
are all sites that have become spaces in which people share ideas, perspectives,
and other resources with each other. It can be very difficult to enter into these
spaces in ways that support complexity and grounded racial analysis, but
there are organizations that are seeking to do so. Some of the most effective,
in terms of engaging racial history, include the following.

Teaching Tolerance
www.tolerance.org
Use the keyword *history* and then invite your workshop participants to
explore that which has caught their imaginations.

Racism Review
www.racismreview.com/blog/hashtag-syllabus-project/
Particularly note their hashtag syllabus project.

Zinn Education Project
www.zinnedproject.org

American Press Institute
www.americanpressinstitute.org/publications/reports/survey-research/
trust-social-media/

Global Voices Online
globalvoices.org

Colorlines.com
www.colorlines.com

Do a keyword search on *racial history.*
The more generic sites (Facebook, Twitter, etc.) can be rich places to explore but it is very important to remember that all four forms of story (stock, concealed, resistance, counter), whether historical or current, will be found there. It is crucial that you approach these sites with clear and specific pedagogical intent. Helping your workshop, community, or class participants think about what structures authority and authenticity for them in these sites would be a place to begin from. Everyone should know, for instance, about Snopes.com, one of the most trusted sites and a primary source online for investigating the credibility of widely shared assertions.

Religious Engagement With Race and History

If you are working with workshop, community, and class participants whose primary authority source is religious, you can't expect to be successful unless you can find some shared context, some common ground from which to work. This is a moment and a context in which it is very difficult to be an outside teacher/consultant. So if you are invited into an unfamiliar setting, make sure that if at all possible you collaborate with someone from inside that setting. Most religious organizations and communities have strong official statements condemning racism, but it is crucial to keep in mind that predominantly white religious organizations in particular have rarely confronted their own broken and anguished histories.

In the Catholic Church in the United States, for instance, there is history that includes priests owning slaves. Only recently, as one example, have the Jesuits begun to confess, atone, and seek reconciliation for their actions. Georgetown University, a Jesuit university that was built in part using slave labor, has begun to offer a variety of forms of reparation and maintains a history archive (slaveryarchive.georgetown.edu). One of the more substantial and thoughtful theological engagements with the history of racism and Christianity in the United States is Willie James Jennings's (2010) authoritative book *The Christian Imagination: Theology and the Origins of Race.* These are merely brief examples, but they point to the recent interest in dominant religious settings to uncovering and engaging difficult histories.

As you work in designing classes and workshops you will need to pay careful attention to the specific institutional structures of authority in a given religious setting. Roman Catholic, Greek Orthodox, and Episcopalian churches all have hierarchical teaching structures that have issued statements about racism, whereas the Methodist, Presbyterian, Lutheran, Church of God in Christ, as well as other nondenominational churches have more loosely structured approaches to authority and may or may not offer specific kinds of resources. In the Christian setting biblical texts still hold a high degree of legitimacy, although some churches have a more charismatic approach to religious authority.

Recently one arena that shows some promise of bearing fruit for building shared context for white antiracist identity in religious contexts is that of interfaith and multifaith work. Auburn Seminary's multifaith initiative to end mass incarceration, for example, draws on rich and complex historical analysis of the carceral state and racism, and does so with a deep respect for, and investment in, multifaith organizing (auburnseminary.org/end-mass-incarceration/).

Another powerful resource is the journal *Interfaith Observer*, which curates resources from across a vast landscape of diverse faith traditions in the United States (www.theinterfaithobserver.org). If you do a search there around *race* or *racism*, you can find numerous examples of videos, essays, and other assets that draw on specific religious languages and histories to invite engagement with dismantling racism.

Building shared context is crucial, regardless of the institutional constraints your workshop or class might endure, and it is unlikely that you will be able to introduce different histories of race effectively unless you're in collaboration with someone who knows the specific community well.

Practicing Agency

Up to now we've explored the process of igniting curiosity in the histories of race and racism and looked at what it's possible to do with curating and presenting materials. But perhaps the most essential element in building an antiracist identity with white people is helping them to *practice* such an identity. As we consider how to do so in relation to history, we want to explore what it means to learn about the practice of collective agency.

Because there are myriad examples of communities and groups of people who have engaged in collective action against racism, history is a wonderful resource for this kind of learning. These histories, however, have often been hidden from us. In the United States dominant stories of national identity often focus on individual attainment, on historical accounts of "heroic individuals" rather than the movements that lifted them up. The civil rights movement in the United States is a powerful case in point, where dominant narratives have celebrated Martin Luther King Jr. but neglected to tell the stories of all of the decades of work and organizing and discipline that led to a movement that he led. Neither do these narratives acknowledge properly the women such as Ella Baker so integral to this effort (Moye, 2013; Ransby, 2003). We in no way want to take away from legitimate celebration of King's leadership, but we want to remind ourselves and others that it was a *movement* that led to the various transformations occurring during those years, not one individual. Searching explicitly for social histories, for movement histories, for keywords that include *collective action* can begin to unearth these historical accounts.

What processes of story sharing have the most impact on our practices of collective action when we turn specifically to questions of history? The Facing History and Ourselves (n.d.) project has decades of experience answering this question, and their resource library is both immense and globally responsive. In that resource bank you will find examples of working with timelines, exercises that explore legislative/legal histories, and prompts and processes for doing personal autobiographical work within one's own family. The library also includes media literacy exercises for working with propaganda—and much, much more.

The point of lifting up historical examples of the practice of resistance is to foster collective responses. Our goal is to remember—literally to *re-member*, to *re-embody*—and in doing so to reshape and rebuild shared context. One way to begin the process of re-membering—of asking who constitutes legitimate members and representatives of a particular location—is to start with place. Where are you meeting? What is the building in which you're gathered and whose labor built it? And what about the physical ground on which the building is constructed. Who has credible claim to be the original inhabitants of this land? What's the history of massacres, lynching, forced removal, or genocide that allows whites to be able to claim legal ownership of the land? How does that history demonstrate white supremacy in action?

There are many rich resources available to help you acknowledge collectively the land upon which you meet. The U.S. Department of Arts and Culture (which is not affiliated with any government) has a handbook available for free that explains how to go about honoring land and those people who first inhabited that land (U.S. Department of Arts and Culture, n.d.). In Canada this practice is known as "territorial acknowledgment," and Native Land Digital (a Canadian organization) has a substantial set of resources for doing this kind of acknowledgment (native-land.ca/territory-acknowledgement/). In the United States the Native Governance

Center (nativegov.org/a-guide-to-indigenous-land-acknowledgment/) and the Crooked podcast *This Land* (crooked.com/podcast-series/this-land/) are good starting points. An antiracist acknowledgment will include not only a reference to the original inhabitants but also a pointed reminder of the white supremacist measures—violent and symbolic—that conferred legal legitimacy on its current inhabitants as the current owners.

A vivid example here in Minnesota, where both of us live and teach, comes from the work of the Healing Minnesota's Stories project (healingmnstories.wordpress.com). This project brings people on a Sacred Sites Tour in the Twin Cities that visits places that Native people claimed—and still claim—as sacred, as well as the places from which they were forcibly removed. In the process the storytellers of that project remind people of the racist oppression practiced and also of the actions of people who resisted it.

Part of this specific set of Minnesota stories demands grief and lament over the forced marches and mass executions that followed in the aftermath of the U.S.–Dakota conflict in Minnesota. We quoted Jones (2016) earlier to the effect that we need a national story that weaves pain, failure, violence, and tragedy into its story of progress and goodness, such as the Dakota 38, the story of 38 Dakota warriors who were hanged on December 26, 1862, in Mankota, Minnesota, in the single largest mass execution in U.S. history, as one that has to be told. Learning that story opens us up to asking what led to that conflict, and who resisted it. Those questions in turn invite learning of Bishop Whipple and his church. Whipple was an Episcopal priest who led a community that sided with the Dakota and was partially successful in pleading their case to President Lincoln (originally more than 300 Dakota men were sentenced to death). It is this kind of complex engagement with history that can begin to build the shared context necessary for engaging in profoundly antiracist learning and practice.

After beginning with place you can then move forward by asking about specific stories of your organization that extend into today: What is the history of this organization that has gathered us together today? Cities, states, provinces, and higher education institutions are slowly waking up to their specific racial histories, an exploration that has led to fierce discussions over who is commemorated or memorialized through statuary and other artwork, and whose presence has been obliterated. In doing this work it is crucial to look not only for the histories of those who engaged in racism but also those who resisted it. Although the discussions may feel difficult to people, they are also energizing and help to build a new collective awareness of the possibilities inherent in multiracial collective action focused on fighting racist oppression.

Questions similar to those we asked earlier in relation to the timeline exercise can be asked in a walk around a campus or through the neighborhood of a specific organization:

- Who founded this organization?
- What plaques, portraits, stained glass windows, and other commemorative installations are used to focus my attention in this place? Which identities and histories are deliberately omitted from such representations?
- How are people welcomed into this place, and are some people implicitly—or even explicitly—not welcomed?
- What values, lifestyles, and points of view are represented in, or omitted from, this organizational setting? Who do I see here, and who is missing?
- What is the dominant story of this organization, and what concealed stories might be found here? Are there any stories of resistance that we can uncover?
- If indigenous people were slaughtered, starved, infected, or removed from this land, are their descendants offered free tuition and automatic acceptance into the institution? What acknowledgments are made to these people in terms of institutional policies?

One of the challenges white people need to engage in spaces in which we are clearly the majority is to uncover and transform the structures in place that define us as typical, the norm, and that inform other people that they are only guests or, worse yet, trespassers, in a given space. These messages are all around us forming what Eisner (1994) called the "implicit" and "null" curricula and they need to be engaged and confronted if we are to explicitly transform our racism.

Begin with place, move into learning the history that led up to current times in your organization, draw out examples of resistance from the past, and then choose action steps that build collective resistance to racism. Exercises such as these will inevitably also lift up instances of oppression that have to do with gender, with physical ability, and with economic access and material wealth, thus illustrating of the reality of the intersectional nature of oppression.

Learning the histories of oppression that have been so effectively kept from the consciousness of white people and then discovering the history of resistance to that oppression offer opportunities for moving forward. Case studies of particular initiatives and the heroines, heroes, and role models these throw up also offer much needed hope. When we use history to build both a shared context and an imagination for what can be done together to make a difference, we practice collective agency.

11

RESPONDING TO
INSTITUTIONAL
RESISTANCE AGAINST
ANTIRACIST ACTIVISM

What happens when you design and implement antiracism work in the midst of predominantly white institutions? The short answer is—resistance! The de facto response from "the slightly more than half of white folks who think that racism against POC is no worse than racism against whites" (Campt, 2018, p. v) will be racial skepticism. White colleagues and white students, because of their color-blind perspective, may well feel that race is a nonissue. Colleagues and students of color, however, will shrug their shoulders at what they deem to be another effort to assuage white guilt and to make it look as if something is happening when, in fact, no substantive institutional change is being effected.

By definition, the process of learning to be antiracist requires us to risk our current understandings and that's something most of us much prefer to avoid. This is just as true of leadership, administration, and management as it is true of students and teaching colleagues. In a world engulfed by conflict, polarization, and rapid change, resistance is ubiquitous. Finding ways to identify, name, and then engage resistance is thus a fundamental task. No matter how energetic and creative you might be within the four walls of a classroom, workshop, or meeting, the institution will usually find ways to sabotage any attempt to name white supremacy and racism as a pervasive institutional problem. So you need to be smarter than those who are working against you, to be nimbler and more light-footed in moving quickly before your efforts are closed down or shunted to the sidelines.

This is why early in any antiracist initiative white teachers and leaders will need to pay very detailed attention to the context in which they're working. And, along the way, they'll need to make wise strategic choices. In the current chapter we want to explore how you can respond to the inevitable resistance you'll encounter and think carefully about how to gauge what counts as success in this work. We offer a framework for assessing the context in which you work, some strategies for dealing with institutional resistance, and some stories of how to fail well in dealing with unexpected eventualities.

Charting the Contexts for Antiracist Work

Preparing to launch an antiracist effort requires a clear understanding of the context in which you operate. You need to know the history of any similar efforts that have been conducted in the past, particularly if these were stalled in any way. You need to know as much as you can about the different perceptions of race that exist across the institution and what role the senior leadership team has played in furthering or dismantling white supremacy. It will be important to know the ideological and racial makeup of the trustees or external governing board as well as the identity of those outside of the senior leadership team who have political credibility on campus as well as in the wider community. You'll need to draw a power map of those in the institution who can be viewed as allies and have a good read of the institutional symbols and levers that can be employed when your efforts are sabotaged.

Table 11.1 is a chart we use to convey the spread of possible institutional permutations that people encounter as they do this work. In our experience most antiracist efforts take place in contexts that fall on the left-hand side of the chart. Notice that each category (1–11) in this chart has a different dynamic to which you should pay attention (quality of conversation, level of commitment, motivation, and so on) as you plan an intervention. Moving from left to right provides a sense of how well each element is developed. The further to the right you move in a given row, the more effective are the conditions and practices identified as necessary for antiracist learning. It's almost impossible for institutions to leap from the far left side of a given row in the chart to the far right side. Antiracist work is usually highly developmental, requiring a great deal of scaffolding and exhibiting incremental change, so you'll need to be strategic in your choices as you design your courses, workshops, trainings, and meetings.

To take perhaps the most obvious contextual factor—motivation—there will be an enormous difference in your approach if the participants in a session are there only because they're required to attend as against working

TABLE 11.1
Spectrum of White Antiracist Practice in Workshops

Less effective << --->> **More effective**

	A	B	C	D	E
1. Definitions of racism used (complexity of conversation)	Participants deny that racism exists any longer or is of importance to white people.	Participants talk about racism in nervous ways, seeking to signal their "color-blindness."	Participants talk about racism in tentative ways, but there is real interest in engaging it.	Participants have a clear set of shared language for talking about racism and begin to work collectively to dismantle it.	Participants talk about racism and becoming a white antiracist in generative, shared, and energizing ways.
2. Personal stance/ commitment to the work	Participants' personal experience is the only arbiter for reality, and race does not exist in that reality.	Participants believe only people of color have any information about race or racism.	Participants have begun to see that as white people they "have" a race and are beginning to seek information about it.	Participants' commitments to engaging racism form the heart of a workshop, and they invite conversation across various identities.	Participants' commitments to antiracism are a key wellspring, supporting openness in learning and seeking transformation.

(continues)

TABLE 11.1 (*Continued*)

	A	B	C	D	E
3. Reason for participating in a workshop (motivation)	Participants come to a workshop because they have been mandated to attend and are openly hostile to analysis of racism.	Participants come to a workshop because they are mandated to attend but demonstrate curiosity.	Participants actively show up for a mandated workshop, eager for new ways to work against racism.	Participants help to organize elective workshops and show up eager to learn.	Participants have invited a workshop on specific elements of an antiracist practice and actively seek collective transformation.
4. Participants' understanding of their own agency in the learning	Participants see their role as strictly defined as being "in the wrong" and are hostile to learning.	Participants see themselves as amateurs awaiting expert instruction through transmission of "correct content."	Participants are open to learning and want to take an active role.	Participants bring experience with previous workshops to the learning.	Participants are colearners with workshop facilitator and other constituencies.
5. Evaluation methods in use	No evaluation envisioned.	End-of-workshop evaluation used to document attendance.	Pre/during/ post workshop evaluation, occasionally for formative as well as summative use during the workshop.	Critical incident reports, participant involvement in formal assessment, primary emphasis on formative evaluation of the workshop.	Continual assessment by all participants, portfolio development for lifelong learning; participants voice and share future goals for action.

TABLE 11.1 (*Continued*)

	A	B	C	D	E
6. Participants' definition of learning/teaching	Workshop participants expect teaching that is largely transmissive and didactic in format.	Workshop participants expect teaching that is largely about input, with workshop leaders as content experts.	Workshop participants expect teaching that takes several forms, and there is some team-teaching (shared leadership).	Workshop participants expect teaching that takes several forms and is done with shared leadership, in which workshop teachers are the designers of an environment where antiracist identity is grown and nurtured.	Workshop participants expect teaching that is aimed at participant discovery; facilitators take on the role of expert guides, with intent to foster collective action.
7. Role of questions and questioning in the workshop	Questions from participants are pertinent only for purposes of clarification.	Questions from participants are allowed if they fall within clear parameters, but they tend to "signal" competition for "wokeness."	Questions arise from genuine curiosity, although competition for air space still lurks.	Participant and leader questions arise as shared attempts to negotiate meaning and clarify truth.	Energized, engaged context of "deconstructive criticism," in which questions come from a place of deep humility, vulnerability, and willingness to lean in to antiracist work.

(*continues*)

TABLE 11.1 (Continued)

	A	B	C	D	E
8. Understanding of the role context plays	Racial/ethnic contexts of participants deemed irrelevant or problematic.	Racial/ethnic contexts of participants mostly irrelevant to learning.	Racial/ethnic contexts of participants are a key element of the workshop and drawn on in useful ways.	Racial/ethnic contextualization is a key element of learning and teaching.	Racial/ethnic contextualization is not only a key element of the learning but thoroughly embedded in how the workshop unfolds.
9. Place in which workshop occurs (structure)	Online teaching format that is purely transmissive, with no ability to evaluate as the workshop progresses.	Online teaching format that has some ability to differentiate and links out to other resources.	Workshop held in person.	Workshop held in person with ongoing feedback from participants as it continues.	Workshop held in person with loose timeline and ability to expand as necessary.
10. Length of workshop	Workshop time less than 90 minutes.	Workshop timed half day.	Workshop given at least a day in format.	Workshop timed in some form of ongoing way.	Workshop format expanded to lifelong learning.
11. Relationship of workshop to existing power structures	Formal online Human Resource workshop done individually in a prepackaged curriculum.	Formal online HR workshop done in a synchronous format with other participants.	In-person workshop led by HR professionals as a "tick off" requirement.	In-person workshop led by collaborative, multiracial, or multiethnic team.	In-person workshop led by leaders from a local organization grounded in antiracism and collective action.

Less effective << --->> More effective with those who have reached out to you and are collaborating in designing the event with you. In the former instance you can pretty much guarantee certain kinds of resistance, hostility, anger, or apathy that won't be present if people are already committed to going deeper into race. Similarly, if an institution you are working with is pushing you to design a self-paced online course or workshop in which progress is assessed by individuals successfully completing quizzes, it'll be much harder for you to work on collective and systemic approaches to antiracism work.

Gathering necessary information and discerning the shape of what's possible in a given setting is not something you can do alone. From the very beginning of institutional or departmental contact you'll need to evaluate what an institution is seeking and how you can respond to an invitation. That will involve speaking to as many people as possible, researching the history of previous efforts, and checking out past institutional responses to racist incidents.

At times we have both turned down invitations to develop a program or run a workshop because the initial contact makes it clear that an institution is only interested in the kind of window dressing typical of repressive tolerance (Marcuse, 1965). But there are occasions when we accept an invitation even though it's clear that the institution resides primarily toward the left side of this chart. Most institutions are caught in unacknowledged white supremacy, so to refuse to work with them would mean we'd never do any work at all! Even in organizations with a less developed racial consciousness there will be energy and commitment among certain people that you can build on, support, and encourage.

When we receive an external invitation to develop a particular course, workshop, or training there is a set of questions we always pose:

- Why have we been invited to do this work?
- Who are the learners who will be present?
- Why are they attending?
- What are the institutional constraints we will face?
- What is the current awareness and analysis of racism in various parts of the institution?

Asking these questions helps make visible the specific forms of institutional power that exist. Organizationally power flows in multiple ways, some more hidden than others, and Bolman and Deal (2017) have helpfully categorized this in terms of structures, human relationships, political constituencies, and symbolic narratives. In answering each of the five questions outlined previously we are pointed to a different focus for perceiving how power flows.

For example, when we ask why we've been invited to do antiracist work, we sometimes receive a response that is primarily structural—in other words, the invitation to us springs from a perception of our academic credibility. We're told that the institutions we've worked for, and our titles within them, give us assumed standing and prestige. At other times, however, the response to our question is primarily relational. People have heard we work well with practitioners, that we walk our talk, have a degree of necessary humility, and don't talk down or condescend. In Bolman and Deal's (2017) terms, our power and authority now derive from the human relationships we have developed over time with activists, teachers, students, and each other.

Asking questions about institutional constraints or levels of awareness of racism helps us understand how some constituencies long for this work and others resist it mightily. This is a political constituency lens. Using this lens requires us to find out who initially asked for a program or workshop and the reasons behind that request. Institutions are so often reactive about race, scrambling to mount classes, workshops, and town meetings only after a racist incident threatens their reputation. Taking a frantic series of ill thought through steps, such as requiring everyone to take a compulsory multicultural competency test and share their results publicly, only increases resentment and sabotages the chances for good antiracist work to occur. Nevertheless, even in the most reactionary institutions, there are usually people wanting to do this work and that constituency needs to be supported.

We also always consider the symbolic frames operating in a given setting. We have both held faculty appointments in institutions with specific religious identities (Brookfield at a Catholic university, Hess at a Lutheran seminary) and that inevitably frames how we present the need for antiracist work in our own contexts. For us the task is always made easier if we can find support from the religious traditions honored in our communities to justify the importance of a specific initiative. In the United States there is fierce contestation over the meaning of religious identity, and that means that power flows are always operating in the symbolic arenas we inhabit.

In Table 11.1 we try to show how specific organizational power flows inform learning designs. When we ask about the degree to which potential participants either deny that racism exists (far left side of the chart) or are already talking about how to become white antiracists in generous, shared, and energizing ways (far right side of the chart), we listen carefully to the kinds of power being described. Asking how people currently perceive racism often produces answers that are solely interpersonal ("The KKK is racist and I don't support them"; "I never use racist epithets"). Here the power that's visible is located in human relationships. However, if someone expresses the belief that racism is a social construct that derives from white supremacy, or that racism is pervasive and permeates institutional practices and policies, then structural, political, and symbolic frames are in play.

An always pertinent question to pose concerns the way in which someone imagines the workshop will proceed. On the one hand, if the people asking you to set up an antiracist program describe a limited, online, transmissive format, you can be pretty certain that the institution is privileging a form of structural power that is hierarchical and controlling. On the other hand, if they prefer an open-ended, flexible, and participatory design, that's evidence that relationships matter in the institution, that structures shape meaning, and that the design for a workshop in this setting can draw fully on all four frames of power analysis. As with any learning event, the more you can learn in advance, the better your design will be, and the more transformative potential your course, workshop, or program will contain.

Using the Chart for Design

We suggest using the chart as a list of outcomes for which to strive. If, after your initial gathering of information, you find the institution to which you have been invited is near the middle of these columns, then you can structure a workshop that will move one column to the right. If the institution is still far to the left, you might choose just one row of intentions upon which to focus. If the institution has already achieved most of the outcomes we specify, then you may find yourself in the energetic place of creating new horizons for this work.

One clear thread that runs through the chart concerns the kinds of communication present in the institution, particularly those voices that are heard most powerfully and that exert the greatest influence. Institutions that place on the far left side of the chart are likely only to value the voices of those in positional power and authority. They will probably lack any mechanism by which to hear less powerful voices, and may even actively silence them. Institutions who cluster on the far right side, however, already have specific structures that are intended to ensure that minoritized voices are lifted up. These institutions probably already have an active antiracism coalition or some established forum for discussing how white supremacy is manifesting itself and how best to contain it. If that's the case, then you want to be in communication with these groups about their analysis of the institution's commitment to this work and its previous history with it, as well as exploring potential routes of collaboration.

If you are working with an institution on the far left side of the chart, it's crucial to figure out which of the frames of power might have openings for potential movement. Even if the structures of the institution are very hierarchical, there may be informal constituencies such as BIPOC affinity groups with whom you can be in conversation. Or there may be a symbolic narrative—an institutional mission statement, for instance—that might be more ignored than practiced but that still constitutes a potential "hook" upon which to attach antiracism work. Many mission and value statements emphasize the common good and contributing to community and societal well-being, so it's not much of a stretch to link efforts to eradicate racism to those public declarations.

Dealing With Institutional Resistance

Institutional resistance takes many different forms, everything from slow responses to email messages and a refusal to provide necessary contextual information to explicit sabotage on the part of faculty or staff who spread false information or give spurious reasons for not addressing race. It's crucial to identify where resistance is arising from and what its central characteristics are before choosing specific processes for any planned learning.

Hess remembers a time when, with the help of a small faculty development grant, she was able to bring to campus a young but already renowned scholar who had just published an important book on theology and race. The night before the scholar was to lecture, one of her senior colleagues circulated a very long email to the faculty decrying the event, making false statements about the guest scholar's work, and urging people not to attend.

In that instance Hess's institution was not far enough along the development chart for any structural authority figures to respond. She was left to fend for herself and hope that people would come anyway. In that instance many more students attended than faculty, but the lecture was recorded and since then has been viewed many, many times. At the time of the workshop Hess felt that it was a near total failure; however, the long-running use of the video recording and the slow but persistent conversations that it prompted over time have had an important impact on the institution. In this case structural power (a dean who did nothing) and political constituencies (senior faculty making their displeasure known) bolstered the resistance. Yet human relationships (students who came and kept asking questions long after) and symbolic narratives (newly articulated theology shared through a video recording of the event) contributed to underlying change.

With racism rooted in white supremacy, any antiracist initiatives that lay clear the existence of that ideology or that trace racist actions and policies back to it are bound to produce serious pushback. The challenge is in finding creative ways to engage that resistance and, in an aikido-like move, transform it into energy for change. Making this kind of subversive shift can be one of the delights of doing antiracist work in a predominantly white institution because it releases good energies and invites imagination for a just and life-giving future.

Consider Category 2—"Personal stance/commitment to the work"—in Table 11.1. That row considers participants' current awareness of race as a social construct. In columns A and B there is little if any understanding of systemic racism. If this is what you're facing, then one approach could be to invite participants into exercises that move them to seek information about what it means to be white, or how we decide that someone has a raced identity. This is where we begin in this book. Over time the intent is to move incrementally into helping people start to see racism as a systemic reality and to understand that confronting it is a collective rather than individual project. When you get to that point, the exercises we shared in chapter 5 such as the autobiographical essay and the power flower offer opportunities for shifting awareness. These activities each draw on personal stories and thus evoke both relational power and cultural/symbolic power.

The more that it's possible to create spaces in which genuine curiosity can be expressed and questions asked without fear of retribution, the greater are the chances that personal resistance can be respected without an event being sabotaged. In the microenvironments of classrooms, workshop gatherings, retreat centers, church halls, and community centers we can do a lot pedagogically to respond in diverse ways to people's curiosity. The problem is that the good effects of what's done inside specific spaces is then often mitigated by the external institutional culture. Institutional resistance is a powerful force and can only be confronted if we are vigilant about sustaining any collective spaces that do exist for continuing this work.

Hess began her appointment at Luther Seminary at a time in which as an institution it had a structural committee addressing racism. On that specific committee were representatives from multiple spaces in the institution, each of which were interested in antiracism work. Over time, as the administrative structures of her school changed, that committee fell out of alignment. As the structures changed, representatives from specific leadership structures who were initially tasked with sitting on that committee gradually disappeared.

Hess remembers working with several colleagues to reorganize that committee. Their proposal was met with apparent support by the president of the school at the time, who argued that something more was needed than a committee and promised a higher level task force. Hess and her colleagues agreed that such a task force might be able to pivot more nimbly and accomplish more than a representative committee could. But that was a false hope. The new task force had no specific structural representation, no clear accountability structure (as the earlier committee had had), and rarely met.

Over time administrative leaders at her school paid less and less attention, rather than more, to the issues at hand. It was only after two successive leadership transitions, several painful incidents, and the collective work of students, alumni, and faculty that structural attention was once more paid to issues of racism and other forms of identity oppression. The lessons Hess took from that experience were that structural power matters and that it requires constant attention to develop such representation and to ensure that it has substantive effects.

In Hess's case the negative structural power flows were only interrupted and turned to positive gain when there was concerted, collective action focused through the other three flows of political constituencies (activating alumni as well as students), human relationships (lifting up stories of ways people had been hurt by the institution), and cultural/symbolic power (drawing on the institution's mission statement and ritual practices).

Brookfield has had extensive experience of how institutions try to manage and sometimes deflect clear evidence of white supremacy and racism. In 2007 at the University of St. Thomas, the then president rescinded an offer for Bishop Desmond Tutu to speak at a 2008 youth peace conference to be held at the school. The withdrawal of the offer was explained by concerns regarding the bishop's views on the Israeli government's treatment of Palestine. The chair of the university's justice and peace studies program kept pressing to reextend the invitation to Bishop Tutu and informed him as chair as to what was happening. She was removed from her position. Subsequently the president reversed his decision and acknowledged he had made a mistake. Bishop Tutu did speak to the 2008 youth peace conference but St. Thomas was not involved. Instead another St. Paul university, Metropolitan State University, cosponsored the conference.

In this instance the structural power of the institution was used to undermine antiracist efforts. The university declared itself as supporting that part of Catholic teaching affirming the dignity of all people but acted in a way that exposed a double standard of advocating for justice but denying a forum for a Nobel Peace Prize winner and champion of the South African antiapartheid movement. The political constituencies that mobilized in protest of this decision, however, succeeded in bringing this double standard to the world's attention and did severe damage to St. Thomas's hope of building relationships with local communities of color. Individuals and groups within and without the university expressed outrage at these events and helped those involved realize that allies existed and that forcing change was possible.

Resistance to antiracism work needs to be confronted in collective ways. If this is not done (and sometimes even when it is) institutions can single out individuals who are scapegoated and discredited. This is why it's so important to be personally grounded and to draw on human relationships and networks that keep you sane when you suspect you are being gaslighted.

There are protective tactics worth following that are based on good communication and the development of thoughtful relationships. The following list of "do's and don'ts" is offered here as prompts for your own work. In some ways these are forms of self-defense and respond to the current state of human resource management many institutions rely upon.

Some Do's and Don'ts

Do ask for and receive written communication that includes logistical details and a specific set of designated outcomes.

Do communicate via a professional email address, and be particularly thoughtful about the tone and content of your emails—write them as if they were postcards that anyone in the institution could read.

Do make sure that you have a solid group of peer colleagues in this work who are not from the institution with which you are working, colleagues who can help you sort through difficult situations and compose thoughtful responses.

Do maintain a professional level of discretion when planning and implementing an event—racism provokes very difficult feelings, and the degree of ignorance that participants can display as events get underway is particularly frustrating. Little is accomplished by venting personally about such ignorance.

Do remember that one of the benefits of being an outside consultant offering a course, program, or workshop is that you have the room to state ideas and pose questions that otherwise would be silenced.

Do remember that if you're an outsider that you are a guest and that the people working with you in a learning setting will remain at the organization. Try to model open and nondefensive communication that invites ongoing learning and collective action.

Do make as much of the workshop's content and resources available in public ways as you can. Using the institution's website is most efficient, but even a basic space on your own professional website can be a way to be transparent about the work of the learning event.

Do consider putting a Creative Commons (CC) license on your materials. Such a license allows you to maintain copyright, while still making your materials available (you can make choices about what kind of such license you want to use).

Do record an event if it is appropriate and will not detract from open communication. Such recordings often prove useful long after the workshop has concluded.

Don't assume that the institution defines words in the same way that you do. Seek clarification and a written trail of definitions.

Don't assume that people of color in the institution share the same commitments with each other, let alone the stated goals of the workshop or course. Know what you want to teach and support, and recognize that you may find yourself in lonely situations because of it.

Don't assume that an institution using you as a consultant has your best interests at heart.

Failing Well

We're both thoroughly conscious of how often we "get it wrong" and how frequently we think we've failed in a given situation. We urge each other, and you our readers, to move past this false epistemological bifurcation of success or failure. Try to think of what you would previously categorize as failure (people not talking, feeling clueless, anger breaking out, feeling you've lost control, leaving an event wishing you could have a do-over) as just the necessary and predictable dynamics of developing an antiracist identity. To paraphrase what a friend told Brookfield, "There are two ways you can do antiracist work—imperfectly or not at all."

What most people take as a signal of failure is really a catalyst for learning. Discerning what to learn from failure, however, is challenging and, again, should not be done in isolation. A support group of friends and colleagues engaged in this work is essential to help you understand that what you think is evidence of your incompetence or unpreparedness is really just a central dynamic of this work. All too often an institution will attempt to place blame for people's dissatisfaction with, and dislike of, antiracist workshops on individual instructors and facilitators. Doing this means the institution can conveniently avoid identifying real challenges that must be addressed systemically.

A very vivid example of failing for Hess came in the 2018 international meeting of her scholarly guild, the Religious Education Association.

The meeting theme was "Beyond White Normativity, Creating Brave Spaces." At first glance, this was a very constructive and potentially trans-formative focus for a group of scholars. But from the beginning of the planning for this conference, things began to go awry. Rather than seeking to embody a learning frame that was more toward the far right of the chart described at the beginning of this chapter, the association's default struc-tures vested the planning of the program in the hands of a very small group of people (something seen in the far left columns of the chart). Limited time, busy scholars, and a multitude of other structural challenges led to a meeting that explicitly claimed to be creating a brave space, but which in many ways embodied its opposite.

Hess played one specific role in that overall failure that is worth explor-ing. She is the networking coordinator for this association, and in that role manages their website that designs the look and feel of a given conference's materials. She gave the conference program chair a number of images to choose from that would carry the meeting's theme, and the chair chose a CC-licensed photograph of a group of people of multiple races untangling a large white rope. The meaning that the chair and Hess intended with the image was to highlight multiracial engagement in untangling the white rope of white supremacy. But both Hess and the program chair are white women, and neither grasped that it was also possible to see in that image further enslavement, to see the rope as constraining and limiting. Further, the two of them were oblivious to the echoes of lynching that could arise from using an image of ropes.

As the meeting began, small groups of people began murmuring about the image, particularly because it was placed on name tags and conference folders that people picked up as they checked in.

Pause for a moment and imagine possible responses to this emerging conflict.

Could the murmurs be ignored? Could check-in table volunteers deny the problem and assert that the image could not possibly be understood in that negative a way? Could the registration table throw away all of the mate-rials, which would immediately cause problems with check-in and previously prepared information folders? Who might explain what was intended by the image? Should they even try? Would any of these responses be failing well in that they might lead to constructive transformation? Or might they dig the problem in more fully?

The answers to these questions are deeply contextual, and likely would vary from organization to organization. In this case the members of the asso-ciation took the challenge into their own hands. While the registration table simply kept handing out tags and folders, people began turning their name tags over, refusing the image and writing their names by hand instead. As the meeting went on, more and more frustration was expressed, the conference image becoming a catalyst for lifting up long-standing concerns.

This could have been a moment for defensiveness and Hess certainly remembers her own self-justifications welling up. But she worked hard to breathe deeply and slowly, to swallow the immediate words that came to mind, and instead to listen carefully to what people were saying. Her intent was to do her best to respect the meanings attendees were making. She asked for concrete proposals and constructive responses, and encouraged scholars who were upset to share their feelings in public ways in the midst of formal plenary sessions.

In the aftermath, as the association's leadership sought to make sense of what had gone wrong and what to do about it for future meetings, Hess consistently urged people not only to listen to what was being said but to express methodological belief—that is, to believe and respect the criticisms expressed. That process, in turn, led to some major governance changes being adopted at the next annual meeting.

This story is a lively example of the ways in which collective responses—the improvised, on the spot actions of turning name tags over and then speaking up in plenary gatherings (both cultural/symbolic moves)—led to major structural changes. In this case, failing well for Hess meant recognizing her own ignorance, defensiveness, and self-justification, while working to ensure there was space for people with different experiences to contribute to the analysis and offer recommendations for the future (a human relations and political constituency invitation). And finally it meant advocating for those changes in the spaces Hess had access to that others might not have (structural shifts).

Brookfield remembers many instances in which he has run workshops and sessions where the backchannelchat.com feed has lit up with multiple complaints and criticisms. A very frequent one is that he is white bashing. Another is that he is seeing race where it doesn't exist. A third is that he focuses too much on himself. A fourth is that he's talking too much.

Brookfield has two chief ways of responding in these situations. The first is to tell himself that describing these as failures is to misunderstand the complexity of this work. If there were only one clear singular path to success that worked for everyone, then perhaps terms like *failure* and *success* would make sense. But when we deal with diverse racial identities, assorted histories and experiences, different levels of readiness for learning about race, and a variety of learning styles and types of information processing, then it clearly makes no sense to talk about uniform best practices. White supremacy twists and contorts itself in our consciousness and actions in ways that are endlessly variable. So what Brookfield used to think of as failures he now regards as inevitable complexities, necessary contradictions.

Like Hess, Brookfield tries to use these so-called "failures" to probe deeper into the nature of racism. If he's accused of white bashing, or told he is seeing race where it doesn't exist, he can ask people to speak or post what they see as examples of him doing those things. In showing how he listens to their responses he can try to use them to teach about the way that white supremacy is so pervasive that most have great difficulty recognizing when it's in play. If he's told that he's using his autobiographical experiences too much, he switches to more of a focus on external sources, videos, and research. If he's told that people need less of Brookfield, he can move to a discussion protocol, ask for responses to a question that somebody's posed on backchannelchat.com, or engage participants in a chalk talk.

It can be very difficult in higher education settings where we are incentivized to be experts who hold a monopoly on knowledge to let go of the desire to be in the right, to occupy the role of the specialist who holds the only valid forms of knowledge. Part of developing an antiracist white identity is deliberately acknowledging our humility and difficulties in doing this highly emotional work. Failing well means problematizing what are labeled as mistakes, owning up to gaps and omissions in our knowledge, and recognizing how one's actions have contributed to furthering racism.

Finding a Center in the Midst of Conflict

When institutional resistance takes a highly personal form, it's crucial that you are grounded as an activist, teacher, change agent, or professional developer in practices that help you develop resilience in the face of such challenges. Such practices run the gamut from individual introspection to developing a local support group to participation in national and international collectives.

On a personal level, Hess draws on centering prayer, an ancient form of religious practice that involves sitting in silence and attending to breath. Even if you are not a religious person, practices of mindfulness have been shaped to support such attention in highly secular settings. She finds Margaret Wheatley's (2010) small book *Perseverance* a resource to which she returns again and again.

There is also transformative research being explored in the area of somatic or body awareness. Resmaa Menakem, a somatic therapist in Minneapolis, has developed a series of practices that take seriously the trauma caused by racism (Menakem, 2017). He urges attention to what our bodies know that our conscious minds might not, whether we inhabit white bodies, Black bodies, police bodies, and so on. In each instance there is trauma, and unless we intentionally seek to heal that trauma, we inevitably recreate it. This is yet another way in which we are coming to understand how racism replicates itself.

Brookfield draws his center from an ontological understanding that this work is beyond simple classifications of good and bad, right and wrong, correct and incorrect. In his soul he knows the complexity and difficulty of it means he will always feel unsatisfied, always want to turn the video back and do an exercise or activity all over again, and will always finish a session leaving some people dissatisfied and maybe angry. These realities are his constant companion and knowing of their inevitability and omnipresence takes the burden off his shoulders of having to "succeed" or be the expert.

He also draws on the support and experiences of colleagues and peers engaged in this work. You can't do antiracist education without a community in which you can vent frustration, confess to feelings of failure, celebrate good days, and share insights and advice. On the collective level, there are a growing number of organizations and other collectivities that invite shared engagement of these issues. Most scholarly and professional organizations have some kind of venue within which issues of racism are being addressed. Just as you can use Table 11.1 to assess an institution for which you are designing a workshop, you can use the same chart to assess your professional organization. Is there a committee devoted to doing antiracism work? Is it participatory and collaborative? Does it prioritize structural power over relational, constituent, and symbolic forms of power? If not, are there affinity groups or other more loosely organized ways in which people can connect together in this work?

There are also national and international organizations that focus on antiracism work. White Privilege Conferences (www.whiteprivilegeconference.com), held annually, draw together people who are working on these issues and highlight emerging resources. The YWCA, both globally and in the United States, has focused on human rights and overcoming racism, and Showing Up for Racial Justice (SURJ) is an organization with chapters in many local communities. Many national religious organizations also have specific committees focused on these issues.

We urge people doing this work to find ways to develop networks of support and encouragement. No one individual, no one institution, can do this by itself. Collective insight and collective action are essential.

12

BEING AN ANTIRACIST WHITE ALLY

An antiracist white identity can really only be realized through action. Putting yourself on the line with all the consequences that entails is essential to white antiracism. Engaging in extended self-reflection on one's racial identity and enactment of white supremacy is obviously important. But it can also be an escape route out of action, a way to avoid the failures and necessary mistakes that will always accompany white activism. So although we understand the importance of self-work, we know that becoming fully antiracist requires dangerous actions. It means leveraging your power and privilege to raise the questions white leaders avoid addressing; risking institutional marginalization and exclusion as you keep forcing people to focus on race, racism, and white supremacy; and being physically willing to form the front and side lines in a phalanx of demonstrators confronting the police.

Most of us who want to be allies in a multiracial struggle start by thinking we will act in a way that feels helpful to people of color. But as with everything else surrounding antiracism, this is a lot more complex than it at first seems. We must remember that the notion of allyship has embedded within it some potentially problematic colonialist notions. As Singh (2019) acknowledged, "Self-appointment of allyship can mean we are off the mark of being a good racial ally" (p. 173). In fact, simply declaring oneself an ally will be seen by people of color as a form of virtue signaling, something you do to make yourself feel better. Real allyship is not something you claim for yourself, but confirmed on you by others. It's earned through sustained commitment and dangerous action.

It's all too easy to slip into the white savior stance in which the patronizing question "What can we do for you?" carries the implicit understanding that people of color need whites to solve their problems for them because BIPOC communities are too marginalized or demoralized to act purposefully on their own behalf. The assumption is that these communities by definition lack the skills and resources to organize, advocate, and push effectively for racial change. White saviors are people who "see themselves as superior in capability and intelligence" and have "an obligation to 'save' BIPOC from their supposed inferiority and helplessness" (Saad, 2020, p. 149). This orientation further sediments white supremacy. What looks like "caring" conceals a form of what Matias and Zembylas (2013) called thinly veiled disgust.

So whites offering help to communities of color should expect to be treated with skepticism and outright mistrust. This is because there is a lot of performative or optical allyship around. This is glaringly evident in corporations that proclaim their support of Black Lives Matter but then continue to employ child slave sweatshop labor to make their products. Latham Thomas (2018) defined this as "allyship that only serves at the surface level to platform the 'ally', it makes a statement but doesn't go beneath the surface and is not aimed at breaking away from the systems of power that oppress" (para. 1).

Optical allyship does not just show up in corporate speak. It's seen in the efforts of whites who want to be considered "woke" and see themselves as "social justice warriors" who put quotes from MLK at the bottom of their emails, display antiracist posters on their office doors, and wear the right signifiers (BLM buttons, T-shirts, and hats) without really committing to the hard work of rigorous self-examination and then painstakingly building, one by one, antiracist coalitions that push for institutional change. As Gyasi Lake (2019), a student at Buffalo State University, observed,

> White people don't exist in line with the liberation of Black people. Whiteness and the ideologies that were brought upon by whiteness must be eradicated for the freeing of Black bodies, making the possibility of white allies incongruous with the goals of said liberation. The sooner we rid our minds with the concept of white allies, the sooner we can strategize for the society devoid of whiteness. (para. 9)

A good place to begin our analysis of allyship is Yancy's (2015) opinion piece for the *New York Times* titled "Dear White America," in which he offers to whites "a form of love that enables you to see the role that you play (even despite your anti-racist actions) in a *system* that continues to value black lives on the cheap" (para. 25). Yancy reminded whites that even as they work in antiracist ways, this neither absolves them of their racism nor means that they are somehow free of white supremacy. Both of us recognize a tendency in ourselves to want to be acknowledged as moral allies in the midst of our activism, to receive the "good white" medal (Hayes & Juarez, 2009). So we have to keep reminding ourselves that the focus should be on supporting the interests of people of color in whatever way they direct us.

One of the founding principles of allyship that is frequently mentioned is that of mutual interest. In a variant of critical race theory's notion of interest convergence (substantive change only happens when it benefits whites), the idea of mutual interest emphasizes how whites see the benefits to them of an antiracist stance. Wise (2011) recounted that when he as a white man is asked by justifiably suspicious people of color why he is involved in the work he does, he always replies that it's for his own benefit as much as anything else. A white supremacist consciousness is harmful to whites who live infected by a pervasive fear of the "other" and the threat to white safety that people of color supposedly represent. The most productive way to be rid of that fear is to develop an antiracist white identity.

The SURJ (n.d.) website makes a similar point:

> When those of us who are white realize that racial justice is core to our liberation as well, then masses of white people will withdraw support from white supremacy. Together, as part of a powerful multi-racial, cross-class movement for collective liberation we can force the system of white supremacy to crumble. (para. 4)

SURJ quotes Alice Garza, the cofounder of Black Lives Matter, saying that people of color need whites to defect from white supremacy, and that that can only happen when whites become aware of how its pervasive organizing presence circumscribes their own lives. In similar terms Kivel (2017) wrote that "racial justice work must be based on our understanding of mutual interest—we all have a tremendous stake in building a society based on inclusion, equity, caring and justice" (p. 131).

Allies and Accomplices

The group Indigenous Action Media (2014) published what they called a "provocation" titled "Accomplices not Allies." They claimed the term *ally* had been rendered ineffective and meaningless and co-opted by any whites who simply wished to appear to be antiracist. It's certainly true that we've sometimes viewed white friends, students, and colleagues describing themselves as allies as earnest virtue signaling. Saying "I'm your ally" or "I want to be your ally" doesn't cost anything and is almost expected from whites working in any organizational or community setting that claims to prize diversity and inclusion. There is a danger that the discourse of allyship thus becomes ritualistic, requiring no serious commitment or effort.

In a further complicating critique of ally politics, an author named only as "M" (2015) argued that the notion of allyship is based on the following thesis: "The only way to act with integrity is to follow the leadership of those who are oppressed . . . support their project and goals, and always seek out their suggestions and listen to their ideas when you are not sure what to do next" (p. 66). The problem with this thesis, M observed, is

> that there is no singular mass of people of color—or any other identity-based group—to take guidance from, and that people within a single identity will not only disagree about important things but also will often have directly conflicting desires. (p. 67)

The film and subsequent TV series *Dear White People* illustrate this well. Based on writer/director Justin Samien's experience as a student at a predominantly white institution, the mainly African American characters display a range of different ideologies, identities, and political projects. So something that seems superficially simple—white activists resolving only to take direction from leaders of color—becomes highly complex once we deconstruct the notion that "people of color" comprise a single category, all of whom think the same.

Because of these and other criticisms of the notion of "ally," Indigenous Action Media and websites like www.whiteaccomplices.org advocate using the term *accomplice* to urge whites to weaponize their privilege in attacking unjust laws and structures. An accomplice is someone who helps another person commit a crime. Pushing back against institutionalized white supremacy sometimes requires illegal acts such as demonstrating without a permit, marching after curfew, and being arrested. Accomplices are ready to break the law, get fired, and lose status and privilege as part of their antiracist work. In demonstrations whites act as accomplices when they are at the front and sides of a march, offering to be the first to be beaten or arrested. Here the intent is to make police think twice about the optics of beating up large numbers of white demonstrators on TV and social media.

For the two of us how you label certain actions is less important than the actions themselves. If we see any difference in how these terms are used it has to do with where the locus of control lies in antiracist work. An alliance is usually between two separate entities who decide that they have a mutual interest in fighting for a particular change. Critical race theory argues that alliances are at the base of major progressive changes around race. Hence, major legislation to advance the interests of communities of color typically only occurs when that same legislation benefits whites. An accomplice, however, is usually acting at the express direction of others to help those others realize certain ends defined as illegal or criminal. In antiracist work white accomplices are directed by people of color in terms of how they can act in ways that are most helpful. Of course, as M (2015) stated earlier, sometimes there are multiple agendas and desires being advanced and whites then need to decide which faction they will work with and support.

Indigenous Action Media (2014) stated that "an accomplice as academic would seek ways to leverage resources and material support and/or betray their institution to further liberation struggles" (para. 11). Because the two of us are white academics, that means we need to embarrass our institutions publicly, make them squirm, and say the unsayable to trustees, presidents, provosts, and deans when their antiracist rhetoric is contradicted by their actions. In public and private forums, we need to name explicitly the white supremacy that lies behind institutional policies, new organizational initiatives, and the individual words and actions of senior leaders. We must be prepared to lose friends, be pilloried on social media, and be fired.

In the rest of this chapter we explore how we can act as allies and accomplices. Despite the critiques of the term we will use the shorthand expression *ally* as an umbrella label, because that's the word that most whites choose to describe how they wish to act as they take the journey to becoming antiracist. But as we think of what it means to work as an ally we incorporate the whole range of accomplice practices.

We should acknowledge, of course, that context plays an enormous role in determining the range of actions open to you at any particular moment. Institutions that openly resist attempts to uncover and challenge white supremacy offer a very different range of possibilities than those trying to do the right thing, no matter how uninformed or naïve their efforts might be. Privately funded or state-sponsored organizations differ in terms of the legal mandates they are under. A faith-based institution will connect race work to religious doctrine in a way that's unfamiliar in a secular organization. Additionally, your intersectional gender and class identity, history at the institution, status as full-time or contract employee, past experience of activism, and the racial makeup and mission of your organization all frame how you judge which of your actions will have the greatest effect. But, notwithstanding all these caveats, let's look at a range of actions and behaviors you might consider.

Saying the Unsayable

A working assumption that lies at the heart of an antiracist consciousness is that the ideology of white supremacy is so pervasive and powerful that institutions, organizations, and communities will always be organized in ways that benefit whites. This is an inconvenient truth for many whites to hear. As we argued at the beginning of this book, whites will believe that they stand against racism by not thinking overtly racist thoughts and by not engaging in individual acts of name calling. In this way of thinking racism is an individual act of symbolic or physical violence that breaks out in isolated instances.

So anytime a white person names the fact that we live and work in a racist system in which white supremacy legitimizes whites' positions of privilege, they are acting as an antiracist ally. If you're in a meeting in which you're considering a new program or policy initiative, you can ask the group to identify the implicit assumptions about race embedded in the proposal. You can be the person who says, "Let's look at the elements of white supremacy in here," or the one who asks, "In what ways does this proposal reduce active and passive racism at our institution?"

The quicker that we make identifying white supremacy a normal and habitual practice, the better we will get at pushing back against it. Every meeting needs people who will foreground race and in predominantly white institutions those individuals really need to be white. A white person leading or encouraging a group to uncover racism takes some of the pressure off people of color who feel wearily obliged always to be the ones doing this. One way we as whites can be allies is to normalize the practice of uncovering racism, to make talking about white supremacy an unremarkable fact of life. "How is our whiteness getting in the way of us seeing what's really going on here?" "What are we missing because we're white?" "What's blinding us to recognizing white supremacy?" These are all questions whites can be the first to pose.

Whenever resources are being allocated we should take the lead in asking how any proposed allocation disproportionately benefits white members of the organization. The two of us adapt variants of the ideology critique approach (Brookfield, 2007) to ask the following questions of any new proposal:

"Who most benefits from this decision?"
"Who is most harmed by it?"
"Whose interests are missing?"
"How could this action be changed to be more socially just?"

In a predominantly white environment with a BIPOC minority, whites should be the first ones to raise questions of how specific actions enact white supremacy. If we want to critique what we see as instances of unacknowledged racism, we'll often begin by quoting examples where we have enacted the same blindness that we're observing in superiors. We'll quote relevant research and theory on racial microaggressions or white fragility to lead into our criticism and, whenever possible, we'll ground our analysis in what people of color have already documented about their experiences in the organization or community.

These approaches are designed to remove the aspect of personal shaming or blaming from our comments. It's important that we keep defensive white decision-makers open to listening to what we have to say and this won't happen if we adopt a disdaining or preaching stance (European American Collaborative Challenging Whiteness, 2010). If people feel you're lecturing them from a position of assumed superiority and enhanced racial cognizance, they'll close down. But if you ground your critique of an action by citing similar actions you yourself have taken, similar omissions you've made, credible research, or examples of practices observed in similar institutions, you raise the chances that people will recognize the racism that's in front of their eyes.

Affirming Accounts of Racism From People of Color

One of the most predictable ways that predominantly white institutions deal with criticism regarding their racism is to deny its existence. This is usually done benignly, for example by explaining away white supremacist speech as slips of the tongue, "simple" misunderstandings about language or intent, examples of lines of communication being crossed. The underlying assumption here is that people of color are seeing racism where it doesn't exist, imagining slights when no malice was meant, and basically making things up.

So when an example of racism is brought to the attention of those in power, whites need to make sure they do everything they can to underscore its validity. There are colonialist echoes in this practice of course. After all, testimony regarding racism from people of color should stand as credible without any need for whites to assert its truth. We don't want to imply that accounts are legitimate only when whites support them. Our intent is simply to say that whites can play an important role in ensuring that righteous anger and justifiable complaints are not swept under the rug, dismissed as imaginings or playing the race card.

Let's give a quick example. Brookfield and his colleague Bryana French recently taught a course in which they ran a chalk talk exercise asking students to document the examples of racism they had witnessed at an institution. They wrote the following question in the middle of two large whiteboards in the classroom: "When you have witnessed or experienced racism on campus

what does this look, sound, feel like?" Students were divided by racial affilia-
tion and this produced two boards covered with examples of specific actions
and concrete examples that people provided regarding things they'd seen or
experienced.

The chalk talk board produced by those who identified as students of
color was particularly compelling in the vividness of the specific accounts of
being ignored, demeaned, discounted, and demoralized. When Brookfield
suggested that this would be useful data for the administration to encounter,
the students of color demurred about the advisability of submitting it themselves. They feared reprisal if any of them were seen as the originators of any
message implicitly criticizing the institution for the widespread amount of
racism it was not attending to.

So Brookfield offered to send an image of this powerful chalk talk
graphic to the president and provost, explaining that students of color felt
fearful about submitting it themselves. He committed to share the results
of his approach to these administrative leaders with students in the class
who could then decide if and how they wished to respond. As it happened,
the president and provost expressed gratitude for this information and then
offered a meeting between the students and the vice president for diversity
and inclusion to address the students' concerns. Here Brookfield was trying
to use his privilege and cultural capital to draw leaders' attention to specific
instances of racism that students had experienced.

Whenever people of color submit accounts of the white supremacy they've
observed and the racism they've experienced, whites can support them by
urging that leaders ask for the broadest and deepest information about these
events that they can gather. Institutional leaders will typically assert that racist incidents are individual acts of nastiness committed by unrepresentative,
bad apples in the community. The belief is that they are like individual fires
that can be quickly doused to prevent a wider conflagration.

Although neither of us wants to suggest that individual measures
shouldn't be taken, we do believe that if this is all that happens, then a real
opportunity has been lost. So if an individual instance of racism is reported,
you can urge leadership to send out a request asking for information regarding similar such incidents in an attempt to understand the true, systemic
nature of the problem. Indeed, one thing we'd urge is that on a regular basis
leadership pose the same question to organizational members asked in the
chalk talk exercise: "When you've seen racism and white supremacy in action
in our community, what does this look, sound, and feel like?" If respond-
ents' anonymity is assured and the responses are subsequently shared with
the whole community, this would go a long way to addressing institutional
racism seriously.

A final example of how we can affirm accounts of racism experienced by people of color is via digital technology. Most of us now have in our jackets, bags, and purses a portable film studio in the shape of a smart phone or tablet. So if you are on the street, in a store, or on public transportation and racism breaks out, you can film what's going on. High schooler Darnella Frazier's 2020 filming of the murder of George Floyd in Minneapolis had a worldwide impact by foregrounding the nature of systemic racism and the casual brutality of police behavior. But this practice began in 1992 with George Holliday's video of Rodney King being pulled out of his car and beaten up by Los Angeles police officers. Now we can view our cell phones as social justice weapons.

So if you bump into a colleague of color in the corridor or cafeteria who starts to describe something that's happened to them, ask if it's okay for you to record their testimony on camera (or via audio) for you to be able to submit as firsthand evidence of institutional racism. It's vital that filming this testimony be completely voluntary. There's always the danger of this turning into a form of victim porn, so it must never be done without the person concerned being completely in agreement and supportive of your showing it at a later date. The website library.witness.org has multiple resources for video activists if you're interested in working in this manner.

Identifying Racism as a White Problem

We have both led and participated in a number of DEI initiatives. Most of these are, understandably, focused on how to make people of color feel more welcomed, recognized, and included. Getting whites to complete implicit bias or cultural competence inventories so that they can communicate more effectively with people of color, changing curricula to include more scholars of color, or running workshops on inclusion—all place the emphasis on people of color. Similarly, public announcements about the need to protect all members of a community or policy declarations affirming the dignity of each individual neatly elide the need to face the reality of white supremacy head on.

We don't want to suggest that these DEI efforts should be ignored. But what is equally important is to force people to confront the fact that the ideology of white supremacy is embedded in, and frames, so many institutional structures and policies. If white supremacy is an organizational unsayable, then you can be the one to speak its name, to shout it from the rooftops. As each new DEI initiative is announced, you can do your best to frame discussion of it around its success in confronting white supremacy and in naming whiteness as the overwhelming institutional reality. So if your institution asks everyone to comment on institutional responses to racist speech, fill out a survey, or scrutinize new policies from a DEI point of view, the first thing you ask about is the degree to which these are explicitly intended to unearth and confront white supremacy.

As those of you who've tried to do this know, white leadership is very adept at stopping white supremacy and white racial identity being the central focus of any institutional initiative. So you'll need to be very persistent about this. Keep making the point that people of color invariably say that the way whites can be most helpful to their cause is by recognizing their own whiteness and, by extension, their collusion in white supremacy. If institutions say they want to be more responsive to people of color, tell them that the best way to accomplish this is to be explicit about how to confront the white supremacist practices and policies embedded in institutional culture.

In our experience the white leadership of predominantly white institutions will listen to your entreaties about the need to prioritize whiteness and then quietly ensure that the term *white supremacy* is omitted from program descriptions or policy rationales. Focusing on whiteness is seen as a nonissue, an unnecessary diversion from developing culturally competent habits. One resource we've found helpful is the *Continuum on Becoming an Anti-Racist Multicultural Organization* developed by the Crossroads Ministry (n.d.) in Chicago. This continuum identifies six stages toward becoming a fully inclusive antiracist organization that is explicitly focused on countering white supremacy. The continuum makes very clear the organizational changes that would need to be made for real progress to occur. Institutions invariably place themselves much further along the continuum than is really warranted, so constantly making clear and concrete suggestions as to what antiracist policies and practices look like is one of the best ways you can be a white ally. Institutions that say they're antiracist need to be helped to see that there are very specific practices and policies associated with that orientation.

Showing Up

You don't always have to take a leadership role with other whites to support the struggles against racism and white supremacy. Demonstrating solidarity by being visibly present at rallies, meetings, and demonstrations organized by people of color is an important way of showing that racism is not a problem of people of color, but rather a white problem. Of course you need to be aware that you're there in an ancillary role and that your bodily presence is sometimes all that's required. If a march has been organized by activists of color, you obviously take direction from the designated leaders. If a teach-in or town hall meeting is set up and run by a particular group, then you follow the process designed by that group.

One consequence of lending your bodily presence to events organized by people of color is that you'll quickly learn not to assume that all Black, Latinx, Asian, or indigenous people think the same way. For example, we have been at Black Lives Matter protests where appeals for love coexist with exhortations to kill police. On marches you should join in with chants you support and at meetings you should applaud everything you agree with. When people voice chants or shout things you disagree with, find ways to engage in nonviolent counterstrategies. For example, start singing a song that people can join in with, or put yourself in directly in front of the people— police or counter-demonstrators—making ugly threats.

Our general rule is that we only speak when there is a space deliberately created for white voices to be heard. Otherwise our role is simply to have our bodies present so that onlookers and media have visible evidence that whites are committed to antiracism and believe racism to be a problem affecting whites. Of course, if the protest rally or demonstration is organized by a white organization such as SURJ, then you're encouraged to make your voices as loud as possible!

Don't expect to be thanked for showing up at an event organized by BIPOC folks. Your presence will most likely be viewed skeptically. Perhaps you'll be judged as someone who is a race tourist motivated by curiosity rather than lending support. Maybe your attendance will be taken mostly as an attempt to assuage your white guilt. So don't look for expressions of approval or "good white" medals. Expect suspicion or just to be ignored.

One final point. There are spaces in which historically marginalized groups need to be with others who share that identity to talk easily *without* whites being present. At one of our institutions an affinity group was recently established for faculty of color, indigenous faculty, and allies. At the first meeting it was very clear that the faculty of color and indigenous faculty were desperate for their own space. There was no direct challenge to the whites attending, nor were we made to feel uncomfortable. But it was no surprise to us when, after the first meeting, the term *allies* was removed from the group's title and the group reconstituted itself as a faculty of color and indigenous faculty group.

Misguided whites who stumble into settings where they're clearly not wanted will be resented. People of color need spaces to relax and share things only they have experience of without the worry of including whites or self-censoring their comments because whites are present. This is the purpose of organizations such as Academics for Black Survival and Wellness (2020).

So be wary of being a racial gate-crasher who in a misguided act of allyship actually interrupts people of color who are trying to gain the emotional sustenance and strategic advice they need.

Bringing "Insider" Knowledge From the White World

Whites know how the white world works. We're socialized to speak, dress, argue, and advocate for what we want. We know the language that will open doors and the arguments that will persuade white power brokers to do something for us. We've learned all the communicative tricks, all the physical and verbal modulations, to make sure we're heard and taken seriously. We build networks and connections based on our racial identity, and our whiteness means that in a white supremacist world we're not perceived as innately threatening when we push a particular agenda.

Sometimes it's helpful to share this insider knowledge of how to traverse a white world to help colleagues of color navigate the political and cultural minefield of a predominantly white institution by:

- Providing constant advice on how to frame radical and challenging proposals in terms of achieving the institution's mission. As we've already observed, it's harder for institutional leadership to wriggle out of commitments when they're framed as efforts designed to help the institution realize the values and tasks it publicly states as crucial to its identity. So whenever you're working with people of color to force a white organization to deal with racism and white supremacy, you can provide advice on how to frame press releases, announce demonstrations, and demand specific institutional policy changes in terms that are directly connected to the organization's public mission or value statement.
- Giving "insider" white information on what we know of the individual histories and passions of members of a senior white leadership team. As whites we've probably spent much more informal time with other white colleagues than have our colleagues of color. We know the arguments that have swayed them in the past and the red flags that predispose them to dismiss suggestions. We can tell colleagues of color the best way to present information on raw, challenging, and contentious topics like racism and white supremacy that will keep the attention of whites who we know will be fearful or uncomfortable when dealing with these issues.

- Building multiracial networks and communities so that when radical proposals are made they have the greatest weight of numbers supporting them. If you've spent several years at an institution pushing an antiracist agenda, you'll probably have a good sense of whom among your white colleagues can be trusted as allies and supporters of genuinely antiracist initiatives. This is another valuable piece of insider knowledge you can pass on. In our experience most whites will publicly agree with people of color whenever they bring the need for major systemic change to the table. But you have the benefit of your informal backchannel communications with white colleagues. Over the years you've been privy to their jokes and stories. You've seen them in small committees or lunched with them in the cafeteria when they were at their most relaxed. So you know which colleagues mean it when they say change is necessary, and which are essentially two-faced on this issue—agreeing with the project of antiracism but not being willing to take any risks to support its expansion.

Holding White Colleagues to Account

One of the most important roles white allies play is holding other whites to account, particularly in all-white environments. When whites are alone all the casual racism of jokes, stories, and stereotypes flourishes. Urban legends of welfare queens and gangbangers, generalizations regarding the shortcomings of people of color, and well-meaning exhortations to help what are seen as deficit populations are shared without embarrassment. When whites are together they feel no need to hold back or self-censor and are willing to express racism in a way that would never happen when people of color are present.

Here's an opportunity for those of us trying to develop an antiracist white identity to do the heavy lifting of identifying and calling out the expression of white supremacy. Doing this "backstage" work brings no public recognition or thanks. Indeed, it's probably best to expect only ridicule or hostility for your efforts. You will be seen as a killjoy who is being way too politically correct when people protest that they are just having fun or blowing off steam. People will accuse you of being holier than thou, of acting superior, having no sense of humor, and taking things way too seriously. When you point out the implicit bias embedded in someone's comment, or the way that a joke captures the essence of white supremacy, don't expect white friends and colleagues to thank you for trying to transform their worldviews. But do it anyway.

Of course, there are things you can do in this racial backstage work that raise the chances people will actually hear what you're saying:

- Begin a critical comment by citing yourself as a carrier of racism. For example, as you bring the racist overtones of a comment to someone's attention, describe how you frequently made similar comments until someone called you out on it and you realized its white supremacist nature. Say how you struggled with that realization but how you eventually came around to accepting its legitimacy.
- Ask someone how they think that a person of color both of you know would feel if they were present to hear a joke being made. If your white friend or colleague says that they would never make that joke if a person of color was around, ask why they feel it's legitimate to make it to you.
- Repeat a story someone is telling in which a minority group is portrayed in a certain way, but switch the identities of the groups being portrayed so that characteristics attributed to people of color are now attributed to whites. If people protest that whites would never think or act in the way that's now being attributed to them, ask them where the evidence for their generalizations regarding people of color comes from.
- Make sure that whenever you point out racism you do it in a way that communicates that racism is a system and that white supremacy is a set of ideas that everyone is subject to. Slipping into the "you're a racist" or "there's your white supremacy showing up" discourse, just reinforces the "racism as individual acts of meanness" paradigm.

Being Willing to Lose Something

Sooner or later you'll be punished for your ally work. Perhaps you'll find yourself ostracized by colleagues and friends. The more upfront and critical you are in your antiracist efforts, the more those in power will attempt to exclude you from race-based initiatives at your own institution. So even as your antiracist work might cause you to be invited to address conferences or run workshops at sister institutions, your own organization will probably work to marginalize or diminish your efforts. Expect those in leadership who profess their dedication to inclusion and diversity to recoil once you start talking about white supremacy and racism. Persisting in urging that the institution talk about its racism and white supremacy will make those in power very uncomfortable. In a predominantly white organization, leadership (and also much of membership) will be far happier with a DEI discourse. When you make it clear that you refuse to accept this framing, you'll most likely become an institutional pariah.

You can also anticipate losing white friends and alienating colleagues by insisting repeatedly that the real problem of the community, organization, or institution is the white supremacy and white racism that permeate its culture and functioning. People will become wary of hanging around you if they know that you won't let them off the hook when racial stereotypes and casual jokes start being shared.

Sometimes your antiracist advocacy will cause you to be maneuvered out of the institution. You won't be fired outright because institutions are smart enough to know that firing someone for advocating racial justice is not good public relations. But your contract will not be renewed or your duties will be changed. One very predictable response to being perceived as a racial troublemaker is for the organization to pile on new duties and responsibilities so that your time for advocacy is reduced. The newly assigned tasks will be justified as necessary to institutional survival and no one will say to your face that your antiracist activism should cease. And any instruction to stop calling out racism will most definitely *not* be put in writing. But an institution can radically restructure your work and drown you in new assignments so that your antiracist work takes a back seat. And if you insist on persisting with your antiracist efforts even as you are overwhelmed with reassignments, you'll perhaps find yourself exhausted and depressed, which, of course, means you're far less effective in your activism.

Conclusion

If you choose to work as an ally or accomplice, you need to know what you're getting into. Anyone who sees this as morally admirable charity work or anyone who expects to receive thanks, recognition, or even acclamation for their efforts will flame out early when these things aren't forthcoming. Ultimately, the reason to take on ally and accomplice work is because you feel it's the right thing to do and you know you wouldn't feel right about yourself if you didn't commit yourself in this way.

Some of the greatest problems facing the United States right now are income inequality and environmental destruction. Racism both frames and intersects with these problems in an undeniable way. BIPOC folks are disproportionately the poorest in our country and disproportionately affected by climate change. You can't say that you want a better world without addressing the way that white supremacy does its best to enforce a racial divide in employment, incarceration, education, health care—in fact, in every dimension of our lives. So if you have any belief in the principle of fairness enshrined in most notions of democracy, you're impelled to develop an antiracist identity.

But we want to end this book by reiterating the argument with which we began. Becoming a white antiracist is psychologically crucial for your mental health and peace of mind. White privilege and white supremacy dehumanizes whites (Sullivan, 2019), causing deep psychic wounds. If you grow up without questioning the myth that your skin color bestows greater intelligence on you, that the genocide of indigenous people was warranted, and that people of color deserve to be enslaved and incarcerated because they're the undisciplined, uncontrolled, and violent "others" who threaten your security, then two things happen. First, you live a lie that, at some deep, preconscious level you know is false. Your whole life is based on an unsustainable illusion and you have to expend a lot of psychological energy convincing yourself that it's actually the truth.

Second, you live in fear of people of color someday being so pissed off, so frustrated, so feeling that they have nothing to lose, that they will rise up and claim the piece of the American pie that whites have worked assiduously to deny them. Each day you wake up feeling that a race war is imminent, that riots, looting, gunfire, and people driving into groups of demonstrators will become your daily reality. You lock your car door as you drive through the inner city, cross the street if a BIPOC group is coming down the sidewalk, clutch your purse to yourself as you ride an elevator with a person of color.

Living a life based on a lie and constantly anticipating a race war will slowly kill you emotionally, spiritually, and mentally, as well as taking a physical toll. So it's really in your own best interests to realize just how effectively white supremacy has tricked you into assuming this is a normal state in which to live. Of course most of us deny this reality and believe we are good whites who are on the right side of history. But when events like the 2020 outrage of George Floyd's murder overtake us, the psychic façade we've erected to convince us that we live a morally responsible life is shattered. That's when, as a matter of sheer survival, becoming a white antiracist is your best hope for the future.

REFERENCES

Academics for Black Survival and Wellness. (2020). *Home page.* https://www.academics4blacklives.com/

Aelabouni, M. (2018, July). *You might be a Lutheran if your VBS snack is tostadas.* Paper on mediated nostalgia and counter aesthetics in #DecolonizeLutheranism" presented at the International Society of Media, Religion and Culture meeting, Denver, CO. meh.religioused.org/web/assets/ISMRC%202018%20paper_Aelabouni.pdf

Anderson, C. (2016). *White rage: The unspoken truth of our racial divide.* Bloomsbury USA.

Arao, B., & Clemens, K. (2013). From safe spaces to brave spaces: A new way to frame dialogue around diversity and social justice. In L. Landreman (Ed.), *The art of effective facilitation: Reflections from social justice educators* (pp. 135–150). Stylus.

Arnold, R., Burke, B., James, C., Martin, D., & Thomas, B. (1991). *Educating for a change.* Between the Lines Press.

Aronson, B. A. (2017). The white savior industrial complex: A cultural studies analysis of a teacher educator, savior film, and future teachers. *Journal of Critical Thought and Praxis, 6*(3), 36–54. https://doi.org/10.31274/jctp-180810-83

Baldwin, J. (1962). *The fire next time.* Vintage International.

Baldwin, J. (1984). *Notes of a native son.* Beacon Press.

Barnett, P. (2019). Building trust and negotiating conflict when teaching race. In S. D. Brookfield & Associates (Eds.), *Teaching race: Helping students unmask and challenge racism* (pp. 109–130). Jossey-Bass.

Barnett, S. (2013). The myth of the lone hero. In J. M. James & N. Peterson (Eds.), *White women getting real about race: Their stories about what they learned teaching in diverse classrooms* (pp. 141–154). Stylus.

Bazelon, E. (2018, June 13). White people are noticing something new: Their own whiteness. *New York Times.* https://www.nytimes.com/2018/06/13/magazine/white-people-are-noticing-something-new-their-own-whiteness.html

Beckert, S. (2014, December 12). Slavery and capitalism. *Chronicle of Higher Education.* https://www.chronicle.com/article/slavery-and-capitalism/

Bell, L. A. (2010). *Storytelling for social justice: Connecting narratives and the arts in anti-racist teaching.* Routledge.

Bell, L. A., Roberts, R., Irani, K., & Murphy, B. (2008). *The storytelling curriculum project: Learning about race and racism through storytelling and the arts.* Storytelling Project, Barnard College. http://www.columbia.edu/itc/barnard/education/stp/stp_curriculum.pdf

Boal, A. (1979). *Theater of the oppressed.* London: Pluto Press.

Bohm, D. (1996). *On dialogue.* London: Routledge.

Bolman, L. G., & Deal, T. E. (2017). *Reframing organizations: Artistry, choice, and leadership* (6th ed.). Jossey-Bass/Wiley.

Bonilla-Silva, E. (2003). *Racism without racists: Color-blind racism and the persistence of racial inequality in the United States.* Rowman and Littlefield.

Bonilla-Silva, E., & Zuberi, T. (Eds.). (2008). *White logic, white methods: Racism and methodology.* Rowman and Littlefield.

Boyd, D. (2014). *It's complicated: The social lives of networked teens.* Yale University Press.

Brackett, M. (2019). *Permission to feel: The power of emotional intelligence to achieve well-being and success.* Celadon.

Brookfield, S. D. (2003a). Racializing the discourse of adult education. *Harvard Educational Review, 73*(4), 497–523. https://doi.org/10.17763/haer.73.4.a54508r0464863u2

Brookfield, S. D. (2003b). Racializing criticality in adult education. *Adult Education Quarterly, 53*(3), 154–169.

Brookfield, S. D. (2004). *The power of critical theory: Liberating adult learning and teaching.* Jossey-Bass.

Brookfield, S. D. (2007). Reclaiming critical thinking as ideology critique. In J. L. Kincheloe and R. A. Horn (Eds.), *The Praeger handbook of education and psychology: An encyclopedia.* Greenwood Press.

Brookfield, S. D. (2012). *Teaching for critical thinking: Tools and techniques to help students question their assumptions.* Jossey-Bass.

Brookfield, S. D. (2013). *Powerful techniques for teaching adults.* Jossey-Bass.

Brookfield, S. D. (2018). Repressive tolerance and the management of diversity. In V. Wang (Ed.), *Critical theory and transformative learning* (pp. 1–13). IGI/Information Age.

Brookfield, S. D. & Associates. (2019). *Teaching race: Helping students unmask and challenge racism.* Jossey-Bass.

Brown, B. (2017). *We need to keep talking about Charlottesville* [Video]. Facebook. https://www.facebook.com/brenebrown/videos/1778878652127236/

Campt, D. W. (2018). *The white ally toolkit: Using active listening, empathy, and personal storytelling to promote racial equity.* I Am Publications.

Cavalieri, C. E., French, B. H., & Renninger, S. M. (2019). Developing working alliances with students. In Brookfield, S. D., and Associates (Eds.), *Teaching race: Helping students unmask and challenge racism* (pp. 151–170). Jossey-Bass. https://doi.org/10.1002/9781119548492.ch8

Center for Courage and Renewal. (n.d.). *Practices of the circle of trust approach.* http://www.couragerenewal.org/PDFs/7practices.pdf

Chandler, J. L. S. (2016). *Colluding, colliding, and contending with norms of whiteness.* Information Age.

Chenoweth, E., & Stephan, M. (2011). *Why civil resistance works: The strategic logic of nonviolent conflict.* Columbia University Press.

Cranton, P. (2016). *Understanding and promoting transformative learning: A guide to theory and practice* (3rd ed.). Stylus.

Crass, C. (2013). *Towards collective liberation: Anti-racist organizing, feminist praxis, and movement building strategy.* PM Press.

Crass, C. (2015). *Towards the "other America": Anti-racist resources for white people taking action for Black Lives Matter.* Chalice Press.

Crossroads Ministry. (n.d.). *Continuum on becoming an anti-racist multicultural organization.* https://www.aesa.us/conferences/2013_ac_presentations/Continuum_AntiRacist.pdf

Daumeyer, N. M., Rucker, J. M., & Richeson, J. A. (2017). Thinking structurally about implicit bias: Some peril, lots of promise. *Psychological Inquiry, 28*(4), 258–261. https://doi.org/10.1080/1047840X.2017.1373556

Davis, M., & Wiener, J. (2020). *Set the night on fire: LA in the sixties.* Verso Press.

Delgado, R., & Stefancic, J. (2017). *Critical race theory: An introduction* (3rd ed.). NYU Press.

Denning, S. (2007). *The secret language of leadership: How leaders inspire action through narrative.* Jossey-Bass.

Dessel, A., & Rogge, M. (2008, Winter). Evaluation of intergroup dialogue A review of the empirical literature. *Conflict Resolution Quarterly, 26*(2), 199–238, https://doi.org/ 10.1002/crq.230

DiAngelo, R. (2016). When nothing's lost: The impact of racial segregation on white teachers and students. In N. M. Joseph, C. Haynes, & F. Cobb (Eds.), *Interrogating whiteness and relinquishing power: White faculty's commitment to racial consciousness in STEM classrooms* (pp. 27–42). Peter Lang.

DiAngelo, R. (2018). *White fragility: Why it's so hard for white people to talk about racism.* Beacon Press.

Dunbar-Ortiz, R. (2015). *An indigenous people's history of the United States.* Beacon Press.

Eddo-Lodge, R. (2017). *Why I'm no longer talking to white people about race.* Bloomsbury Circus.

Eisner, E. (1994). *Cognition and curriculum reconsidered.* Teachers College Press.

Elbow, P. (1986). *Embracing contraries: Explorations in teaching and learning.* Oxford University Press.

Ellington, R. (2016). Mathematics teacher education as a racialized experience. In N. M. Joseph, C. Haynes, & F. Cobb (Eds.). *Interrogating whiteness and relinquishing power: White faculty's commitment to racial consciousness in STEM classrooms* (pp. 211–222). Peter Lang.

Essed, P., Farquharson, K., Pillay, K., & White, E. J. (Eds.). (2018). *Relating worlds of racism: Dehumanization, belonging, and the normativity of European whiteness.* Palgrave Macmillan.

European American Collaborative Challenging Whiteness. (2010). White on white: Developing capacity to communicate about race with critical humility. In V. Sheared, J. Johnson-Bailey, S. A. J. Colin III, E. Peterson, & S. Brookfield (Eds.), *The handbook of race and adult education: A resource for dialogue on racism* (pp. 145–158). Jossey-Bass.

Facing History and Ourselves. (n.d.). *Teaching strategies.* www.facinghistory.org/resource-library/teaching-strategies

Farber-Robertson, A. (2000). *Learning while leading: Increasing your effectiveness in ministry.* Rowman and Littlefield.

Feagin, J. R. (2013). *The white racial frame: Centuries of racial framing and counter framing* (2nd ed.). Routledge.

Feagin, J., & O'Brien, E. (2003). *White men on race: Power, privilege, and the shaping of cultural consciousness.* Beacon Press.

Flynn, A., Holmberg, S. R., Warren, D. T., & Wong, F. J. (2017). *The hidden rules of race: Barriers to an inclusive economy.* Cambridge University Press.

Flynn, J. E. Jr. (2015). White fatigue: Naming the challenge in moving from an individual to a systemic understanding of racism. *Multicultural Perspectives, 17*(3), 115–124. https://doi.org/10.1080/15210960.2015.1048341

Foste, Z. (2020). The enlightenment narrative: White student leaders' preoccupation with racial innocence. *Journal of Diversity in Higher Education, 13*(1), 33–43. https://doi.org/10.1037/dhe0000113

Foucault, M. (1980). *Power/knowledge: Selected interviews and other writings, 1972–1977.* Pantheon Books.

Fox, H. (2014). *When race breaks out: Conversations about race and racism in college classrooms* (2nd ed.). Peter Lang.

Fund for Theological Exploration. (2012). *The FTE guide to VocationCare.* http://fteleaders.org/uploads/files/GUIDE%20TO%20VOCATIONCARE%202012%20Low.pdf

Furie, M. (2016, September 13). It's not easy being meme. *The Atlantic.* https://www.theatlantic.com/politics/archive/2016/09/its-not-easy-being-green/499892/

Gallman, S., Pica-Smith, C., & Rosenberger, C. (2010). Aggressive and tender navigations: Teacher educators confront whiteness in their practice. *Journal of Teacher Education, 20*(10), 1–12. https://doi.org/10.1177/0022487109359776

Gandbhir, G., & Foster, B. (2015, March 17). A conversation with my black son. *New York Times Op Doc.* https://www.nytimes.com/2015/03/17/opinion/a--conversation-with-my-black-son.html

Gillespie, D. (2003). The pedagogical value of teaching white privilege through case study. *Teaching Sociology, 31,* 469–477. https://stonehill-website.s3.amazonaws.com/files/resources/privilege-case-study.pdf

Gorski, P. (2015). Foreword. In E. Moore Jr., M. W. Penick-Parks, & A. Michael (Eds.), *Everyday white people confront racial and social injustice: 15 stories* (pp. ix–xiv). Stylus.

Grandin, G. (2015). Capitalism and slavery. *The Nation.* https://www.thenation.com/article/capitalism-and-slavery/

Habermas, J. (1987). *The theory of communicative action. Vol. 2. Lifeworld and system—A critique of functionalist reason.* Beacon Press.

Habermas, J. (1990). *Moral consciousness and communicative action.* MIT Press.

Hall, S. (2003). The whites of their eyes: Racist ideologies and the media. In G. Dines and J. M. Humez (Eds.), *Gender, race and class in the media* (2nd ed.). SAGE.

Haney Lopez, I. (2006). *White by law: The legal construction of race.* New York University Press.

Haney Lopez, I. (2014). *Dog whistle politics: How coded racial appeals have reinvented racism and wrecked the middle class.* Oxford University Press.

Hayes, C., & Juarez, B. (2009). You showed your Whiteness: You don't get a 'good' White people's medal. *International Journal of Qualitative Studies in Education, 22*(6), 729–744. https://doi.org/10.1080/09518390903333921

Heaven, C., Clegg, J., & Maguire, P. (2006). Transfer of communication skills training from workshop to workplace: The impact of clinical supervision. *Patient Education and Counseling, 60*(3), 313–325. https://doi.org/10.1016/j.pec.2005.08.008

Helms, J. E. (2019). *A race is a nice thing to have: A guide to being a white person or understanding the white persons in your life* (3rd ed.). Cognella Academic Publishing.

Hobbs, R. (2019). *Teach the power of propaganda.* Media Education. https://mediaedlab.com/2019/06/29/teach-the-power-of-propaganda/

hooks, bell. (1994). *Teaching to transgress: Education as the practice of freedom.* Routledge.

Horton, M. (1990). *The long haul: An autobiography.* Doubleday.

Horton, M., & Freire, P. (1990). *We make the road by walking: Conversations on education and social change.* Temple University Press.

Ignatiev, N. (1995). *How the Irish became white.* Routledge.

Indigenous Action Media. (2014, May 4). *Accomplices not allies: Abolishing the ally industrial complex.* http://www.indigenousaction.org/accomplices-not-allies-abolishing-the-ally-industrial-complex/

Jennings, W. (2010). *The Christian imagination: Theology and the origins of race.* Yale University Press.

Jensen, D. (2004). *The culture of make believe.* Chelsea Green.

Jones, K. (2020, May 30). *How can we win?* [Video]. YouTube. www.youtube.com/watch?v=sb9_qGOa9Go&t=219s

Jones, K., & Okun, T. (2001). *White supremacy culture.* http://cwsworkshop.org/PARC_site_B/dr-culture.html

Jones, S. (2016, September 7). How to heal the spiritual pain of America. *Time Magazine.* https://time.com/4477582/heal-the-spiritual-pain-of-america/

Katz, J. H. (2003). *White awareness: Handbook for anti-racism training* (2nd. ed.). University of Oklahoma Press.

Kay, M. R. (2018). *Not light, but fire: How to lead meaningful race conversations in the classroom.* Stenhouse.

Kendall, F. E. (2013). *Understanding white privilege: Creating pathways to authentic relationships across race* (2nd ed.). Routledge.

Kendi, I. X. (2017). *Stamped from the beginning: The definitive history of racist ideas in America.* Bold Type Books.

Kendi, I. X. (2020). *Be antiracist: A journal for awareness, reflection, and action.* One World Books.

Kernahan, C. (2019). *Teaching about race and racism in the college classroom: Notes from a white professor.* West Virginia University Press.

Kivel, P. (2017). *Uprooting racism: How white people can work for racial justice* (4th ed.). New Society Publishers.

Klein, M. (2019). Teaching intersectionality through "I am from." In S. Brookfield and Associates (Eds.), *Teaching race: Helping students unmask and challenge racism* (pp. 87–108). Jossey-Bass.

Knobel, M., & Lankshear, C. (Eds.). (2007). Online memes, affinities, and cultural production. In *New literacies sampler* (pp. 199–228). Peter Lang.

Lake, G. (2019). *I have no interest in "white allies."* Black Youth Project. http://blackyouthproject.com/i-have-no-interest-in-white-allies/

Lara-Villanueva, M. (2018). Talking to the wall: Whiteness and white resistance in the classroom. In G. J. Sefa Dei & S. Hilowle (Eds.), *Cartographies of race and social distance* (pp. 133–148). Springer.

Lawrence Lightfoot, S. (2000). *Respect: An exploration.* Basic Books.

Lensmire, T. J., McManimon, S. K., Dockter Tierney, J., Lee-Nichols, M. E., Casey, Z. A., Lensmire, A., & Davis, B. M. (2013). McIntosh as synecdoche: How teacher education's focus on white privilege undermines white privilege. *Harvard Educational Review, 83*(3), 410–443. https://doi.org/10.17763/haer.83.3.35054h14l8230574

Lewis, V. (2013, September 13). *What it means to be American* [Video]. YouTube. www.youtube.com/watch?v=2nmhAJYxFT4&t=59s

Lindeman, E. C. L. (1926). *The meaning of adult education.* New Republic.

Lipsitz, G. (2018). *The possessive investment in whiteness: How white people profit from identity politics* (20th anniv. ed.). Temple University Press.

Loewen, J. (2018). *Lies my teacher told me: Everything your American history textbook got wrong.* The New Press.

Loewen, J. W. (2003). Challenging racism, challenging history. In C. Thompson, E. Schaefer, and H. Brod (Eds.), *White men challenging racism: 35 personal stories* (pp. xv–xxix). Duke University Press.

Lopez, I. (2014). *Dog whistle politics: How coded racial appeals have reinvented racism and wrecked the middle class.* Oxford University Press.

Lorde, A. (1984). *Sister outsider.* Crossing Press.

Love, B. (2020). *We want to do more than survive: Abolitionist teaching and the pursuit of educational freedom.* Beacon Press.

M. (2015). A critique of ally politics. In C. Milstein (Ed.), *Taking sides: Revolutionary solidarity and the poverty of liberalism* (pp. 64–83). AK Press.

Mangino, R. (2008). Teaching the "ism" in racism, or, how to transform student resistance. In L. Guerrero (Ed.), *Teaching race in the 21st century: College teachers talk about their fears, risks, and rewards* (pp. 35–48). Palgrave Macmillan.

Marcuse, H. (1965). Repressive tolerance. In R. P. Wolff, B. Moore, & H. Marcuse (Eds.), *A critique of pure tolerance* (81–123). Beacon Press.

Marx, K., & Engels, F. (1998). *The German ideology.* Prometheus Books.

Matias, C. E., & Zembylas, M. (2013). When saying you care is not really caring: Emotions of disgust, whiteness ideology, and teacher education. *Critical Studies in Education, 55*(3), 319–337. https://doi.org/10.1080/17508487.2014.922489

Maye, C. (2020). *I really did want this to be a poem* [Unpublished manuscript]. Department of Art and Art Education, Teachers College.

McIntosh, P. (1988). *White privilege: Unpacking the invisible knapsack.* Wellesley College Center for Research on Women.

McIntosh, P. (1998). White privilege and male privilege: A personal account of coming to see correspondences through work in women's studies. In R. Delgado & J. Stefancic (Eds.), *Critical white studies: Looking behind the mirror* (pp. 291–299). Temple University Press.

Menakem, R. (2017). *My grandmother's hands: Racialized trauma and the pathway to mending our hearts and bodies.* Central Recovery Press.

Mezirow, J. (1991). *Transformative dimensions of adult learning.* Jossey-Bass.

Mezirow, J., & Taylor, E. W. & Associates. (2009). *Transformative learning in practice: Insights from community, workplace, and higher education.* Jossey-Bass.

Michael, A. (2015). *Raising race questions: Whiteness and inquiry in education.* Teachers College Press.

Mosley, D. V., Hargons, C. N., Meiller, C., Angyal, B., Wheeler, P., Davis, C., & Stevens-Watkins, D. (2020). Critical consciousness of anti-black racism: A practical model to prevent and resist racial trauma. *Journal of Counseling Psychology.* Advance online publication. http://dx.doi.org/10.1037/cou0000430

Moye, T. J. (2013). *Ella Baker: Community organizer of the civil rights movement.* Rowman and Littlefield.

Nexstar Media Wire. (2020). *Trump announces "1776 commission" to promote "patriotic education."* https://fox40.com/news/political-connection/trump-announces-1776-commission-to-promote-patriotic-education/

Nordell, J. (2017, May 7). Is this how discrimination ends? *The Atlantic.* https://www.theatlantic.com/science/archive/2017/05/unconscious-bias-training/525405/

Okun, T. (2010). *The emperor has no clothes: Teaching about race and racism to people who don't want to know.* Information Age.

Oluo, I. (2018). *So you want to talk about race.* Seal Press.

Ontario Institute for Studies in Education. (n.d.). *The power flower. Reflection on our social identities.* https://www.oise.utoronto.ca/edactivism/Activist_Resources/The_Power_Flower.html

Ortiz, P. (2018). *An African American and Latinx history of the United States.* Beacon Press.

Outlaw, L. T. J. (2004). Rehabilitate racial whiteness? In G. A. Yancy (Ed.), *What white looks like: African American philosophers on the whiteness question* (pp. 159–172). Routledge.

Painter, N. I. (2015). *The history of white people.* Norton.

Palmer, P. (2011). *Healing the heart of democracy: The courage to create a politics worthy of the human spirit.* Jossey-Bass.

Pawlowski, L. (2019). Creating a brave space classroom. In S. D. Brookfield & Associates (Eds.), *Teaching race: Helping students unmask and challenge racism* (pp. 63–86). Jossey-Bass.

Paxton, D. (2010). Transforming white consciousness. In V. Sheared, J. Johnson-Bailey, S. A. J. Colin III, E. J. Peterson, & S. D. Brookfield (Eds.), *The handbook of race and adult education: A resource for dialogue on racism* (pp. 119–132). Jossey-Bass.

Perez, A. (2018). *Love while challenging racist behavior*. Interaction Institute for Social Change. https://interactioninstitute.org/love-while-challenging-racist-behavior/

Preskill, S. J. (2021). *Education in black and white: Myles Horton and the Highlander Center's vision for social justice*. University of California Press.

Racial Equity Tools. (2020). *Compilation of racial identity models*. https://www.racialequitytools.org/resourcefiles/Compilation_of_Racial_Identity_Models_7_15_11.pdf

Ransby, B. (2003). *Ella Baker and the black freedom movement: A radical democratic vision*. University of North Carolina Press.

Reinsborough, P., & Canning, D. (2017). *Re:imagining change: How to use story-based strategy to win campaigns, build movements, and change the world* (2nd ed.). PM Press.

Resendez, A. (2016). *The other slavery: The uncovered story of Indian enslavement in America*. Houghton Mifflin Harcourt.

Rodriguez, D. (2008). Investing in white innocence: Colorblind racism, white privilege, and the new white racist fantasy. In L. Guerrero (Ed.), *Teaching race in the 21st century: College teachers talk about their fears, risks, and rewards* (pp. 123–136). Palgrave Macmillan.

Roediger, D. R., & Esch, E. D. (2012). *The production of difference: Race and the management of labor in US history*. Oxford University Press.

Ross, K. M. (2020, June 4). Call it what it is: Anti-Blackness. *New York Times*. https://www.nytimes.com/2020/06/04/opinion/george-floyd-anti-blackness.html

Saad, L. F. (2020). *Me and white supremacy: Combat racism, change the world, and become a good ancestor*. Sourcebooks.

Saini, A. (2019). *Superiority: The return of race science*. Beacon Press.

Saito, N. T. (2020). *Settler colonialism, race, and the law: Why structural racism persists*. New York University Press.

Saslow, E. (2018). *Rising out of hatred: The awakening of a former white nationalist*. Anchor Books.

Shor, I. (1997). *When students have power: Negotiating authority in a critical pedagogy*. University of Chicago Press.

Shor, I., & Freire, P. (1987). *A pedagogy for liberation: Dialogues on transforming education*. Bergin and Garvey.

Showing Up for Racial Justice. (n.d.). *Why SURJ?* https://www.showingupforracialjustice.org/why-surj.html

Singh, A. A. (2019). *The racial healing handbook: Practical activities to help you challenge privilege, confront systemic racism and engage in collective healing*. New Harbinger Publications.

Singleton, G. (2014). *Courageous conversations about race: A field guide* (2nd ed.). Corwin.

Singleton, G. E. (2012). *More courageous conversations about race*. Corwin.

Singleton, G. E., & Linton, C. (2005). *Courageous conversations about race*. Corwin.

Sleeter, C. E. (2016). Learning to work while white to challenge racism in higher education. In N. M. Joseph, C. Haynes, & F. Cobb (Eds.), *Interrogating white-*

ness and relinquishing power: White faculty's commitment to racial consciousness in STEM classrooms (pp. 13–26). Peter Lang.

Smith, B. (2019). Forming classroom communities to help students embrace discomfort. In S. D. Brookfield & Associates, *Teaching race: Helping students unmask and challenge racism* (pp. 171–190). Jossey-Bass.

Smith, D. T., Juarez, B. G., & Jacobson, C. K. (2011). White on Black: Can white parents teach Black adoptive children how to understand and cope with racism? *Journal of Black Studies, 42*(8), 1195–1230. https://doi.org/10.1177/0021934711404237

Smith, H. (2009). The Foxfire approach to student and community interaction. In L. Shumow (Ed.), *Promising practices for family and community involvement during high school* (pp. 89–103). Information Age.

Solomon, A., & Rankin, K. (2019). *How we fight white supremacy: A field guide to black resistance.* Bold Type Books.

Stevenson, B. (2014). *Just mercy: A story of justice and redemption.* Random House.

Stevenson, B. (2019). *We can't recover from this history until we deal with it* [Video]. YouTube. https://youtu.be/YRJX5jvORzQ

Sue, D. W. (2010). *Microaggressions in everyday life: Race, gender, and sexual orientation.* Wiley.

Sue, D. W., Alsaidi, S., Awad, M. N., Glaeser, E., Calle, C. Z., & Mendez, N. (2019). Disarming racial microaggressions: Microintervention strategies for targets, white allies, and bystanders. *American Psychologist, 74*(1), 128–142. http://dx.doi.org/10.1037/amp0000296

Sullivan, S. (2006). *Revealing whiteness: The unconscious habits of racial privilege.* Indiana University Press.

Sullivan, S. (2014). *Good white people: The problem with middle-class white anti-racism.* SUNY Press.

Sullivan, S. (2019). *White privilege.* Polity Press.

Tatum, B. (1997). *Why are all the black kids sitting in the cafeteria? And other conversations about race.* Basic Books.

Taylor, E. W., & Cranton, P. & Associates. (2012). *The handbook of transformative learning: Theory, research, and practice.* Jossey-Bass.

Thomas, L. [@glowmaven]. (2018, May 1). *We are not interested in optical allyship* [Image]. Instagram. https://www.instagram.com/p/BiPDZkbFJFY/?hl=en

Tilley, S. A., & Powick, K. D. (2015). Radical stuff: Starting a conversation about racial identity and white privilege. In D. E. Lund & P. R. Carr (Eds.), *Revisiting the great white north? Reframing whiteness, privilege, and identity in education* (2nd ed.). Sense.

Tochluk, S. (2010). *Witnessing whiteness: The need to talk about race and how to do it* (2nd ed.). Rowman and Littlefield.

Traister, R. (2018). *Good and mad: The revolutionary power of women's anger.* Simon and Schuster.

Truman, L. J. [@LauraJeanTruman]. (2018, October 7). *Keep my anger from becoming meanness* [Tweet]. Twitter. https://twitter.com/laurajeantruman/status/10491 31455778119681?lang=en

U.S. Department of Arts and Culture. (n.d.). *Honor native land: A guide and call to acknowledgment.* https://usdac.us/nativeland/

Visions Inc. (2018–2020). *About.* https://www.visions-inc.org/who-we-are.html

Vogt, E., Brown, J., & Isaacs, D. (2003). *The art of powerful questions: Catalyzing insight, innovation and action.* https://www.scribd.com/document/18675626/Art-of-Powerful-Questions

Wah, L. M. (Director). (1994). *Color of fear* [DVD]. Stir Fry Productions.

Warren, M. R. (2010). *Fire in the heart: How white activists embrace social justice.* Oxford University Press.

Wesch, M. (2008). *Context collapse.* https://krex.k-state.edu/dspace/handle/2097/6302

Wheatley, M. (2010). *Perseverance.* Berret-Koehler.

WhiteHouse.gov. (2020). *Remarks by President Trump at the White House conference on American history.* https://www.c-span.org/video/?475934-1/president-trump-announces-1776-commission-restore-patriotic-education-nations-schools

Wieder, A. (2013). Ruth First and Joe Slovo in the war against apartheid. *Monthly Review Press.*

Wilkerson, I. (2010). *The warmth of other suns: The epic story of America's great migration.* Random House.

Wilkerson, I. (2020). *Caste: The origins of our discontents.* Random House.

Wise, T. (2011). *White like me: Reflections on race from a privileged son* (rev. ed.). Counterpoint.

Wright Mills, C. (1959). *The sociological imagination.* Oxford University Press.

Yancey, G. (2003). *Who is white? Latinos, Asians and the new black/nonblack divide.* Lynne Rienner.

Yancy, G. (Ed.). (2004). *What white looks like: African American philosophers on the whiteness question.* Routledge.

Yancy, G. (2012). *Look, a white! Philosophical essays on whiteness.* Temple University Press.

Yancy, G. (2015, December 24). *Dear white America.* https://opinionator.blogs.nytimes.com/2015/12/24/dear-white-america/

Yancy, G. (2018a). *Backlash: What happens when we talk honestly about racism in America.* Rowman and Littlefield.

Yancy, G. (2018b, October 24). *#IAmSexist.* https://www.nytimes.com/2018/10/24/opinion/men-sexism-me-too.html

Yep, G. A. (2007). Pedagogy of the opaque: The subject of whiteness and diversity courses. In L. M. Cooks & J. S. Simpson (Eds.), *Whiteness, pedagogy, performance: Dis/placing race* (pp. 87–110). Lexington Books.

Yoon, I. (2016). Why is it not a joke? An analysis of internet memes associated with racism and hidden ideology of colorblindness. *Journal of Cultural Research in Art Education, 33,* 92–123. https://pdfs.semanticscholar.org/fd07/488fbe610d24cd84e8511642c7d25bdbe8fb.pdf?_ga=2.25570301.1924798441.1566663171-2015481151.1566663171

Zinn, H. (2017). *A people's history of the United States.* Harper.

ABOUT THE AUTHORS

Stephen D. Brookfield is Distinguished Scholar at Antioch University, adjunct professor at Teachers College, Columbia University, and Professor Emeritus at the University of St. Thomas (St. Paul, MN). Since beginning his educational career in 1970, he has worked in England, Canada, and the United States, teaching and consulting in a variety of adult, community, organizational, and higher education settings. His overall project is to help people learn to think critically about the dominant ideologies they have internalized and how these can be challenged. He is particularly interested in methodologies of critical thinking, discussion and dialog, critical reflection, leadership, and the exploration of power dynamics, particularly around racial identity and white supremacy. To that end he has written, cowritten, or edited 19 books on adult learning, teaching, critical thinking, discussion methods, critical theory, leadership, and teaching race, six of which have won the Cyril O. Houle World Award for Literature in Adult Education (in 1986, 1989, 1996, 2005, 2011, and 2012). His academic appointments have included positions at the University of British Columbia, Teachers College, Columbia University (New York), Harvard University, and the University of St. Thomas in Minneapolis-St. Paul. He has consulted with numerous organizations and institutions across the world and delivered multiple workshops and conference keynotes. He can be contacted via his website (www.stephenbrookfield.com/).

Mary E. Hess is professor of educational leadership at Luther Seminary, where she has taught since 2000. During the 2016–2017 year she held the Patrick and Barbara Keenan Visiting Chair in Religious Education at the University of St. Michael's College in the University of Toronto. She is affiliated faculty at the School of Theology and Ministry at Seattle University, as well as at the San Francisco Theological Seminary/Graduate School of Theology in the University of Redlands. Hess has degrees from Yale, Harvard, and Boston College, and has directed a number of projects focusing on the challenges of media culture for communities of faith. As an educator straddling the fields of media studies and religious studies, she has focused her research on exploring ways in which participatory strategies for knowing and learning are constructed and contested amid digital cultures. She is particularly interested in dialogic forms of organizational development and the challenges posed to communities by oppressive systems such as racism, classism, sexism, and so on. Hess publishes regularly in academic journals and is a past president of the Religious Education Association. She was a core member of the International Study Commission on Media, Religion, and Culture. She is a consultant with the Wabash Center on Teaching and Learning in Theology and Religious Studies, is a member of the Faculty Development Committee of the Association of Theological Schools, and serves on the editorial boards of several journals. Hess has created and maintains a number of websites (indexed at meh.religioused.org).

INDEX

as, 87–89, 93; social media and, 91; victimization within, 36–37
empathy, 2, 3, 38–39
employment, 21, 64, 126
empowerment, 144–145
environmental law, 21
Episcopal Church USA, 103
epistemology, 29, 32, 58–59
equality, movements for, 161–162
Equal Justice Initiative, 103
European American Collaborative Challenging Whiteness, 69
Evangelical Lutheran Church of America, 103
evidence-based practice, 59
exceptionalism, Black, 125–126
Eyes on the Prize (film), 77

Facebook, emotion within, 91
facilitators: anger and, 91; boundaries and, 151–154; chalk talk exercise and, 115–116; circle of voices exercise and, 112–113; circular response exercise and, 118; discussion prompts of, 96; ideology critique exercise and, 137–141; instructions for, 80–81; interventions by, 150–151; productive dissonance and, 154–155; racial autobiographies of, 94; racial discussions structuring by, 106–107; rational clarification and, 147
Facing History and Ourselves project, 165, 176
factual listener, 81
faculty of color, within higher education, 26–27
failure, success within, 192–195
fairness, 2, 45–46
family, racism within, 159
Farber-Robertson, A., 72, 94–95
Farley, Margaret, 9

fear, 17–18, 68, 86
feedback, 148, 149–151. *See also* Backchannel Chat
feelings listener, 81
5 Tips for Being an Ally (film), 76
Floyd, George, 13, 77, 169, 205
Flynn, J. E., Jr., 128
Foste, Z., 37
Foucault, M., 28, 135
"four corners" exercise, 80
Fox, H., 56
Frazier, Darnella, 205
Freire, P., 145–146
French, Bryana, 203–204
Fruitvale Station (film), 79
Fund for Theological Exploration, 71–72
Furie, Matt, 173

Gallman, S., 94
Garza, Alice, 199
gaslighting, 167, 168
Georgetown University, 174
Get Out (film), 79
Gillespie, Diane, 101
Global Voices Online, 173
golden rule, 1–2
Goodman, Andrew, 162
"Grassy Narrows, Home to Me" (song), 100
The Great Debaters (film), 55
Green Book (film), 79
guilt, 45, 87–89

Habermas, J., 24–25, 110
Haggerty, Benjamin Hammond (Macklemore), 100
Harris, Duchess, 79
Harvard University, 101
hashtag syllabus movement, 102
Healing Minnesota's Stories project, 177
health, people of color and, 126

When I First Became Aware of Race
lesson, 69
"Where Is the Love?" (song), 100
Whipple, Bishop, 177
white advantage, 31, 43, 46. *See also*
white privilege
white antiracist identity: activism
through, 40–41, 65; characteristics
of, 25; embracing, 35–36;
importance of, 18–20; positive
development of, 47–48; practice
of, 175–178; teaching of, 20
White By Law (Lopez), 169
white fragility, 36, 84, 106
White Like Me (Wise), 16
whiteness/whites: awareness of,
42, 62; beliefs and behaviors
exercise within, 97–100;
benefits to, 15; day to day life
of, 42–43; demographics of,
19; dominance of, 14, 20, 22;
economic exploitation of, 64–65;
entrenchment of, 25; guilt
and, 45; identity of, 6, 18–19,
44–45, 76–77; ideology of,
208–209; learning about, 47;
microaggressions and, 168; as not
a racial identity, 51–52; parental
communication by, 60; possessive
investment in, 20; power of, 31,
33, 42, 45, 124–125, 126, 161;
pride and, 45; race mask of, 10;
racial identity of, 13, 14; racial
justice fight by, 162; savior stance
of, 197–198; teaching of, 44
white normativity, 51
white privilege: awareness of, 15,
95; case studies of, 101–102;
defined, 65; dehumanizing of,
212; ideology of, 29, 36; law
enforcement and, 60; leveraging
of, 5–6, 19, 41, 155–157, 197,
200; personal testimony and, 58,

86; power and, 46; The Privilege
Walk exercise and, 128–129; social
justice leveraging of, 47; term
use of, 31, 32, 46, 63–65; white
supremacy and, 17
"White Privilege" (song), 100
White Privilege Conferences, 196
white racial frame, 33
White Rage (Anderson), 169
white students, confession of, 38
white supremacy: alternate names
for, 32; assumptions of, 3–4;
The Brain Fart exercise and,
132; characteristics of, 19;
conversations regarding, 85;
culture of, 32; defection from,
199; defined, 22; dehumanizing
of, 212; discussion question
regarding, 114; fear within,
17–18; as humanly created, 142;
ideology of, 1, 15, 17, 21–23,
27, 32–33, 47, 49, 89, 126, 128,
194–195, 201–202; institutions
and, 143; leadership viewpoint of,
4; march of, 76; myth of, 17–18;
normativity within, 51; norms of,
92–93; police and, 124; politics
and, 24; power and, 33, 51, 161;
racism continuance and, 13;
resistance to, 162; savior stance of,
197–198; as self-sustaining, 134;
socialization into, 85–86; term use
of, 63–65; threat to, 127; within
United States, 32–33; war against,
15; worldview of, 14
*Why Are All the Black Kids Sitting in the
Cafeteria? And Other Conversations
About Race* (Tatum), 34
Wiener, J., 162–163
Wilkerson, I., 169
Wisconsin, indigenous people within, 6
Wise, Tim, 16, 77, 199
working class, demonization of, 37